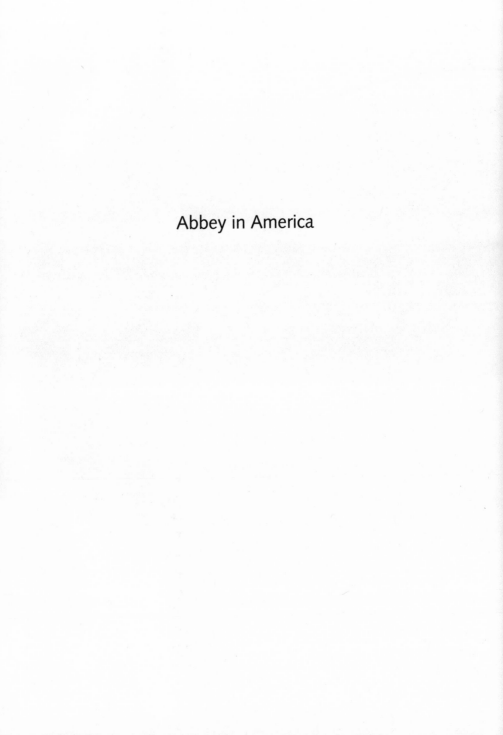

Abbey in America

Abbey in America

A Philosopher's Legacy in a New Century

EDITED BY JOHN A. MURRAY

UNIVERSITY OF NEW MEXICO PRESS   •   ALBUQUERQUE

© 2015 by the University of New Mexico Press
All rights reserved. Published 2015
Printed in the United States of America
20 19 18 17 16 15   1 2 3 4 5 6

Library of Congress Cataloging-in-Publication Data
Abbey in America : a philosopher's legacy in a new century / edited by John A. Murray.
    pages cm
  Includes bibliographical references and index.
  ISBN 978-0-8263-5517-1 (cloth : alk. paper) — ISBN 978-0-8263-5518-8 (electronic)
  1. Abbey, Edward, 1927–1989—Criticism and interpretation. I. Murray, John A.,
  1954– editor.
  PS3551.B2Z55 2015
  813'.54—DC23

                        2014033717

"Abbey's Road," by Edward Hoagland, first appeared in the New York Times (1990)
and was later included in Hoagland on Nature: Essays (New York: Lyons Press, 2003).
"On the Edge with Edward Abbey, Charles Ives, and the Outlaws," by Charles Bowden,
was published in excerpted form in High Country News (October 13, 2014). John A.
Murray's book review of Abbey's last book The Fool's Progress, included in the appendix,
was published in the Bloomsbury Review (March/April 1989). Material from Doug
Peacock's "Desert Solitaire Revisited" previously appeared as the preface to the French
edition of Edward Abbey's Desert Solitaire published by Gallmeister in 2010.

All photographs by John A. Murray were taken on traditional film and developed in a
darkroom, in large format (4 × 5), medium format (6 × 4.5), and 35 mm. All photographs
were provided by John A. Murray, except for the Wendell Berry photograph at the 1989
Abbey memorial, taken by Charles W. Murray Jr.; the photograph of John A. Murray with
the state record mule deer, taken by Charles W. Murray Jr.; the self-portrait by Genoa
Alexander; and the photograph of Esther Rose Honig in the Atacama desert, which was
taken by Ali Zadmehr.

Cover image: A detail of a 6 × 6-inch engraving of Edward Abbey entitled The River Rat
by John A. Murray © 2014.
Designed by Lisa Tremaine

Composed in Sabon text and Syntax display

This book is dedicated to the memory of

Dr. Maria Santos Gorrostieta Salazar (1976–2012)

of Tiquicheo, Michoacán, Mexico, and all those

courageous activists, journalists, and authors

around the world who have been silenced in recent years

for speaking the truth to power, as Edward Abbey,

a great humanist, consistently did

throughout his life and literary career.

Contents

Preface   **IX**

Introduction: Edward Abbey, Yesterday and Today   **1**

Part 1. Scholarly Perspectives

1. Equal Parts Anger and Love: A Posthumous Interview with
    Edward Abbey   **27**
    KATHLEEN DEAN MOORE

2. One Man's Terrorist: Reclaiming Edward Abbey for the
    Post-9/11 Era   **35**
    MICHAEL BRANCH

3. Edward Abbey on Immigration   **43**
    JOHN ALCOCK

4. Abbey in the Anthropocene   **51**
    CURT MEINE

5. Abbey's Secret   **57**
    BEN A. MINTEER

Part 2. Independent Authors

6. The View from Alaska   **65**
    NANCY LORD

7. A Meditation on Two Works by Ed Abbey   **71**
    GLENN VANSTRUM

Part 3. Friends, Acquaintances, and Colleagues

8.   Abbey's Road   **83**
     EDWARD HOAGLAND

9.   *Desert Solitaire* Revisited   **91**
     DOUG PEACOCK

10. Abbey Following His Own Truth   **97**
     JACK LOEFFLER

11. On the Edge with Edward Abbey, Charles Ives,
     and the Outlaws   **107**
     CHARLES BOWDEN

12. The Age of Abbey   **123**
     JOHN A. MURRAY

Part 4. A New Generation

13. Faraway   **167**
     GENOA ALEXANDER

14. Valle de la Luna   **171**
     ESTHER ROSE HONIG

Afterword   **181**

Appendix. *The Fool's Progress:* An Honest Novel
     A Review by John A. Murray   **197**

Further Reading   **201**

Contributors   **207**

Index   **213**

Preface

As I gathered the contributors for this book, I recalled the early scenes of *The Magnificent Seven*, as Yul Brynner searched Tombstone for a band of gunslingers to make one last trip into the back of the beyond. It was an enjoyable process, as I made contact with old friends, as well as established communications with authors and scholars I had not met before, but whose works I had long admired. I would like to thank each of them for joining me on this saddle-creaking, extended journey of exploration and understanding. I must express my gratitude to Ted Hoagland, who urged me in a February 2014 phone conversation to make an extra effort in my search for the reclusive Charles Bowden, who I finally was able to track down through one of his publishers (much thanks to Kristen Buckles, an editor at the University of Arizona Press, for her kind assistance!). It was with great sadness that I learned of the death of Charles Bowden at his home in Las Cruces, New Mexico, on August 30, 2014, shortly after I received a final email from him that spoke of his enthusiasm for the book. I would also like to thank Gavin Van Horn, the director of Culture Studies at the Center for Humans and Nature in Chicago, for his thoughtful and detailed critique of the work, which greatly improved the book. Many additional writers, scholars, and public figures were invited to join the book with a reflective essay that gave fresh consideration to Abbey but had to reluctantly decline because of other obligations. They are here in spirit and include Gary Snyder, Craig Childs, Cheryl Strayed, Gary Nabhan, David Quammen, Tom McGuane, Linda Hogan, Robert Redford, John Macrae (Abbey's editor at Holt), Bill McKibben (Middlebury), Scott Russell Sanders (emeritus, Indiana University), Paul Hutton (University of New Mexico), Durwood Ball (University of New Mexico), and Patricia Limerick (University of Colorado).

A book of this type can sometimes seem like a banquet from which the guest of honor is absent. This volume was conceived with that adage in mind. It offers readers a collection of essays that the author would, conceivably, have been pleased with and honored by. I would like to thank John Byram, his gifted staff, and the editorial board of the University of New Mexico Press for their enthusiastic support of the project from the beginning. My history with the press goes back a third of a century, to an early work on the Gila Wilderness, and, later, a nature-writing textbook, both of which I published in another literary age with David Holtby and Elizabeth Hadas. It was a wonderful experience to collaborate again with such consummate professionals and such a fine academic institution. In his journals, Abbey commented on his relationship with his alma mater, the University of New Mexico: "All these letters, speaking invitations, etc. But never have I received any letters from old friends at UNM, or any kind of invitation from that school. Letters from strangers every day, but never a word from those I'd most like to hear from."[1] Hopefully this book will help in part, if only symbolically, to return Abbey to the institution of higher learning at which he began his intellectual pilgrimage.

Abbey in America examines the case for accepting the author's works into the English and American prose canon. While pursuing a thesis regarding the merits of Abbey's writings first advanced by Thomas J. Lyon of Utah State University in 1987, the work also addresses arguments to the contrary. The author's legendary drinking, and its destructive effect on his life and later writings, is frankly addressed, as are his often-contentious literary and personal relationships with other members of the guild. The uneven nature of Abbey's published fiction is acknowledged in the introduction and afterword. Abbey was a complex and polarizing figure, with a mixture of assets and liabilities. He has proven to be endlessly fascinating, both as a prolific author and as an outspoken advocate for his beliefs. In that spirit, both informed praise and judicious criticism, by the editor and the thirteen contributors, can be found in these pages.

This new examination of the author's legacy may be seen by future scholars as the first step, in the new century, toward a comprehensive evaluation of the late twentieth-century figure, much as, a century ago, our predecessors began the process of reappraising Thoreau. Thoreau was increasingly classified not as a poet and lecturer, as he perceived himself and was thought of by his contemporaries, including Emerson and Hawthorne, but as a unique and gifted essayist and as the author of an essential philosophical work. Similarly, Abbey can now be regarded not as a major fiction writer or even as a major minor fiction writer, as he preferred to view himself, but, rather, as an essayist of the first rank. The consensus appears to be that two of Abbey's works—*Desert Solitaire: A Season in the Wilderness* and *Abbey's Road*—are as accomplished as anything in the English and American prose canon, and that is no small achievement for this distinguished UNM graduate.

Note

1. Edward Abbey, *Confessions of a Barbarian: Selections from the Journals of Edward Abbey,* 1951–1989, ed. David Petersen (New York: Little, Brown and Co., 1994), 81.

Introduction
Edward Abbey, Yesterday and Today

*A civilization, nearing its end, may burst into all the transient and
melancholy glory of a cottonwood in autumn.*

—EDWARD ABBEY, *JOURNALS* (ALBUQUERQUE, DECEMBER 27, 1954)

1

Twenty-six years after his passing, Edward Abbey (1927–1989) remains a
central figure in the literature of nature. From a humble stone hut on the
side of a desert wash, Abbey became one of the most influential champions
of the environment in his era. He set out to produce a collection of essays
documenting his service as a seasonal ranger at a national monument in
Utah, during a period of isolation and despair as a novelist. By the time
he was done, he had created a work to place on the shelf beside those by
Henry David Thoreau, Rachel Carson, and Joseph Wood Krutch. One
recalls Jonathan Swift, who, disillusioned with the age of Restoration, sat
down to write *Gulliver's Travels* (1726) as a satiric allegory of contemporary events and, in the end, left posterity a humorous book for children
of all ages. Or Richard Henry Dana, who set out to document the abuse
of sailors in a humanitarian tract and instead created a timeless classic
of the sea, *Two Years Before the Mast* (1840), that inspired Herman
Melville to write *Typee* (1846) and *Moby Dick* (1851). Abbey was not just
another plain-speaking and philosophizing denizen of the Far West, or a
stock regional commentator, trained in the conventional dialectics of his
century and selected by scholars to fill out a national collection. He was
the natural spirit of the American landscape expressing itself in a language
that resonates with truth.

The essence of Abbey's literary craft was the art of division, of setting in
opposition distinct ideas or points of view, which he methodically explored.
Part of this process resulted from six years of academic training in philosophy at the University of New Mexico. Since the classical period, the truth

1

has been carefully pursued through the systematic application of rigorous logic. Quite often the search has proceeded, as can be seen emerging in the Socratic dialogues, from thesis to anti-thesis to synthesis. This well-organized approach is evident throughout *Desert Solitaire* (1968) in Abbey's analysis of the natural and supernatural ("Down the River"), society and solitude ("Havasu"), and culture and civilization ("Episodes and Visions"). Later in his career (1988), Abbey's characteristic method can be seen in his examination of humanized versus natural landscapes ("Thus I Respond to Rene Dubos"), in his separation of conventional political systems and less formally structured political associations ("Theory of Anarchy"), and in his discussion of civil laws and civil disobedience ("Of Protest"). That the author made these potentially esoteric discussions so easily accessible to lay people is a tribute to his literary genius. Thomas J. Lyon of Utah State University expressed it this way, in his book *This Incomparable Land* (2001): "Abbey is able to breathe life into some of the hoariest dilemmas of philosophy, such as the ancient conflict in epistemology between realism and idealism, and he is able to present his own search for meaning in the desert in personal, accessible terms."[1]

Like other rationalists, from Aristotle to René Descartes to Bertrand Russell, Abbey kept his distance from any system of inquiry that was not based on strict empiricism. He was allied with the cause of reason, as he states in his 1979 essay "Science with a Human Face": "In this embrace of easily reconcilable opposites I wish to stand apart, alone if need be, and hold up the ragged flag of reason. . . . By 'reason' I mean intelligence informed by sympathy, knowledge in the arms of love."[2] Consonant with this, Abbey provided a reappraisal of the nineteenth-century nature writer Ralph Waldo Emerson, who owns the distinction of being the only major intellectual to have met Wordsworth (1833), Thoreau (1843–1862), and John Muir (1871), claiming that Emerson "could not abide the dichotomies of life—those troublesome divisions between reality and illusion, mind and nature, religion and science, moral law and physical law, the temporal and the eternal, the spiritual ideal and the mundane actual."[3] Abbey, who embraced a Jeffersonian rigor on matters of the mind and spirit, regarded Emerson's transcendentalism, derived from Kant's idealism, as he did the occult and organized religions (sometimes in the same discussion), as a "tortured and tortuous metaphysical hallucination."[4]

Death, to Abbey, was not the first question, as it was for the French philosopher Albert Camus, who made that statement the opening sentence of *The Myth of Sisyphus* (1943), but rather the last. In that affirmative spirit, Abbey chose Thoreau's deathbed observation, "One world at a time, please" as the title for his last collection of essays (1988). In life he could have embraced any creed, but he chose one congruent with the radiant spirit of his literary exemplar Montaigne, who in his essay "The Affection of Fathers for Their Children" writes that "even if I were able to make myself feared, I would rather make myself loved."[5] Abbey chose his literary exemplar well—Shakespeare was also a close reader of Montaigne's book (1588) and borrowed from him freely. Scholars have linked phrases and passages in *The Tempest* (1610) and *Hamlet* (1599) to Montaigne's essays. Like Montaigne, Shakespeare, and Thoreau, Abbey was committed to apprehending the truth and communicating whatever objective certainties could be established by reason to his readers, who he considered his friends.

Abbey's relationships with the authoritative hierarchies of his era—political, social, economic, literary, religious, academic—are best summarized in Aleksandr Solzhenitsyn's observation in *In the First Circle* (1968): "A great writer is, so to speak, a second government in his country. And for that reason no regime has ever loved great writers, only minor ones."[6] Abbey, who referred to Solzhenitsyn as his "hero" in "A Writer's Credo" (1988), quoted Ernest Hemingway in the same essay: "A writer is like a gypsy. He owes no allegiance to any government. If he is a good writer he will never like any government he lives under. His hand should be against it and its hand will always be against him."[7] Solzhenitsyn's predecessor Tolstoy similarly wrote, in a letter to his colleague Vasily Botkin, that "the truth is that the State is a conspiracy designed not only to exploit, but above all to corrupt its citizens. . . . Henceforth, I shall never serve any government anywhere."[8] In his quest to expand the boundaries of human understanding and improve the human condition, Edward Abbey was adhering to a well-established tradition in modern literature.

Abbey's writing was as economical as the simple apothegms at the core of his beliefs. There is scarcely a line in any of his essays that does not conduce to the progress of a passage. He revered the old masters and studied and learned from them. If his fellow insurgent during the 1970s and 1980s, Hunter S. Thompson, was essentially a tragic writer who imposed comedy upon the calamities of human experience, then Edward Abbey was a neo-humanist who schooled himself in the ethics and rigor of contemporary science. His word-pictures rivaled, in terms of their literary quality, those of the nineteenth-century frontier writers Francis Parkman and Mark

Twain. Some of his finest descriptive writing can be found in his four Australian essays, when he was confronting the unknown and unfamiliar and had to invent a new vocabulary and system of metaphors. This is evident in his memorable sketch of Ayers Rock in "Back of Beyond" (1979): "It resembles a pink—or in different light—a rust red worm or grub, hairless and wrinkled, that has succumbed, through petrifaction, to the prevailing inertia of Being. A Being that Was—and may, someday, in some future geological epoch, stir its stumps and writhe once more toward Canberra to be recognized."[9] Similarly, Abbey's resonant portraits of the native Australians in "The Outback" (1979) evokes the renderings of Parkman and Twain in the Old West: "Some of the [aboriginal] men had faces like Socrates, others like Darwin and Tolstoy. . . . The old men had white hair, white beards, a certain dignity and beauty."[10]

The author of *Fire on the Mountain* and *Black Sun* was a complex individual compounded of an unusual gift, a natural propensity for kinetic thought and action, and universal human qualities. If his dependence on alcohol impaired his health, diminished his cognition, and shortened his life, as critics point out, such was also the case for half the American Nobel laureates of his century (the literary Mount Rushmore of O'Neill, Faulkner, Hemingway, and Steinbeck), as well as his brother-in-arms in the West during the 1970s and 1980s, Hunter S. Thompson. The habit was not uncommon in the Imperial age, or any human age for that matter, and Abbey was always in excellent and quite immortal company. He was keenly aware of his affliction. He attempted as best he could to manage it, as did many members of the modern guild, from James Joyce, who Hemingway had to carry home from their Parisian outings in the early 1920s (according to biographer Jeffrey Meyers), to Jack Kerouac, who hemorrhaged and died from the effects of drinking in 1969. Fifteen years before his death Abbey wrote: "Drinking too much again: insulting cell tissues, all them brain cells rotting away, cirrhosis of the liver, kidney stones, the shakes—Jesus Christ! Gimme a drink!"[11]

Abbey understood the nature of the underlying condition, and that he was treating it with the world's oldest anodyne: "Dejection. Loss of nerve. Awake at four in the morning, full of fear. A manic-depressive, I am now in the depressed phase."[12] One of his favorite books, both for his search for self-knowledge as well as for his study of prose models, was Robert Burton's *Anatomy of Melancholy* (1623). There is no indication in his journals or letters that the author ever sought formal medical treatment for this affliction. Abbey apparently preferred the intensity of a natural life and the vagaries of fate and genetic inheritance to the alternative states of mind, and being, that are sometimes induced by the pharmaceutical regimes of modern science. Freedom was central to Abbey's philosophical system. The ability to choose without constraint on matters of personal or public concern, and to embrace the individual spirit with all of its inherent contradictions was, to the author, of paramount importance, as was his cheerful acceptance of that which made him uniquely human. Viktor E. Frankl, who wrote *Man's Search for Meaning* (1945), expressed it this way: "Everything can be taken from a man but one thing: the last of the human freedoms—to choose one's attitude in any given set of circumstances, to choose one's own way."[13] Frankl, a Holocaust survivor, elsewhere quotes a statement by Anton Wildgans that speaks to Abbey's travails: "What is to give light must endure burning."[14]

Those who write about him on this and other matters now, as we do here, do so with an assurance that he likely never felt. Some who had close interactions with him noted a measured reserve in social settings. Others had contrary impressions, as people can present themselves in different ways depending on the company. Marilyn Auer, who has been my editor for the past thirty years at the *Bloomsbury Review*, met Abbey on his final book tour through the West (March 1988), when he stopped by our Denver editorial offices (then at 17th and Emerson). She later expressed her surprise at his subdued presence, which contrasted with the outspoken character she knew from his books. Her late brother Tom, the publisher of the literary review, had breakfast with Abbey at the Mercury Café, then located on Capitol Hill, during the same visit and related a similar impression.

Abbey addressed the nature of his personality in his journals: "The real Edward Abbey? . . . A shy, retiring, very timid fellow, obviously. Somewhat of a recluse, emerging rarely from his fictional den only when lured by money, vice, the prospect of applause."[15] Robert Redford noted the same characteristic when writing of their Utah horseback trip in his 1978 book *The Outlaw Trail*: "Ed is a large man with an Abe Lincoln beard and a cool eye. . . . He's an observer who carefully reserves his strong feelings for the printed page."[16] That humility, of course, was part of his nature, and it contributed to his success as a philosopher and writer. He was a close student of nature, wild and human, and took note of every *thing* in his ken. The author was, at his core, intensely aware that our vision presents us with an earthly paradise greater than any that can be conceived by the human imagination, that a Heisenberg-like state of uncertainty is essential to apprehending the truth, and that to have the curiosity and wonder of a child is no disgrace.

Abbey had his forgettable moments and mistaken theories, as every individual does, but he always wrote with a controlled eloquence that drew readers near and infuriated those who, out of envy for his literary gifts or discomfort with his uncompromising candor, disliked him. Above all, he was one of those happy souls for whom "yes" always triumphed over "no." He was committed at all times to helping his readers see the world around them more clearly. Like his predecessors Emerson and Thoreau, he was at heart a reformer and wished to liberate and empower the human race. On that mission, he was one of the great truth tellers of his century. He understood that most forms of work are a kind of enforced idleness (as evidenced in his long "career" as a seasonal fire lookout), that our first duty is to live (in 1987 he turned down a national literary award because he had a river to run in Idaho), and that our finest moments occur when we show compassion and charity, especially toward the natural world (as demonstrated by his impassioned, lifelong defense of the North American wilderness).

From his earliest efforts to his latest works, Abbey was unique among his peer-group with respect to his extraordinary sense of humor. The effect of this was, as Lyon points out in his "The Nature Essay in the West" (1987), to "democratize and personalize the complaint."[17] Lyon compares Abbey favorably to America's greatest humorist: "Abbey surpasses other nature writers by expressing his dismay in sardonic, self- and species-reducing humor, the like of which has not been seen in the West since Mark Twain."[18] As a member of a nature-writing guild whose members are often pious to the point of self-parody, Abbey's penchant for the comic absurdities of life gave him a special ability to edify the masses and influence public discussion. Nothing was safe from his pen. When his first child, Joshua Abbey, was born, he wrote playfully, in a Swiftian ("A Modest Proposal") mode, "Babies . . . you can always eat them, can't you?"[19] Lyon observes that "his mingling of prophetic depth with outrageous exaggeration and satire gives him a unique literary voice, a standing in a wholly separate category from other nature essayists."[20]

Like Twain ("Fenimore Cooper's Literary Offenses" [1895]), Hemingway (*A Moveable Feast* [1960]), and many American authors before him, Abbey was fond of satirizing fellow members of the guild. This pursuit made his life as socially interesting at times as that of the outspoken Lord Tyrion in *Game of Thrones*. Of Tom Wolfe (*The Electric Kool-Aid Acid Test*), he observed in his journal that he was "a pretentious fad-chaser and apologist for the techno-tyrants."[21] That passing statement was mere preparation. Five years later Abbey thoroughly eviscerated Wolfe in the introduction to *Abbey's Road*. Abbey's withering 1987 piece on John Updike in the *Bloomsbury Review* was equally colorful, and also grew from an earlier piece of writing: "Updike cannot rise or be raised above the mediocrity of his origins, training, ambition & nature. His work lacks vision—he cannot see beyond the suburbs. He lacks passion—has nothing of interest to tell us of anything important. A smug, fatal complacency has stunted his growth; his books are essentially trivial. Like so many writers of that little pre-school Ivy League coterie, a streak of servility flaws his outlook; he has the soul of a sycophant."[22] Like his literary heroes—Solzhenitsyn and Marquez—Abbey waged endless war against the cultural bureaucrats who operated in the guise of writers.

Some of his most entertaining criticism can be found in his correspondence with Gretel Ehrlich, Alston Chase, Barry Lopez, and others whose literary works or pretensions he found amusing. In the introduction to *Abbey's Road*, the author makes light of himself on the issue: "Long ago, returning a friendly greeting from the poet Gary Snyder, I wrote: 'Dear Gary, I admire your work too, except for all that Zen and Hindu bullshit.' One potentially lengthy correspondence craftily nipped in the bud."[23] In the same fiery introduction he rants against Gloria Steinem, Annie Dillard, and other contemporaries. Alston Chase, the Macalester philosophy professor and author of *Playing God in Yellowstone* (1986), eventually became another target: "Saw your reply to my letter in the January 'Outside.' You ought to be ashamed of yourself. Such cowardly and dishonest weaseling. You're supposed to be an educated man; you know very well that sabotage and terrorism are two widely different things. . . . If you ever come to the Tucson area, give me a call; it would be a pleasure to say these things to you face to face."[24] In fairness to Abbey, he often and openly criticized himself (the letters humbly seeking advice from authors and editors on *The Fool's Progress*) and also lavished praise on living authors for whom he had genuine respect, among them Peter Matthiessen, Edward Hoagland, Wendell Berry, Colin Fletcher, Ann Zwinger, and Hunter S. Thompson.

The author lived and wrote in another social and historical age, when the country and the world were quite different. He died before the Cold War

Abbey memorial service, Arches National Park (May 1989)

ended, before the 9/11 attacks, before the rise of the Internet, before the ascent of China, before the wars in Iraq and Afghanistan, before the global and national economic collapse, before the Arab Spring, before the effects of climate change were documented and appreciated by leaders in the world community, before the emergence of a new, capitalistic, and dynamic Russian state, and before the end of what will be known in history as the American century. His peaceful and prosperous epoch represented, in retrospect, a golden age for letters, before the Internet and the digital realm changed the nature of book publishing forever and also fundamentally altered the dynamics of the published book as a unit of expression and discourse.

The age of Abbey was, by contrast with the current era, an innocent time, when privacy rights and intellectual property rights were still widely honored, and literary works had not been yet been devalued commercially through e-book publication. National Book Award winner George Packer provides a lengthy, cogent analysis of these developments in a recent *New Yorker* article.[25] Author Tony Horwitz subsequently published an insightful personal account on the same theme in the *New York Times*.[26] In the 1970s, 1980s, and 1990s authors like Edward Abbey, working on now-archaic typewriters, could still make a modest living from their books and published articles. All of this—a deep equilibrium of the printed word that had persisted for six centuries in Western civilization—was undone by a series of monumental events in the aughts, as the literary marketplace was transformed by new technology, including the explosive growth of the Internet, and published books lost much of their historic value as marketable commodities. David Carr, writing of the annual BookExpo America convention in the *New York Times*, summarizes the radically changed landscape of the post-Abbey era as follows: "Books, we are told, are relics that have reached their sell-by date, put out by an industry that is a desiccated shell of its former self."[27]

The final blow to many of Abbey's former colleagues in the literary world, as well as those in related guilds (journalism, publishing, graphic arts), was the great recession, which has been categorized by the Nobel Laureate Paul Krugman as the lesser depression.[28] The economic upheaval, which began with a banking liquidity and housing market crisis in 2007 caused by deregulation and rampant speculation, constituted the most serious economic calamity to befall the nation since the 1930s. The sudden loss of traditional industries and job markets, coupled with mass long-term unemployment that continues to this day (2015), visited great destruction upon the United States and many other developed nations. This was especially true for those working in the literary arts. When the federal government failed to honor the social contract, as it had with the federal writers and artists programs in the Great Depression (and ironically with both a Democratic president and Congress in place from 2009–2011), a generation of hardworking, once-prolific writers in Edward Abbey's inner and outer circle essentially disappeared. The administration's support of Wall Street and big business, which would provide campaign contributions for the 2012 reelection, instead of Main Street, which had been thoroughly undone by the collapse, had many direct and indirect consequences. As a result of this policy decision, the vibrant literary world to which Edward Abbey had devoted his life essentially became a thing of the past.

2

Edward Abbey was an academic philosopher turned independent writer. With two degrees in philosophy from the University of New Mexico, he was primarily absorbed with the chief question of his original guild, as expressed in Pilate's question to Jesus: "What is truth?" (John 18:38), as well as with the focused secular mission of the earlier martyr Socrates: "It is no ordinary matter that we are discussing, but the right conduct of life."[29] At all times Abbey embraced Montaigne's motto: "Que sais-je?" (What do I know?). In one of his last and most insightful essays Abbey asks, "Truth, truth, what is truth? The word drops easily from the mouth but what does it mean? I venture to assert that truth for one thing is the enemy of Power, as Power is the enemy of truth."[30]

The focus of this book is similar, in its questioning nature, to the approach of our author—Who was Abbey? What did he believe? Where does he stand among his peers, living and dead? How will his works affect American literature, world literature, and the history of ideas? Are there aspects of his life, literary age, and books that have not been noted before? *Abbey in America: A Philosopher's Legacy in a New Century* examines these questions through a number of prisms. Each essayist presents a unique perspective on Abbey and adopts a different literary, personal, or scholarly approach. The contributors range across four generations and, geographically, the length and breadth of the country. They include university professors, a field scientist, an environmental historian, Abbey's personal friends, a medical doctor, a science educator, a professional journalist, and independent scholars, authors, and commentators.

Both Doug Peacock and Jack Loeffler, who knew Abbey well, provide close portraits of the man they experienced for many decades. Edward Hoagland, another Abbey confrere, provides a personal reflection on the man, as does Charles Bowden, who frames his discussion in terms of the immigration issue. John Alcock, an emeritus professor of biology at Arizona State University, also focuses on immigration, a subject of social and political importance in his state. Philosophical aspects of Abbey's legacy are addressed by Michael Branch, a literary scholar at the University of Nevada, and Kathleen Dean Moore, a philosophy professor at Oregon State University. Curt Meine and Ben A. Minteer, two noted environmental scholars, explore the meaning of Abbey in the current century. Glenn Vanstrum, the physician/author of *The Saltwater Wilderness* (2003), and Nancy Lord, a former Alaskan state writer-laureate, examine the author in terms of their life experience. The millennial writers Genoa Alexander and Esther Rose Honig, both born after Abbey's death, take us far outside the Southwest, as they view, respectively, a tropical desert in the Caribbean and a high-altitude desert in Latin America in terms of Edward Abbey's works and beliefs.

My essay, "The Age of Abbey," provides a broader intellectual and literary context for the author, in the manner of Giorgio Vasari's *Lives of the Artists* (1550) or William Drummond's recorded conversations with Ben Jonson (1619). In the spirit of those Renaissance writers, I focus on Abbey and related western authors in his milieu. I remain as fascinated by the development of literature in my time as the Florentine and Elizabethan were by the rapid growth of the visual arts and literary arts in their respective eras. My perspective on Edward Abbey is similar to that of Vasari on Leonardo da Vinci, who describes him as follows: "In the normal course of events many men and women are born with various remarkable qualities and talents; but occasionally in a way that transcends nature, a single person is marvelously endowed by heaven . . . and with talent in such abundance that he leaves others far behind."[31]

Collectively, the essays in *Abbey in America* are part of a universal historical process, as a major author is evaluated by peers and successors and absorbed into the canon. The analogy would be a mountain range, which is best observed, as a single unified entity, at a distance, where its full relationship to its geographic environs becomes apparent. Twenty-five years has provided sufficient time for Abbey to settle into spatial and temporal relief. The initial, and necessary, period of hagiography, eulogies, and paeans has passed, and a more sober and objective analysis can now proceed. At a similar period after their deaths, the process of clinical evaluation of Henry David Thoreau and John Muir likewise commenced. Abbey can now be seen in clear relation to other prose writers of his age and cultural province who are deceased, including Hunter S. Thompson, Wallace Stegner, and John Haines, as well as in relation to those talents who emerged after him, such as Craig Childs and Cheryl Strayed.

3

Abbey was much affected by the natural history and human history of his adopted province, the desert Southwest. His first foray into the region, in the summer of 1944 (at the age of seventeen), represented a turning point on his life journey. He glimpsed the country of his personal future, and returned as soon as circumstances permitted. In "Hallelujah on the Bum" (1977) he wrote about the three-month excursion during which one memorable day followed another: "Brightest New Mexico. The sharp, red cliffs of Gallup. Mesas and mountains in the distance. . . . And over all a golden light, a golden stillness."[32] One is reminded of what Herman Melville wrote to Nathaniel Hawthorne in an often-quoted 1858 letter: "From my twenty-fifth year [when Melville returned from his Pacific voyage] I date my life."[33] Abbey's youthful introduction to the Southwest was as momentous an event for the future bard of the desert.

The relationship between landscape, society, and literature has long been a subject of interest to scholars and writers. The British classicist Maurice Bowra (1898–1971) observes in *The Greek Experience* (1957) that "a people lives by its geography [and] . . . nature remains in the end what it was in the beginning, a school which by its prizes and its penalties fashions its children to a special pattern. In Greece the configuration and the character of the landscape have been a primary influence in shaping the destiny of its people." Bowra continues with this mode of thought:

> Greek light played a part in the formation of Greek thought. Just as the cloudy skies of northern Europe have nursed the huge, amorphous progeny of Norse mythology or German metaphysics, so the Greek light surely influenced the clear-cut conceptions of Greek philosophy. If the Greeks were the world's first true philosophers, in that they formed a consistent and straightforward vocabulary for abstract ideas, it was largely because their minds, like their eyes, sought naturally what is lucid and well defined. Their senses were kept lively by the force of the light, and when the senses are keenly at work, the mind follows no less keenly and seeks to put in order what they give it.[34]

To Bowra, ancient Greece became a center of progress in art, science, government, and technology in part because of the close relationship between landscape and human consciousness. The same was true of the American Southwest through the twentieth century. The sprawling region, with its open spaces, public domain, and three-hundred-plus days of sunshine annually, inspired writers (John Van Dyke, Mary Austin, Zane Grey), artists (Maynard Dixon, the Taos Society, Georgia O'Keeffe), photographers (Ansel Adams, Eliot Porter, Imogene Cunningham), philosopher/commentators (Joseph Wood Krutch, Edward Abbey), architects (Frank Lloyd Wright [Taliesen West in Scottsdale], Richard Neutra [Kaufmann House in Palm Springs]), musicians (from Marty Robbins to Jim Morrison), and the scientists who worked at Los Alamos and China Lake, as well as engineers and administrators who designed the highway system, the water diversion and dam projects, and the great cities. Abbey emerged as a chief figure in the province, as the radiant countryside, in the manner described by Bowra, stirred him to create his literary works. In *The Journey Home: Some Words in Defense of the American West* he writes: "In my case it was love at first sight. This desert, all deserts, any desert. No matter where my head and feet may go, my heart and my entrails stay behind, here on the clean, true, comfortable rock, under the black sun of God's forsaken country. When I take on my next incarnation, my bones will remain bleaching nicely in a stone gulch under the rim of some faraway plateau, way out there in the back of beyond."[35]

A generation before Abbey arrived in New Mexico and made his way to Taos, the English modernist writer D. H. Lawrence (1885–1930) resided in Taos for three productive years (1922–1925). After he died, his ashes were brought from Europe and buried in a nearby chapel. Before moving to the Southwest, Lawrence wrote a seminal essay ("The Spirit of Place" [1918]) about the relationship between landscape and the human experience. It was a subject that fascinated him. He composed his *Studies in American Literature* (1923) during the Taos period, when he lived in a creative community that included the Taos Society, a group of artists that flourished between 1912 and 1927. Lawrence frequently wrote letters to literary and artistic colleagues in Europe, spreading the good word about the unique cultural province that would, a generation later, figure so powerfully in the life of Edward Abbey. These correspondents included Harriet Monroe (patron of James Joyce), Alfred Steiglitz (husband of Georgia O'Keeffe, who would soon visit Taos and then move permanently to the Chama basin), Aldous Huxley (who eventually settled in Los Angeles), and the novelist E. M. Forster. On December 30, 1922, Lawrence wrote to John Middleton Murry, the Bloomsbury group literary critic in London, from the Del Monte Ranch near Questa, south of Taos. The young British writer found New Mexico, only ten years a state, just as exciting as the young American writer Edward Abbey would when he arrived in the next generational wave: "It is good fun on this ranch—quite wild—Rocky Mts.—desert with Rio Grande Canyon away spreading below—great and really beautiful landscape—looking far, far west."[36]

Forty years before Edward Abbey, Dennis Hopper (who film-optioned *The Monkey Wrench Gang*), and their counterculture milieu came to Taos, Lawrence considered creating an alternative community—a western version of social experiments like Brooks Farm—while living on a ranch near Questa, a then-remote Taos outlier. The ranch featured the distinctive ponderosa tree ("the Lawrence tree") that Georgia O'Keeffe immortalized in an oil painting in the summer of 1929, during her initial reconnaissance trip after Lawrence departed to explore Mexico. In a letter to Mabel Dodge Luhan dated August 1929, O'Keeffe made reference to the Lawrence tree and the painting: "I had one particular painting—that tree in Lawrences [sic] front yard as you see it when you lie under on the table—with stars—it looks as tho it is standing on its head—I wanted you to see it—Will send you photographs."[37] That same year Ansel Adams made a pilgrimage to Taos to illustrate his first published book, which was devoted to the Taos Pueblo (1930), as did Paul Strand, who also worked in the area. Eliot Porter soon followed, and settled with his family near Tesuque. All of this modern history provided a strong foundation for Edward Abbey, who made his way to Taos in the early 1950s. For much of the twentieth century, from the age of Lawrence through the age of Abbey, Taos functioned as a kind of latter-day Florence in the American Southwest. The area attracted many of the best minds and talents of the era, including the world-class scientists, engineers, and program administrators at the nearby Los Alamos National Laboratory.

In his seminal essay on place, Lawrence explores the relationship between landscape and the human imagination. "All art," he observes, "partakes of the Spirit of the Place in which it is produced." Lawrence specifically recalls the literature of northern Africa, a desert region similar to northern New Mexico, "and the mysterious religious passion . . . which, voicing itself in Latin, utters the . . . cry of Tertullian, Augustine, Athanasius, the great saints of the African Church. These are not Romans. They are the prelude to a new era. It is not only that they utter the *ideas* [his emphasis] which made Europe. Chiefly in them is felt the first throb of the great mystic passion of mediaeval life. . . . Africa, seething in Roman veins, produces these strange pulses of new experience, incipient newness within the old decadence."[38] The philosopher Albert Camus, who Edward Abbey often quotes in his essays and books, was five years old and living with his French-born parents in his native Algeria the year that Lawrence's essay was published in the *English Review*. In works such as "The Wind at Djemila" (1937), Camus celebrates the exhilarating light and stark beauty of the desert along the southern Mediterranean littoral. Camus, who studied the anarchist movement in his youth, was a significant influence on Abbey, who wrote his master's thesis at the University of New Mexico on the subject of anarchism.

Both Camus and Abbey were deeply affected by the philosophers of Greece and placed the lucidity and rationality of the sunny Mediterranean philosophers at the core of their belief systems.

Edward Abbey could have chosen to live anywhere—Sigurd Olson's Voyageur's Country, Adolph Murie's Alaska, Edwin Way Teale's New England—but he established himself in the Southwestern province—northern New Mexico—which seemed to him the opposite of all those other places, and the area most likely to inspire him, as it had kindred spirits who came before. Over time, the outer and inner landscapes converged and became a single living and creative entity. Abbey later wrote that "Of all the western states I love New Mexico best. . . . Brightest New Mexico, fairest of them all."[39] He resided in northern New Mexico for five years, during his earliest and most formative period in the Southwest. In Albuquerque and Taos, at the headwaters of the Rio Grande, the views that would carry him through adulthood were shaped. It was during this energetic youthful period that he formed a permanent allegiance to the much larger desert province. Evidence of that bond can be seen in his journal entries from the Taos period, as in this one: "Great cumuli thunderheads above us. . . . Rita [Abbey's first wife] sits on a rock a few yards away, sketching. Chickens complaining from down below, at the San Geronimo. I can see for fifty miles or more into the 'strange mystic unknown' Southwest. There's a mesa out there on the horizon, a beautiful high steep-sided flat-topped mesa. Blue, purple, dark, far-away, never-to-be-known-looking."[40]

After many years of geographic and personal exploration in the "never-to-be-known-looking" country, Abbey produced his signature work, *Desert Solitaire.* The book, on one level, replicated the universal flight to nature narrative. Earlier examples include Christ's forty-day sojourn in the deserts of Judea (after meeting the desert prophet John, between 27 and 29 AD), the three far-ranging pilgrimages to the Far North of Matsuo Bashō (1687–1691), and Thoreau's twenty-six–month sabbatical at Walden Pond (July 4, 1845–September 6, 1847). In this universal pattern of escape and return, a restless spirit, disillusioned with the shortcomings of an overly materialistic culture, retreats to the wilderness in search of a vision, obtains enlightenment, and then comes back to society to liberate and empower it. Two thousand years ago, the Nazarene, adapting Psalm 49, summarized this process and perspective in a well-known observation (Luke 9:25): "For whosoever will save his life, will lose it. . . . For what is a man profited, if he shall gain the whole world, but lose his soul?" Abbey returned from the desert with an impassioned critique of his society's consumer and tourist culture and an eloquent argument for the saving graces of wild nature. His book offers both a modern treatment of a primary thesis of *Walden* (that happiness is to be found by living in accordance with nature), and a significant expansion of the traditional nature-writing genre, in terms of the often raucous humor.

Throughout his career Abbey continually pursued the elusive literary ideals of truth and beauty. At his best, in the majority of the essays and at least two of the novels (*The Brave Cowboy* and *Black Sun*), Abbey achieved or came close to realizing that goal. In his Taos journal Abbey wrote frankly of the universal creative challenge: "The more [art] strives toward purity, the nearer it comes to failure and disaster. . . . The *scherzo* from Beethoven's F Major Quartet: What a clean clear fresh and celestial piece of music that is. . . . [T]here is an art which escapes all categories and that is an example of it. . . . The past that can never be recovered, the future that never can be known, the elusive mystery of the quivering present—no wonder our existence is so fraught with poignancy, pathos, tragedy."[41] As a philosopher with a natural allegiance to the Renaissance humanists, Abbey blended the rigorous empiricism of Aristotle and the comprehensive methodology of Plato in roughly equal amounts. As a social critic, he often and ironically (considering his beliefs regarding organized religions) employed the jeremiad rhetorical form of the Puritans. As a prose stylist, he combined the narrative innovations of literary rebels like Hunter S. Thompson with the controlled realism of venerated masters like Hemingway. Over a literary career that spanned three decades, Edward Abbey produced a resonant body of prose writing that continues to exert an influence on American letters and thinking.

4

In his last collection of essays *One Life at a Time, Please* (1988), Edward Abbey wrote about his chief precursor in twentieth-century America, Joseph Wood Krutch. The Columbia English professor, following in the footsteps of another eastern professor, John C. Van Dyke (*The Desert* [1901]), enriched American literature with such works as *The Desert Year* (1951), *Grand Canyon* (1957), *The Forgotten Peninsula: A Naturalist in Baja California* (1961), and *Baja California and the Geography of Hope* (1967). As authors often do when choosing subjects about which to write, the creator of *Desert Solitaire* and *Appalachian Wilderness: The Great Smoky Mountains* (1970) was obliquely commenting on himself when he recalled his extended conversation with Krutch, who he interviewed in 1968 at the professor's home in Tucson: "He was a humanist and one of the last of an endangered species. He believed in and he practiced the life of reason. He never submitted to any of the fads or ideologies or fanaticisms of the twentieth century."

For his part, Krutch observes in *The Modern Temper: A Study and a Confession* (1929), a landmark work of social criticism that Abbey was familiar with, that, "I have no mandate to speak for anyone but myself."[42] A year before his death, Abbey made the same observation in his journals: "In writing, I speak only for myself. But in speaking only for myself, I have discovered, through the years and to my delight, that I speak also for hundreds of thousands of *others* [author's emphasis]. Every one of my books since *Brave Cowboy* has stayed in print, and every single one has sold by now at least fifty thousand copies. Not bad for the most hated, reviled and ignored of modern American writers."[43] Indeed, part of Abbey's attraction was, and still is, that in refusing to censor himself or become another literary shape-shifter, as writers sometimes do for social or guild reasons, he articulated the reader's private thoughts and feelings and became the expressive voice for a much larger group of people. Each essay published by him was as open and direct as a letter to a trusted friend, in the congenial spirit of his model, Montaigne. Abbey's truthful and provocative writings went on to stimulate public debate, which was part of his purpose as a writer—to cause change and make the world a better, or at least a more interesting, place.

Abbey offered a unique voice of dissent among American intellectuals, who tend, as a group, to operate in support of the primary assumptions of the society, as with the perennial utopian theme that began, along with the rhetoric of moral apostasy and declension, with the Puritans. Only Abbey's fellow literary rebel from the 1970s and 1980s, Hunter S. Thompson, exceeded his sense of secular mission in this regard. One could see Abbey, in response to the human-caused global warming thesis, reminding colleagues that as recently as eleven thousand years ago the Laurentide ice shield covered the Midwest, with boreal vegetation extending past the Cumberland Plateau, and that the continental formation vanished rapidly, in geological time, as a result of atmospheric cycles. That was his nature—to examine a subject in a clinical light, acknowledging only established facts, and then draw rational conclusions that would, to his delight, cast popular dogma asunder.

Part of Abbey's attraction was his life-affirming approach to the larger journey. This personal set of beliefs is reflected as much in what he chose to write about as what he chose not to write about. On July 4, 1970, for example, Abbey's twenty-seven-year-old wife Judy died from leukemia in a New York hospital. The author did not draw the blinds, remain in seclusion, and write a first-person narrative of injustice and suffering, with an ironic title like *Independence Day*, but instead left the steel and concrete city and returned to the sunny western deserts. There he produced, with the photographer Philip Hyde, a tribute to, and defense of, the Four Corners region, in *Slickrock* (1971). That strategic choice—embracing life, health, and happiness over death, sadness, and prolonged mourning—represented one of the author's most attractive qualities. He was an eternally questing spirit who, throughout his life, kept moving steadily from the darkness toward the light.

Abbey stood in contrast to many of the nature writers of his time, who often composed essays and books in a gothic mode of anxiety and personal introspection. Representative examples of this melancholy, humorless, and inward-dwelling school can be found in Terry Tempest Williams's graphic family death narrative *Refuge: An Unnatural History of Family and Place*, which David Quammen contemporaneously reviewed in "Palpitating the Tumor" (*Outside* magazine), as well as in the intense psychological essays, such as "Recovering Memory" and "Sliver of Sky," of Barry Lopez. Both authors influenced the genre in their formal roles at the Milkweed Society and the Orion Society during the last decade of the twentieth century and the first decade of the twenty-first century. Their writings represent a significant departure from the mainstream activist traditions of the literary form.

Many other post-Abbey writers similarly veered from the author after his death. When the ethnobotanist and MacArthur fellow Gary Paul Nabhan was asked to contribute to this collection, he replied in an e-mail (August 15, 2013) that Abbey was "an old lech" who was "emotionally dysfunctional and wrong ideologically" and "set back nature writing and environmental conservation by three decades." To Abbey's advocates, the opposite is true—the free-spirited author breathed refreshing life and broader meaning into a senescent literary genre. He also actively led a successful environmental movement that achieved many concrete objectives, a movement that was continued by writers who sometimes failed to reach the literary and political bars that he and others of his generation set.

Readers instinctively look to writers for guidance in the form of affirmation and hope. Keats, on this topic, observes in "The Fall of Hyperion" (1819)
that the poet is a physician. Abbey knew that the best medicine, however
harsh in its elements, is most effectively delivered with an equal measure of
sweetness. He understood, as every schoolchild does with a skinned knee,
that if an injury—whether physical or psychic—is not left alone to heal, it
will continue to bleed and eventually become infected. With those principles
in mind, Abbey kept his reflections on the passing of his third wife for his
journals, where he quietly achieved a confessional catharsis: "During the last
few terrible days, she seemed to me somehow more beautiful than ever—more
sweet and good and brave. She wanted so much to live!"[44] Abbey understood,
as have others in the nature-writing guild (Theodore Roosevelt and Peter
Matthiessen), that the general's courage is not tested until he stands at his
wife's open grave, that grief in extremis can become a journey into solipsism,
and that the greatest tribute a person can make to a loved one lost is to
re-engage with the central currents of life, nature, and society.

By walking away from this catastrophic event, and embracing the source
of his power and freedom—the Southwestern deserts—with the *Slickrock*
project, Abbey saved himself and, once again, his readers. Abbey realized
that each person's state-of-mind represents a conscious choice. The condition of being miserable or, conversely, the opposite of that involves a
philosophical as much as a personal decision. The author knew that our
salvation is in love—love of family, friends, nature, the arts, and country.
This belief was expressed in the epigraph he selected from St. Francis for
his final essay collection: "O Lord, make me an instrument of thy peace.
Where there is hatred, let me sow love, where there is darkness, light; and
where there is sadness, joy." With such thinking and writing, Abbey offered
readers the twin lights of reason and hope.

From his earliest to his last works, Edward Abbey represented a contin-
uation of the Wordsworth-Thoreau-Krutch line. Thoreau was continually
inspired by the revolutionary writings of Wordsworth, who departed the
world on Shakespeare's birthday in 1850, when Thoreau was thirty-three
and preparing to embark on his historic expedition to eastern Canada.
Seventeen years earlier Thoreau's literary and philosophical mentor, Emerson, had made a pilgrimage across the Atlantic to meet Wordsworth at
Rydal Mount. Energized and uplifted by his conversations with the British
laureate, Emerson soon commenced work on his seminal essay "Nature."
Like Wordsworth, the original nature rebel who dreaded, in Rousseau-like

fashion, the coming of modern progress from London to the pristine Lake District (the express train), Thoreau saw industrial society as, quite often, an artificial purgatory. He inveighed against the "quiet despair" of urban life. One of his final acts was to travel to Minnesota, in order to explore a new country. Had the naturalist and philosopher continued westward he would have eventually reached the Upper Missouri of Lewis and Clark, George Caitlin, and John James Audubon. Granted a normal life-span, Thoreau might have produced a significant work on the Yellowstone headwaters and the northern Rockies, as the restless, eastern-raised Muir later did on the Range of Light.

A century later, Krutch, who wrote an influential biography of Thoreau (1948), similarly stood opposed to what he called the "secular Calvinism" of the contemporary era. Like his predecessors, Abbey, who wrote an essay in 1982 entitled "Down the River with Henry Thoreau," had little regard for the forced conformity and anthill drudgery of modern existence. He recoiled from the prevailing belief systems of his time and embraced the principles of Renaissance humanism, which are based upon human rationality, the dignity of the human spirit, and the saving grace of human values.

In a letter to a University of New Mexico Press editor, Abbey stated that if his books had a common theme it was "human freedom in an industrial society."[45] Had he lived, Abbey would have likely emerged as one of the strongest critics of the Internet technology culture, with its hive mentality, new forms of addiction, abandonment of privacy and intellectual property rights, handheld mobile communication devices, trivialization of human interaction (texts, tweets, and e-mails), and ever-dehumanizing products (the new generation of implanted electronic devices that will by the end of the decade quite literally computerize people). The man who considered television a waste of time would have agreed with the statement that people do not own their computers but are rather owned by their computers. He understood that an overload of multitasking and information saturation destroys the ability of the mind to empty itself of nonessential trivia, concentrate on deep ideas, form alternative lines of inquiry, build new conceptual structures, and create unified organic works. It is no coincidence that three of the greatest advancements in the history of science were made by individuals removed by circumstance from their demanding academic routines: Newton, who spent two years isolated in the country at Woolsthorpe during the Great Plague (1665–1667); Darwin, who took a five-year voyage (1832–1836) as chief naturalist on the *Beagle*; and Einstein, who had an eight-year stint (1901–1909) at the Swiss patent office when he was unable to find work as a professor. The same has been true for writers, as with William Wordsworth's productive years at his Lake Country cottage, Thoreau's liberating sojourn at his rustic cabin, and Abbey's restorative time at his Sonoran desert retreat.

For these reasons, Abbey took jobs, well into his forties, as a fire lookout, in order to escape the distractions of the modern world. In books such as *The Journey Home* (1977) and *Beyond the Wall: Essays from the Outside* (1984), Abbey rebelled against the absurdities of regimented society. He saw that those who thought they had been liberated by technology were actually in bondage to another form of master. Like Mark Twain, Abbey believed that humor was a powerful weapon in the eternal war against those who would oppress humankind with new forms of servitude, illusory systems of thought and belief, and false constructs regarding what constitutes the good life. He also believed that one brave act was worth a thousand books, as Dave Foreman reminded everyone in his prepared remarks at Abbey's wake, held at Arches National Park on May 20, 1989.

5

When I reflect upon the totality of Edward Abbey's legacy and his restless, lifelong search for truth and certainty, I recall what Whitman wrote of Thoreau after the two writers had met at the poet's attic residence in Brooklyn: "One thing about Thoreau keeps him very close to me: I refer to his lawlessness—his dissent—his going his own absolute road let hell blaze all it chooses."[46] The same observer who took careful note of Abraham Lincoln—"I see the President almost every day. . . . I saw him this morning about 8 1/2 coming in to business, riding on Vermont avenue, near L street. . . . Mr. Lincoln on the saddle generally rides a good-sired, easy going gray horse, is dressed in plain black, somewhat rusty and dusty, wears a black stiff hat, and looks about as ordinary as the commonest man"—saw in the self-effacing cabin dweller from Walden Pond another kind of American Everyman who was also making a singular contribution to humanity.[47] Like those other two American icons, Whitman and Thoreau, Edward Abbey was both an ordinary citizen and an outspoken nonconformist. He never ceased to contemplate, and vigorously question, the cosmos near and far.

On his journey of sixty-two years, the independent son of self-sufficient Pennsylvanian farmers skeptically examined and discarded one system after another in a determined quest to find what was durable and absolute. At all times the author of *Desert Solitaire*, like the author of *Walden*, was a rationalist in the Greek, Renaissance, and Enlightenment traditions. Abbey understood, as did St. Francis, whose writings provided the prefatory quotation for *One Life at a Time, Please* (1988), that our nature is best revealed in the reverence and love we show for that which is irreplaceable. That is the case whether the object of our devotion is a sun-washed Arizona canyon where the last American jaguars still leave their tracks, or a pair of raptors constructing a nest of twigs and branches on the side of the National Cathedral.

Jamque vale!
J. A. M.
Denver, Colorado

Notes

1. Thomas J. Lyon, *This Incomparable Land: A Guide to American Nature Writing* (Minneapolis, MN: Milkweed, 2001), 112.
2. Edward Abbey, "Science with a Human Face," in *Abbey's Road* (New York: Plume, 1991), 127.
3. Edward Abbey, "Emerson," in *One Life at a Time, Please* (New York: Holt, 1988), 211.
4. Ibid., 212.
5. Michel de Montaigne, "On the Affection of Fathers for Their Children," in *The Essays: Selections*, trans. M. A. Screech (London: Penguin, 1993), 157.
6. Aleksandr Solzhenitsyn, *The First Circle* (London: Collins Press, 1970), 513.
7. Edward Abbey, "A Writer's Credo," in *One Life at a Time*, 165.
8. Qtd. in A. N. Wilson, *Tolstoy* (London: Hamish Hamilton, 1988), 46.
9. Edward Abbey, "Back of Beyond," in *Abbey's Road*, 53.
10. Edward Abbey, "The Outback," in *Abbey's Road*, 40.
11. Edward Abbey, *Confessions of a Barbarian: Selections from the Journals of Edward Abbey, 1951–1989*, ed. David Petersen (Boulder, CO: Johnson Books, 2003), 255.
12. Ibid., 261.
13. Viktor E. Frankl, *Man's Search for Meaning* (New York: Simon and Schuster, 1984), 86.
14. Viktor E. Frankl, *The Doctor and the Soul: From Psychotherapy to Logotherapy*, trans. Clara Winton and Richard Winton (New York: Vintage, 1986), 67–68.
15. Abbey, *Confessions of a Barbarian*, 264.
16. Robert Redford, *The Outlaw Trail: A Journey through Time* (New York: Grosset and Dunlap, 1978), 107.
17. Thomas J. Lyon, "The Nature Essay in the West," in *A Literary History of the West*, ed. Western Literature Association (Ft. Worth: Texas Christian University Press, 1987), 1247.

18. Ibid.

19. Abbey, *Confessions of a Barbarian*, 134.

20. Lyon, "The Nature Essay in the West," 1247.

21. Abbey, *Confessions of a Barbarian*, 254.

22. Edward Abbey to Ed Hoagland, October 31, 1982, in *Postcards from Ed: Dispatches and Salvos from an American Iconoclast*, ed. David Petersen (Minneapolis, MN: Milkweed, 2006), 127.

23. Edward Abbey, introduction to *Abbey's Road*, xvi.

24. Edward Abbey to Alston Chase, December 16, 1987, in *Postcards from Ed*, 224–25.

25. George Packer, "Cheap Words," *New Yorker*, February 17 and 24, 2014.

26. Tony Horwitz, "I Was a Digital Best Seller!," *New York Times*, June 21, 2014.

27. David Carr, "Amazon Absorbing Price Fight Punches," *New York Times*, June 2, 2014.

28. Paul Krugman, "Does He Pass the Test?," *New York Review of Books*, July 10, 2014.

29. Plato, *The Republic*, 2 vols., trans. Paul Shorey (Cambridge, MA: Harvard University Press, 1930), 1: 101.

30. Edward Abbey, "A Writer's Credo," 165.

31. Giorgio Vasari, *The Lives of the Artists*, vol. 1, trans. George Bull (New York: Penguin, 1965), 255.

32. Edward Abbey, "Hallelujah on the Bum," in *The Journey Home: Some Words in Defense of the American West* (New York: Plume, 1991), 10.

33. Qtd. in Hershel Parker, *Herman Melville: A Biography*, vol. 1 (Baltimore, MD: Johns Hopkins University Press, 1996), 842.

34. Maurice Bowra, *The Greek Experience* (Cleveland, OH: World Publishing Company, 1957), 3, 11–12.

35. Edward Abbey, "The Great American Desert," in *The Journey Home*, 12.

36. Qtd. in Joseph Foster, *D. H. Lawrence in Taos* (Albuquerque: University of New Mexico Press, 1972), 51.

37. Qtd. in Flannery Burke, *From Greenwich Village to Taos: Primitivism and Place at Mabel Doge Luhan's* (Lawrence: University Press of Kansas, 2008), 177.

38. D. H. Lawrence, "The Spirit of the Place," in *Studies in Classic American Literature*, ed. Ezra Greenspan, Lindeth Vasey, and John Worthen (Cambridge: Cambridge University Press, 2014), 167.

39. Edward Abbey, "Desert Places," in *The Journey Home*, 65.

40. Abbey, *Confessions of a Barbarian*, 113.

41. Ibid., 115.

42. Joseph Wood Krutch, *The Modern Temper: A Study and a Confession* (New York: Mariner, 1956), xv.

43. Abbey, *Confessions of a Barbarian*, 361.

44. Ibid., 240.

45. Edward Abbey to Ms. Heist, Editor, University of New Mexico Press, November 22, 1977, in *Postcards from Ed*, 81.

46. Qtd. in Robert D. Richardson, *Henry Thoreau: A Life of the Mind* (Berkeley: University of California Press, 1986), 349.

47. Walt Whitman, *Specimen Days and Collect*, in *The Norton Anthology of American Literature*, vol. 1, ed. by Nina Baym et al. (New York: Norton, 1985), 2125.

PART 1

SCHOLARLY PERSPECTIVES

It is not the writer's task to answer questions but to question answers.
To be impertinent, insolent, and, if necessary, subversive.

—EDWARD ABBEY, *A VOICE CRYING IN THE WILDERNESS* (1989)

Newspaper Rock, Utah (May 1999)

CHAPTER 1

Equal Parts Anger and Love
A Posthumous Interview with Edward Abbey

KATHLEEN DEAN MOORE

HOW DESPERATELY THE west—and the wild, and the world—needs
Edward Abbey today. What would he make of the stamper trucks shaking
red rocks off the cliffs? What fine adjectives would he find for the drilling
rigs on fracking pads spattered all the way from the Uinta Basin to the
San Juan River? What would he say to the oil company executives who
are cheerfully taking down the great natural systems that sustain life on
the planet in order to jack up profits that are already the highest since the
pharaohs? How would he grieve for his beloved spotted toads, besieged
by global warming, pipelines, and roads? What would he say when he
climbed to the hidden springs—where for centuries the mountain lions have
lain down with the lizards—to find the water gone, poisoned and forced
underground to fracture the rock to release the natural gas to earn a fat
CEO $22 million a year? What would he say about the silent masses, the
corrupted science, the solipsistic consumers and sociopathic corporations?
What could he tell us gloomy citizens about our moral responsibilities in
a time of global warming and ecosystem collapse?

But Ed's gone, either gently desiccating in a desert grave or swearing
softly in heaven, having ascended with his soul tied tightly to the soul of
Leslie McKee's wife, a kind Mormon woman who promised she would
carry him heavenward when she herself went. All the same, his fierce love
of the world is still with us in his rampaging books and letters. I found
him in Powell's Books in Portland, Oregon, dog-eared and leaning slightly
to the left, in a crowded section labeled "nature." Then, with some serious
slicing and splicing, I deciphered his answers to the questions that have
been haunting me.[1]

Here is what he said:

KDM: If you drove a nail through the center of this decade, all of planetary history would swing in the balance. Global warming, massive extinction, poisonous air and land and water—all these have brought us to a hinge point in history. In this decade, we will lose it all, or we will redeem a just and thriving planet. Just telling you. Do you have words to describe this peril?

EA: Humanity has entrapped itself in the burning splendor of *technikos*.[2] We are cursed with a plague of diggers, drillers, borers, grubbers, of asphalt spreaders, dambuilders, overgrazers, clear-cutters, and strip miners whose object seems to be to make our mountains match our men—to make molehills out of mountains for a race of rodents, for the rat race.[3] My god, I'm thinking, what incredible shit we put up with most of our lives.[4] The present course is one of premeditated suicide.[5] We are befouling and destroying our own home, we are committing a slow but accelerating life murder—planetary biocide.[6]

KDM: You're a well-credentialed philosopher, Mr. Edward Abbey, MA from UNM. Philosophers believe in the power of ideas to shape history. We know that it's a crackpot cosmology that got the world into this scrape—a world view that brags that humans are separate from and superior to the earth, in charge and in control, that the planet and all its lives have no value except in their usefulness to ours. We need a new set of answers to the foundational questions of the human condition. What is the world? What is the place of humans in the world? How, then, shall we live? Do you know the answers?

EA: Though a sucker for philosophy all of my life I am not a thinker but—a toucher. I believe in nothing that I cannot touch, kiss, embrace—whether a woman, a child, a rock, a tree, a bear, a shaggy dog. The rest is hearsay.[7] What else is there? What else do we need?[8]

Religions, all of them, tend to divorce men and women from the earth, from other forms of life.[9] We are obliged to spread the news, painful and bitter though it may be for some to hear, that all living things on the earth are kindred.[10] We are kindred, all of us, killer and victim, predator and prey, me and the sly coyote, the soaring buzzard, the elegant gopher snake, the trembling cottontail, the foul worms that feed on our entrails, all of them, all of us.[11]

KDM: But if all of us are kin, then surely we don't have the right to treat every creature in the whole buzzing world like chattel slaves, as if they belonged to us to ruin or to auction—coyotes and gut-shot cactus, entire fields of mice and crows. What would you call for instead?

EA: Recognition of the rights of other living things to a place of their own, a role of their own, an evolution of their own not influenced by human pressures. A recognition, even, of the right of nonliving things—boulders, for example, or an entire mountain—to be left in peace.[12] In demanding that humans behave with justice, tolerance, reason, love toward other forms of life, we are doing no more than demanding that humans be true to the best aspects of human nature.[13]

KDM: The kinship metaphor suggests that we and our brothers and sisters on the land share a common home. What does that tell us about what we ought to do?

EA: With bulldozer, earth mover, chainsaw, and dynamite, the international industries are bashing their way into our forests, mountains, and rangelands and looting them for everything they can get away with. This for the sake of short-term profits in the private sector and multimillion dollar annual salaries for the three-piece-suited gangsters.[14]

If our true home is threatened with invasion, pillage, and destruction—as it certainly is—then we have the right to defend that home, by whatever means are necessary. We have the right to resist, and we have the obligation. Not to defend that which we love would be dishonorable.[15]

Be of good cheer, the military-industrial state will soon collapse. Meanwhile, we must do all in our power to oppose, resist, and subvert its desperate aggrandizements. As a matter of course. As a matter of honor.[16]

KDM: Really, by whatever means are necessary? Killing?

EA: Not people. We're talking about bulldozers. Power shovels.[17]

KDM: Breaking the law?

EA: Why not?[18] You think this is a picnic or something?[19] The "choice-of-evils" statute allows the intentional commission of an illegal act when the purpose of such act is to prevent a greater harm or a greater crime.[20] "Protest is always justified," said Gofman, "when it is the only means to make a deaf government listen."[21]

KDM: But blowing up a railroad bridge, pushing a loader into the drink, as in *The Monkey Wrench Gang*? These days, people would call that ecoterrorism, and it'd be a long time before any one of your heroes passed a bottle around the campfire again. Police don't like gang members either; they shoot them.

EA: Let's have some precision in language here: terrorism means deadly violence—for a political and/or economic purpose—carried out against people and other living things, and it is usually conducted by governments against their own citizens or by corporate entities against the land and all creatures that depend upon the land for life and livelihood. A bulldozer ripping up a hillside to strip-mine for coal is committing terrorism. Sabotage, on the other hand, means the use of force against inanimate property. The characters in *Monkey Wrench* do this only when it appears that all other means of defense of land and life have failed and that force—the final resort—is morally justified. Not only justified but a moral obligation.[22]

KDM: We've got to talk about moral obligation. You wouldn't believe how many people treat environmental emergencies as just technological or scientific problems, economic problems, or even national security problems. But honestly, taking whatever you want for your profligate life and leaving a dangerous and ransacked world for the next generation is a moral failure, and it calls for a moral response. You're a philosopher: what are some of the moral reasons why we have to push back against the forces of destruction?

EA: What I am concerned about is the world my children will have to live in, and maybe, if my children get around to it, the world of my grandchildren.[23]

KDM: That is a good utilitarian argument for action, based on the hope that it might make a difference to the people you care about. But you write so often about honor and dishonor that I wonder if you are working toward a virtue ethic, judging the rightness of actions not by whether they save the world (they probably won't) but whether they spring from a virtuous character . . .

EA (*interrupting*): And high moral purpose—concern for right and wrong, justice and injustice, truth and falsehood, beauty and ugliness.[24]

KDM: And an obligation to be loyal to the earth?

EA: Loyalty to the earth, the earth that bore us and sustains us, the only home we shall ever know, the only paradise we ever need—if only we had the eyes to see. Original sin, the true original sin, is the blind destruction for the sake of greed of this natural paradise that lies all around us—if only we were worthy of it.[25]

In any case, the beauty and existence of the natural world should be sufficient justification in itself for saving it all.[26]

KDM: Now you're talking as though the natural world has intrinsic value—value in and of itself, not just because it's useful to us. Are you affirming that the natural world should exist for its own sake, for its beauty and mystery and wonder?

EA: You bet, Doc.[27] Its significance lies in the power of the odd and unexpected to startle the senses and surprise the mind out of its ruts of habit, to compel us into a reawakened awareness of the wonderful—that which is full of wonder. For a few moments, we discover that nothing can be taken for granted, for if this ring of stone is marvelous, then all which shaped it is marvelous, and our journey here on Earth, during which we are able to see and touch and hear in the midst of tangible and mysterious things-in-themselves, is the most strange and daring of all adventures.[28]

KDM: What is the special obligation of a writer in this astonishing but desperately wounded world?

EA: I believe that words count, that writing matters, that poems, essays, and novels—in the long run—make a difference.[29] The writer's job is to write, and write the truth—especially unpopular truth.[30] Especially truth that offends the powerful, the rich, the well established.[31] But he also has the moral obligation to get down in the dust and the sweat and lend not only his name but his voice and body to the tiresome contest. How far can you go in objectivity, in temporizing, in fence straddling, before it becomes plain moral cowardice?[32] "It is always the writer's duty," Samuel Johnson said, "to make the world better."[33]

KDM: But what is your vision of a better world? It's easier to imagine the end of the world than the end of business as usual. The financial power of the fossil fuel industry has really done a job on our democracy. But maybe that doesn't matter; Plato didn't think much of democracies anyway. Democracies always turn into plutocracies, the rule of the rich, he said, because rich people can buy votes. And plutocracies always turn into anarchies, because the people won't stand for injustice forever. So that's the vision we're left with? Anarchy?

EA: Anarchy is democracy taken seriously. An anarchist community would consist of a voluntary association of free and independent families, self-reliant and self-supporting but bound by kinship ties and a tradition of mutual aid.[34]

KDM: I just don't know how to get there. It's hard for activists to find a focus these days. Already the world is knocked off kilter—big storms, rising water, starving people on the move. What kept you going? What powered your steadfast efforts to defend the land?

EA: Equal parts anger and love.[35]

KDM: But how did you keep from falling into utter despair?

EA: Thoreau said, "Who hears the rippling of rivers will not utterly despair of anything." That makes sense.[36] Where there is no joy, there can be no courage, and without courage all other virtues are useless.[37] One single act of defiance against power, against the state that seems omnipotent but is not, transforms and transfigures the human personality.[38] The search for transcendence and integrity and truth goes on.[39] Best to march forth boldly, with or without life jackets, keep your matches dry, and pray for the best.[40]

KDM: I don't know where you are now, Edward Abbey. But I hope that maybe some of us citizens (of the U.S.A., of the planet) might find you in ourselves—the bravura, the common sense, the ferocious truth, the anger, and the love that will empower us to save your "unpleasant solpugids" and your slickrock—and maybe even save our own sorry skins.

All the mining and drilling, the burning, burning, the thunder and the roar—all the oily gases, and now the melting planet with its crazy storms—all the dying, dear god, the unnamed creatures, the singing frogs, the children of the future, whose small voices cannot call out to us. It's moral monstrosity on a cosmic scale. We can't allow it. From your place in the stony cycles of the planet, what is your advice to us?

EA: It's time to get fucking back to work.[41]

Notes

1. All of the sentences herein attributed to Edward Abbey are his alone, gleaned from his books and letters, although not all the words in his sentences are herein. That is, I have not changed any words, but I have left some out if the omission doesn't change the meaning. Many of the sentences are wildly out of context, but they seem to make good sense in their new combination, so I think that's OK. I trust that Ed will want to share them, to "let himself be used as the voice for those who share his view of earthly affairs, his emotions and discoveries, aspirations and hopes" (Edward Abbey, "A Writer's Credo," in *One Life at a Time, Please* [New York: Henry Holt, 1988], 163).

2. Edward Abbey, "MX," in *Down the River* (New York: Dutton, 1982), 93.

3. Edward Abbey, "Down the River with Henry Thoreau," in *Down the River*, 34.

4. Edward Abbey, *Desert Solitaire: A Season in the Wilderness* (New York: Touchstone, 1990), 155.

5. Edward Abbey, "Of Protest," in *Down the River*, 105.

6. Edward Abbey, "A Writer's Credo," in *One Life at a Time, Please*, 177.

7. Edward Abbey, "Meeting the Bear," in *Down the River*, 57.

8. Edward Abbey, preface to *Desert Solitaire*, xiii.

9. Edward Abbey, *Postcards from Ed: Dispatches and Salvos from an American Iconoclast*, ed. David Petersen (Minneapolis, MN: Milkweed Editions), 93.

10. Edward Abbey, *Desert Solitaire*, 21.

11. Ibid., 34.

12. Edward Abbey, "River of No Return," in *Down the River*, 119.

13. Edward Abbey, *Postcards from Ed*, 94.

14. Edward Abbey, "Eco-Defense," in *One Life at a Time, Please*, 30.

15. Ibid., 31.

16. Edward Abbey, "Preliminary Notes," in *Down the River*, 4.

17. Edward Abbey, *The Monkey Wrench Gang* (New York: Avon Books, 1992), 58.

18. Ibid., 101.

19. Ibid., 77.

20. Edward Abbey, "Of Protest," in *Down the River*, 103.

21. Ibid., 109.

22. Edward Abbey, *Postcards from Ed*, 129.

23. Ibid., 93.

24. Edward Abbey, "Free Speech," in *Down the River*, 9.

25. Edward Abbey, *Desert Solitaire*, 167.

26. Edward Abbey, "River of No Return," in *Down the River*, 120.

27. Edward Abbey, *The Monkey Wrench Gang*, 79.

28. Edward Abbey, *Desert Solitaire*, 36–37.

29. Edward Abbey, "A Writer's Credo," in *One Life at a Time, Please*, 162.

30. Edward Abbey, *Postcards from Ed*, 214.

31. Edward Abbey, "A Writer's Credo," in *One Life at a Time, Please*, 163.

32. Edward Abbey, *Postcards from Ed*, p. 215.

33. Edward Abbey, "A Writer's Credo," in *One Life at a Time, Please*, 178.

34. Edward Abbey, "Theory of Anarchy," in *One Life at a Time, Please*, 26.

35. Edward Abbey, "A Writer's Credo," in *One Life at a Time, Please*, 176.

36. Edward Abbey, "Preliminary Notes," in *Down the River*, 3.

37. Edward Abbey, *Desert Solitaire*, 125.

38. Edward Abbey, "Of Protest," in *Down the River*, 108.

39. Edward Abbey, "My Friend Debris," in *One Life at a Time, Please*, 216.

40. Edward Abbey, *Desert Solitaire*, 240.

41. Edward Abbey, *The Monkey Wrench Gang*, 123.

CHAPTER 2

One Man's Terrorist

Reclaiming Edward Abbey for the Post-9/11 Era

MICHAEL BRANCH

THIRTY YEARS AGO, near the trailhead of one of the career paths I did not ultimately take, I worked as an antiterrorist specialist at a federal agency in Washington, D.C. I was then finishing college, and I didn't yet have the slightest idea of the difference between the life of a real intelligence agent and that of the glamorous James Bond, who seemed to me an excellent role model for a twenty-one-year-old boy. And while 1984 wasn't a time of the Cuban missile crisis–style Cold War, it was chilly enough just the same. That summer the USSR and thirteen of its Eastern Bloc allies had boycotted the Olympic Games in Los Angeles, and in early September the Soviets downed Korean Airlines Flight 007, killing 269 people including a U.S. congressman. November brought Able Archer 83, a NATO military exercise so expansive that it made us wonder if the folks whose sweaty fingers were on the nuke buttons feared 1984 scenarios far worse than those George Orwell had contemplated. Gorbachev's reforms would soon bring better days, but in 1984 none of us had heard the words "perestroika" and "glasnost." We knew only that those bomb shelters we had in our suburban northern Virginia backyards—shelters that throughout high school we regarded as Khrushchev-era monuments useful only as places to drink beer and make out with girls—started to look like they might need restocking with potable water and beans.

Although I worked with intelligence field agents—men and women whose dedication and sacrifice are still inspiring to me—my own job was incredibly mundane. I was charged with helping to build a database of terrorist incidents in order to establish a useable body of data that analysts could later search for patterns. I'd sit down every morning with a cup of coffee and a banker's box full of classified files, each of which documented a specific terrorist incident. Some were massive, like the 1983 U.S. Embassy bombing in Beirut, in which sixty-three people were killed. Other incidents were, at least by the standards of the job, minor: a diplomatic kidnapping, say, or yet another kneecapping of some guy who had crossed the Irish Republican Army. My job was to turn each file into a little story, a vignette that neatly summarized the event and also employed terms that might later be useful in seeking patterns: *AK-47, letter bomb, RPG, parrilla, strychnine, sniper, decapitation, piano wire.* The files also contained graphic photographs. One day I wrote a narrative about a man who had been walking his dog in his neighborhood when a car slowed down and someone inside it put a bullet through his forehead. As it turned out, the terrorists had assassinated the wrong man. This particular dead father and husband was an accountant who just happened to be in the wrong place at the wrong time. This was my first job as a professional writer. I did it every day, all day long. I even wore a tie.

During this same period my environmental consciousness was being raised, and I found myself deeply concerned about a range of environmentally destructive practices, especially clear-cutting and strip-mining in the central Appalachians. As shocked as I was that these devastating practices were permitted, I was equally surprised at the lack of outrage they triggered. The mainstream media covered these atrocities with antiseptic cost-benefit analyses and, as today, much bemoaning of the jobs that might be lost if sustainable practices were adopted. Worse still, I noted an unaccountable dearth of discussion showing even a hint of ethical concern. Having educated myself about the issues, I was convinced that strip mining and clear-cutting were not only ill advised but in fact wrong, and yet I heard no conversation indicating that, like racial segregation or human trafficking, these acts of environmental violence should be stopped because they were morally unjustifiable.

At about this time some forest activists with whom I was collaborating on a road closure initiative passed along a tattered copy of the newsletter of Earth First!, which had been founded just a few years earlier, in 1980, and was gaining momentum. The newsletter was full of outrage and humor and creativity, but amid the cartoons and editorials were helpful discussions of concepts like biocentrism, deep ecology, and direct activism. I didn't agree with everything I read, but I was gratified to find that somebody somewhere was finally talking about things that mattered so much to me. I soon subscribed to the newsletter—a simple act that I would later discover almost certainly earned me an FBI file—and began to follow with interest the group's activities. When in the spring of 1985 Earth Firsters descended on the Willamette National Forest to protest logging there, it was clear that the beliefs articulated in their rag were more than just talk.

This was also the period in which I discovered the work of Edward Abbey. I was already a devotee of American writers like Emerson and Thoreau—and, later, Wendell Berry, Annie Dillard, and Gary Snyder— whose forceful expression of the aesthetic, ethical, and spiritual value of nature had profoundly influenced my decision to leave the antiterrorism business and instead pursue a life as a writer, teacher, and activist. I wish very much that I could re-experience my first reading of Abbey. I recognize the value of rereading books we admire, but there is something unrepeatably galvanic, fresh, and transformative in that first encounter with a writer whose work touches us deeply. I recall feeling that in Abbey I had finally found a voice that was speaking to my deepest feelings of both love and outrage.

I first read *The Monkey Wrench Gang* during the summer of 1985, while driving my old pickup from the Blue Ridge Mountains toward the wide open American West that Abbey treasured but that I had never before seen. I was at that time deeply naïve about the risks of direct action environmentalism. Only later would I meet committed activists like Dave Foreman and Paul Watson, whose sacrifices in the interest of resistance to environmental abuse made clear the very real costs of that resistance. *The Monkey Wrench Gang*, especially when paired with the sustained philosophical arguments that animate *Desert Solitaire*, exposed me to three core ideas I had never seen expressed so cogently before, and that have profoundly shaped my subsequent thinking and writing about nature.

The first of these ideas is that moral outrage in response to environmental exploitation is warranted and necessary. Abbey once observed that "love implies anger. The man who is angered by nothing cares about nothing." It is a deliberately provocative statement, and one that is useful because it asks us to consider what we love enough to be angry at the prospect of losing. I had felt not only frustrated but actually wounded by the blown-out clear-cuts I observed throughout Appalachia, and like any injured animal I wanted to fight back. But we live in a culture in which intensely passionate expressions of concern are often stigmatized as counterproductive. Reading Abbey made me wonder how often our willingness to keep quiet, to be reasonable, provides effectual aid and support to those few who profit obscenely from the destruction of the places we love. I was reminded, in fact, of that memorable line from Henry Thoreau's *Walden*: "The greater part of what my neighbors call good I believe in my soul to be bad, and if I repent of anything, it is very likely to be my good behavior." Abbey understood that good behavior can sometimes be a form of complicity, and so he offered the emancipatory insight that anger on behalf of the land is justified and that action in response to that anger may be morally required. "Sentiment without action," writes Abbey, "is the ruin of the soul."

The genius of the second idea I derived from reading *The Monkey Wrench Gang* lay precisely in Abbey's ability to show why this second idea does not in fact contradict the first. It is only this: if you love the land, enjoy it. The simplicity of this directive to get outside and recreate in nature is deceptive, for if we are angry as hell about environmental destruction, how are we to simply suspend that fury in order to go have fun? If our cause is as urgent as we claim it is, won't stepping away from activist efforts expose us as selfish or hypocritical? And how are we environmental activists to shake off the grief associated with our fight long enough to achieve the buoyancy of spirit necessary to really enjoy ourselves? Australian philosopher Glenn Albrecht has coined the useful term "solastalgia" to refer to the psychic distress produced by environmental devastation; how then are we to shed this solastalgic anguish for the purposes of outdoor recreation? Despite the apparent contradiction here, Abbey nevertheless insisted that the only true preventative for activist burnout was enjoyment of the land we fight to protect. "Be as I am—a reluctant enthusiast . . . a part-time crusader, a half-hearted fanatic," he advises. "It is not enough to fight for the land; it is even more important to enjoy it. While you can. While it's still here. . . . Enjoy yourselves, keep your brain in your head and your head firmly attached to the body, the body active and alive, and I promise you this much: I promise you this one sweet victory over our enemies, over those desk-bound men and women with their hearts in a safe deposit box and their eyes hypnotized by desk calculators. I promise you this: you will outlive the bastards." I've always appreciated that while Abbey rallied us to fight to save the world, he also gave us permission to make that fight a part-time job.

The third idea I encountered while reading Abbey has been absolutely critical in shaping who I have become as an environmentalist and as a writer. Abbey was the first environmental writer I discovered who was genuinely funny and who therefore seemed to give his blessing to the idea that serious work could and probably should be done with good humor. More than that, he showed that satirical humor, far from simply offering comic relief from the disappointments and defeats inevitably associated with environmental activism, could be a powerful weapon in striking at forms of authority that underwrite the destruction of nature. In his insightful 1957 essay "The Decline of American Humor," Kenneth Rexroth explains that "great humor has a savagery about it," because powerful satirical comedy prompts "the realization that the accepted, official version of anything is most likely false and that all authority is based on fraud" while also fortifying us with "the courage to face and act on these two conclusions." Abbey deployed comedy tactically, even paraphrasing Walt Whitman's benediction to his readers: "This is what you shall do: Be loyal to what you love, be true to the earth, fight your enemies with passion and laughter." Though he certainly wasn't above a puerile joke now and then, Abbey should be regarded as a member of that venerable lineage of satirists who wield laughter in support of the larger ethical imperative of their work. As Wendell Berry puts it in his spirited and elegant defense of Edward Abbey in *What Are People For?: Essays*, "Humor, in Mr. Abbey's work, is a function of his outrage, and is therefore always answering to necessity."

Of course we live in a different age now, and not only because population growth and rampant resource extraction have transformed the American West in many of the ways Edward Abbey feared they would. It is hard not to wonder what Abbey would make of our anemic response to global climate change, our stubborn failure to reform devastating mining practices, our forfeiture of public lands to the fracking boom, or even the collusion of corporate communications companies with the incredible overreaching of the same intelligence gatherers for whom I once wrote small, terrifying stories in exchange for a paycheck. The role of our government in causing these problems—or at least in failing to take responsibility for helping to solve them—brings to mind Abbey's incisive admonition that "a patriot must always be ready to defend his country against his government."

I suspect that in our own historical moment few would regard Ed Abbey as a patriot. One unfortunate consequence of having Abbey on one side of those flaming twin towers and ourselves on the other is that his morally justifiable brand of direct action environmentalism risks being swept up in the wide net of antiterrorist rhetoric that is now being dragged indiscriminately through American culture. Terrorism is the act of coolly firing a bullet into a man's kneecap to deliberately maim him for life. It is firebombing a synagogue full of worshippers because you don't like the god they're praying to in there. It is raping a man's young daughter in front of him before strapping him to a metal bedframe, attaching electrodes to his neck, and slowly turning up the juice. I know because I wrote those stories. We needn't approve of dumping sand into the crankcase of a D9 tractor in order to recognize how different this act is from an act of terrorism. Using a chainsaw to fell a billboard is no more violent than using a welding machine to construct one, just as the removal of a set of surveyor's stakes is no more destructive than having driven them in the first place.

My point here is not that we should endorse the destruction of property but rather that we should acknowledge—as the FBI's explicit definition of "ecoterrorism" importantly does not—that there is both a real and an ethical difference between harming property and harming people. Perhaps it should not be surprising that in a nation where corporations are accorded the rights of individuals and money is a legally protected form of political self-expression we are so easily confused about the distinction between property and people and thus between activism and terrorism. It is important to recognize that Edward Abbey, who once said, "I hate and fear violence," was not similarly confused. "Let's have some precision in language here," he writes. "Terrorism means deadly violence—for a political and/or economical purpose—carried out against people and other living things, and is usually conducted by governments against their own citizens (as at Kent State, or in Vietnam, or in Poland, or in most of Latin America right now), or by corporate entities such as J. Paul Getty, Exxon, Mobil Oil, etc. etc., against the land and all creatures that depend upon the land for life and livelihood." If we must use the term "ecoterrorist" to refer to those who destroy the nonhuman world, it would in fact be more accurate to use it to describe Halliburton, BP, Barrick, Massey, Duke, and Weyerhaeuser. However, my own brief professional experience with terrorism suggests that we would be better advised to reserve the term "terrorist" for a person who engages in the always morally unconscionable use of violence against people. I understand that one man's terrorist is another man's freedom fighter, but surely we can develop a semantics that is sufficiently nuanced to distinguish between a person who murders runners at the Boston Marathon and another who occupies an old-growth redwood in an attempt to prevent its destruction.

In reckoning the rich legacy of Edward Abbey, I am reminded of the important struggles our country has endured. When, in 1773, the Sons of Liberty destroyed the property of the East India Company by dumping it into Boston Harbor, they engaged in a form of direct activism that powerfully asserted American rights and freedoms. To the degree that this bold act helped precipitate the American Revolution, it might even be said that the sovereignty of our nation can be traced to precisely the kind of resistance Abbey endorsed. I think of the immense courage of radical abolitionists during the 1850s, men and women of principle who broke the law by "stealing" slaves from their masters and helping them achieve freedom. I think of the mass incarceration of civil rights protestors a century later, when whites and blacks alike violated segregationist laws in numbers so great as to turn the tide of the fight toward racial justice. While it will certainly take longer than forty years to evaluate Abbey's legacy, I consider him a patriot whose radicalism is absolutely in the American grain. He was a pioneer in offering a compelling, forceful, philosophically consistent articulation of the ethical grounds for resistance to the rampant violence of environmental destruction.

Of course I understand that Abbey was a self-styled provocateur, that irreverence and confrontation were his stock-in-trade as a writer. I strongly disagree with the stance he took on a number of issues, and I disapprove of much that has been done in his name. But the lesson of history is that power is rarely relinquished without a fight and that institutionalized injustice has deep roots. I suspect that posterity will judge us harshly for failing to act decisively in the face of widespread environmental destruction, and so it may be that Abbey's controversial radicalism will ultimately be understood in the tradition of American revolutionaries and progressives such as Thomas Jefferson, Thomas Paine, Harriet Beecher Stowe, Henry David Thoreau, John Muir, Susan B. Anthony, Woody Guthrie, Rachel Carson, and Cesar Chavez. In the meantime, even those of us who live in post-9/11 America, where the dangerous label of "terrorist" is sometimes applied as indiscriminately as "communist" once was, might begin by making an honest attempt to answer the hard question that Henry in Abbey's novel *A Fool's Progress* confronts us with: "But if the end don't justify the means, what can?"

CHAPTER 3

Edward Abbey on Immigration

JOHN ALCOCK

ILLEGAL IMMIGRANTS, PERHAPS especially those from Mexico and Central America, have a hard time of it. Several hundred are known to have died each year since 2000 in the attempt to cross the border into the United States without the required authorization. Others have surely perished unknown to the authorities because their bodies have never been found. Accounts of particular deaths are wrenching, as in the case of Omar, a thirteen-year-old Guatemalan boy, who tried to negotiate the Arizonan desert in the company of others but failed, dying of heat exposure as did an older woman in his group after they were abandoned by the coyote who was taking them and some others into Arizona. Omar's mother was already in Phoenix waiting for the arrival of a son who never came. The gripping story of his short and unhappy life has been told in Terry Greene Sterling's "Death in the Desert—Is Immigration Reform Killing the American Dream?" (*Newsweek*, July 7, 2010).

Sterling suggests that the efforts of the authorities in the United States to block illegal immigration have increased the risks for aliens who seek to cross over in the less populated and relatively unguarded parts of the border, those sections between Texas and California that are direst, hottest, and most dangerous. In Arizona many undocumented persons try to enter the United States by passing through the Tohono O'odham Indian Reservation, a remote and extremely arid part of the Sonoran Desert. Prior to the increase in border security, undocumented migrants generally had one day's walk to the point where they would be picked up and driven to a destination; now they generally have to walk at night for two or even three days before they meet their coyote's associates in a car or van.

Sonoran Desert near the
Mexican border (April
1995)

During the heat of the summer, the journey on foot through southern Arizona is especially perilous, as it was for Omar and his companion.

When Omar died he had been separated from his mother for four years, during which time he begged his mother to let him come to the United States to join her and his older siblings who had preceded him. It is not hard to understand why his mother finally supplied her young son with the money to pay for his trip north. Nor is it odd that a group called Humane Borders has placed water tanks in the Arizonan desert along trails known to be used by undocumented migrants in order to, as the website says, "take death out of the immigration equation."

But most Arizonans vigorously support the goal of blocking illegal entry into the United States. The legislative proposal Arizona SB 1070 (Support Our Law Enforcement and Safe Neighborhoods Act) was signed into law by Governor Jan Brewer in April 2010 to the general approval of the citizens of the state. A Rasmussen poll at the time reported 70 percent support for SB 1070, which was viewed by many elsewhere as a draconian anti-immigration law. Among its provisions was the requirement that all persons who were stopped because they were suspected of being illegal aliens must have their identification papers handy. In addition, police were required to determine the immigration status of the persons they detained for any reason. True, the Supreme Court ruled as unconstitutional many aspects of SB 1070, but the point is that most of the citizens of Edward Abbey's home ground want to keep people from crossing the border illegally. This conclusion receives further support from the reelection of the vehemently anti-immigrant Sheriff Joe Arpaio for the fifth time in 2012 despite a host of damaging claims against him ranging from abuse of power to racial profiling to failure to investigate sex crimes in favor of trying to round up illegal aliens in sweeps through Latino neighborhoods.

Ed Abbey died in 1989, before Sheriff Joe came to be Maricopa County's chief law enforcement officer and long before opposition to immigration, especially of the illegal variety, became an essential part of the policies advocated by Republicans at all levels of government. But Abbey in some sense anticipated the future when he wrote an anti-immigration essay that he intended to publish in the *New York Times*, according to James M. Cahalan in *Edward Abbey: A Life*. After reading Abbey's offering, the *New York Times* withdrew its invitation. In fact, it did not even give Abbey a kill fee for the rejected op-ed piece. But we can read what he had to say about the subject online ("Edward Abbey on Immigration," compassrosebooks.blogspot.com, October 29, 2009).

Abbey's essay is not temperate, not middle of the road, not evenhanded. His position can be deduced from the following excerpt: "It might be wise for us as American citizens to consider calling a halt to the mass influx of even more millions of hungry, ignorant, unskilled, and culturally-morally-genetically impoverished people. At least until we have brought our own affairs into order. Especially when these uninvited millions bring with them an alien mode of life which—let us be honest about this—is not appealing to the majority of Americans."

Abbey's advice to our government was straightforward: "Therefore— let us close our national borders to any further mass immigration, legal or illegal, from any source, as does every other nation on Earth. The means are available, it's a simple technical-military problem. Even our Pentagon should be able to handle it."

In the years that have followed since Abbey wrote this essay, we have seen that Abbey was more than a little optimistic about the possibility that technical-military means exist to solve the issue of illegal immigration. Despite the expenditure of literally billions of dollars on border enforcement, illegal aliens, undocumented workers, desperate Latinos, whatever you choose to call them, still make their way into the United States across the border, some (including Omar) dying in the attempt, others finding work in Phoenix, or Chicago, or New York.

Abbey's views on immigration were, needless to say, controversial, and he was accused more than once of being a racist. But anyone who thinks that Abbey had gone from being a benign nature writer to a professional curmudgeon in the years since he wrote *Desert Solitaire* has not read this superb book. In it he lays the foundation for his later opposition to immigration, particularly in the chapter entitled "Polemic: Industrial Tourism and the National Parks." There he urges that cars be banned from national parks and that visitors be forced to use their own two legs, or bicycles, or horses to explore what these places have to offer rather than rely on automobiles and paved roads. He then poses a couple of rhetorical questions: What about children? What about the "aged and infirm"? Abbey is strongly unsympathetic to the notion that car travel is necessary for the very young and very old, noting that youngsters will grow older and have their chance at a later date to see the parks whereas oldsters had the opportunity to visit the parks at a time when they were less overrun with people than they are at the time of his writing (in the 1960s). Here is a man unafraid to take a stand sure to anger some while causing others of a more politically correct orientation to wince at the very least. I imagine that Abbey would acknowledge the sadness of Omar's death but urge that we accept his fate as a necessary price to pay to discourage unwanted immigrants from entering our country.

And what is the basis for Abbey's willingness to risk offending his readers? He believed that there were already in the 1960s far too many people in the United States. His position is unequivocal. "It will be objected that a constantly increasing population makes resistance [to automotive tourism in the national parks] and conservation a hopeless battle. This is true. Unless a way is found to stabilize the nation's population, the parks cannot be saved. Or anything else worth a damn."

In the years since the publication of *Desert Solitaire*, the population of the United States has continued to grow, despite Abbey's wishes. In 1968, the year in which this book appeared, our nation had about 200 million citizens; today in 2013, there are 315 million of us, an increase of well over 50 percent in less than fifty years. Even by 1989, the year of Abbey's death, the trend was obvious to all, although occasionally those unaware of the fact that populations grow when there are more births than deaths will claim that our population is at or on the verge of stability because we are at or near replacement rate. (Even if couples have only two children, the population will grow when there are more and more women reaching the age of reproduction, as is true in most third world countries and in the United States as well.)

For someone as convinced as Abbey was that the national parks and everything else worth a damn were threatened by a "constantly increasing population," immigration is not good. This viewpoint explains why, long before the current brouhaha about illegal immigration, Abbey began his campaign against permitting more people to enter the United States legally or in any other way. The racist tag as applied to Abbey arises because Mexicans and others from south of the border make up the bulk of the illegal immigrants to the United States.

In the immediate post-Abbey census, the U.S. Census Bureau reported that about 5 percent of our population was Hispanic; currently about 17 percent of the U.S. population falls into this category. Indeed, in one year between 2010 and 2011, the Hispanic population grew by 1.3 million, more than half the total increase for the nation as a whole. Much of this increase was due to births rather than immigration because Hispanic American women are often younger and tend to have more children than women belonging to other census categories. But immigration is at the root of the growth of the Hispanic population in the United States, a point Abbey recognized:

Thus the pregnant Mexican woman who appears, in the final stages of labor, at the doors of an El Paso or San Diego hospital, demanding care for herself and the child she's about to deliver, becomes an "undocumented worker." The child becomes an automatic American citizen by virtue of its place of birth, eligible at once for all of the usual public welfare benefits. And with the child comes not only the mother but the child's family. And the mother's family. And the father's family. Can't break up families can we? They come to stay and they stay to multiply.

If Abbey were alive today and capable of mental activity, I wonder what his thoughts would be about immigration. I am pretty sure that he would be horrified and depressed by the growth of our population and the Hispanic contribution to that growth. But I also suspect that he would be somewhat embarrassed to be considered in league with the current anti-immigration faction, and I cannot imagine that he would be a fan of Sheriff Joe. He liked being a contrarian; at the time he wrote, the anti-immigrant contingent had yet to reach its present large and noisy state. If he were with us today, he might well choose a route that made him a contrarian again.

A starting point for his reorientation might come from the realization that immigration contributes to only part of the growth of the population of our nation and that illegal immigrants represent only a fraction of the total number of immigrants. Furthermore, given that recent immigrants, legal and illegal, tend to be poorer than the rest of us, the negative environmental effects of this subpopulation are smaller than those associated with the wealthier, non-Hispanic population. As biologists are fond of pointing out, a newborn American child will consume thirty to fifty times as much as a typical newborn unlucky enough to be born in a developing nation. The difference between Hispanic and non-Hispanic Americans is much smaller but still significant. If Abbey were to agree with this analysis, he might conclude that although every new American constitutes a drain on our resources and increases the pressure on our national parks, there is ample reason to target more wealthy residents as opposed to less prosperous newcomers. In so doing, he would surely find himself in a minority once again, and so could express an unwelcome position by taking on wealthier Americans of all political persuasions.

If Abbey could survey the United States in 2015, he would certainly be disheartened by the evidence that his policy positions as spelled out so forcefully in print have proven to be largely ineffective. Our population, as noted already, continues to grow steadily with a doubling time of seventy years or so. True, the number of illegal immigrants has fallen but not because of expensive militarized border enforcement, which has proven as much of a failure as our military adventures in Iraq. As Janet Napolitano once said, before she became secretary of homeland security, "You show me a 50-foot wall, I will show you a 51-foot ladder." The recent decreases in illegal immigration almost certainly stem from the grim economic situation in the United States and not because it has recently become more difficult to enter the country illegally.

Abbey's efforts to encourage resistance to the forces of development, population growth, and environmental destruction have also failed. The environmental advocacy group called Earth First!, which was inspired by Abbey's writing, early on staged a number of events such as tree sit-ins designed to call attention to the destructive effects of large-scale logging. The group has also engaged in recent protests against fracking and oil transport by trains, but I think it safe to say that it has had little success in changing the anti-environmental policies of loggers, frackers, or anyone else.

Even the administrators of national parks have failed to follow Abbey's advice for the most part. Yes, there are shuttle busses in some of the larger, more heavily visited parks, but the automobile still rules supreme, and the commercial development of the major parks has continued unabated since 1968. Abbey realized that this would be the case, writing that *Desert Solitaire* was "not a travel guide but an elegy. A memorial. You're holding a tombstone in your hands."

Although Abbey's ideas have not had much effect on the world of politics and law, his worries about the consequences of unbridled population growth are even more legitimate today than they were in the 1980s, given the current evidence all around us that there are too many people on the planet. But in the last analysis, his attempts to ban cars from our national parks and to stop immigrants like Omar from coming to our country may be less important (or less realistic) than an Abbeyesque message he delivered in a speech to a Montanan audience: "It's not enough to fight for the land; it is even more important to enjoy it. While you can. While it's still here."

Amen.

CHAPTER 4

Abbey in the Anthropocene

CURT MEINE

SERENDIPITOUSLY, A SCRAP of notebook paper comes forth just in time for this assignment. I remember writing it but had long since lost track of it, had no idea where I might have filed it. I rummage around for it, but cannot find it. And then, while not looking for it, it surfaces.

Edward Abbey would have scoffed at the hint of Zen in that. But then again . . .

March 15, 1989. (The Ides of March—what would he have made of that?) I am living in a small carriage house in Madison, Wisconsin, on Lake Monona, a few blocks from the university campus. The sun rises over the lake, and the morning news comes on NPR. "Writer and environmentalist Edward Abbey has died." That's how I remember it, anyway. Beyond that, I don't recall what they said, how they described Ed or his writing or his influence. I bet the word "iconoclast" was in there somewhere.

The news rocked me off my feet and into a chair. I didn't know Abbey. I didn't know anything about the health problems that had finally caught up with him. I didn't know much about the actual Abbey at all. I knew he wrote books that I enjoyed, that made me laugh, that blew the staid cover off of nature writing. I knew that his words provided consolation as the nation turned away from uncomfortable self-criticism and toward blustering triumphalism and mindless consumption of the world and of ourselves. I knew that he was a provocateur, inspiring those outrageous Monkey Wrenchers and Earth Firsters, inflaming those threatened by the suggestion that humans are not the center of the universe, nor the only object of value within it. I knew that something in his cri de coeur contributed to my own attempts to make some small difference with actions

51

and with words. I had half-memorized his essay "A Writer's Credo" after a few lines of it brought me to tears in the bookstore aisle: "I write to entertain my friends and to exasperate our enemies. To oppose, resist, and sabotage the contemporary drift toward a global technocratic police state, whatever its ideological coloration. . . . I write for the joy and exultation of writing itself. To tell my story."

I sat dumbfounded for a few minutes and then felt the need to write something. Reading it now, my little private commentary seems a bit lugubrious—a good Abbey word there! It began:

> We learn today that Ed Abbey has passed along (there is no "away") to his next life. Gone, I hope, to meet up with his old, familiar pals— Jefferson, Thoreau, Emerson, Krutch, hosts of brilliant, forgotten women, too—the souls whom he embraced, and who could hardly fail to welcome their kin. Gone, I hope, finally, to get some answers from "the old Bastard." Good, funny, joyful answers.

Yeah, well. I don't know if Abbey believed in a "next life." He did write, "If my decomposing carcass helps nourish the roots of a juniper tree or the wings of a vulture—that is immortality enough for me. And as much as anyone deserves." As for that awkward "brilliant, forgotten women, too": some overcompensation on my part going on there. I suppose every Abbey reader knew something of his predilections in that area.

Then some appreciation of the writer:

> Abbey, for all that made him difficult, was the one voice one could always turn to for solace, comfort, companionship when one questioned one's own instincts. When your own aspirations and dissatisfactions, yearnings and outrages, demanded resonance in the deep, recessed thoughts of another human being, Abbey was there. When one extrapolated the trends in which history has swept us along, and tried to face the situation with dignity, humor, and humanity, Abbey's the one who made it seem meaningful, without seeming Meaningful. If you know what I mean. Truth, courage, and democracy have lost their voice tonight.

I suppose that says more about me, then, than it does about Abbey. But I do think he would have liked that last line.

Then I addressed Ed directly:

Aw, Ed. How could you leave just as this story is reaching its climax? Just like you to get us all worked up, and then absent yourself? You have stripped the human race naked, and forced honest men [where are those "forgotten women"?] to face the image, and now you take away your voice.

If there is crying in the desert, it is that of your friends and family, and that of the wild winds that didn't much care about you one way or the other. And you knew it. Now, finally, you've rejoined the wind, and the animals, and the plants, and the soils and waters and hard, awful bedrock of the world. Now they're free to care for you again. And you're free to assume the place of the . . . what was it? Vulture?

A little melodramatic, but also a little more like it. Vultures and such.

So there is the biological process of decay and decomposition and recomposition and some manner of reincarnation of the elements. Then there is the cultural transmission, the absorption of the words and symbols, the stories and mythologies and meanings, into the ongoing flow of human civilization. (Yes, sayeth Abbey, get your terms right: "Civilization is the vital force in human history; culture is that inert mass of institutions and organizations which accumulate around and tend to drag down the advance of life. . . . Civilization flows; culture thickens and coagulates, like tired, sick, stifled blood.") So I ended my 1989 lamentation:

And we are left to face our own journey, still confined, still obligated. But still able, and still capable of love. There can be no letting up, no letting go. The core of our humanity, and the health of humanity's home, require attention. Yet allow us this moment to exercise our prerogative, and mourn our friend.

Reading back on it, I see the Abbey influence in my Abbey commentary. He did have that effect. But we all grow up, grow older. We see the heroes and inspirations of our earlier selves in new light. I am no longer in Abbey's thrall, but neither do I disavow that particular personal growth ring, now embedded within later layers of life. It remains part of the core, providing shape and structure and support to whoever I've become, and whoever I will yet be.

• • •

And so is he embedded in our evolving civilization (if not culture). Or maybe not quite embedded. His is still coyote, resistant to domestication, coming into the interstitial wilds, even in our cities, yipping from out beyond the circle of our campfire lights, away from our hearths. He is not always tolerated, much less welcomed. His same old adversaries, the high priests of the religion of growth, the drivers of the global techno-industrial machine, still roam and rule, their motives unchanged, their tools sharpened, their wallets fattened, their footprints enlarged, their consciences unburdened, their damaged bequeathed, content (contra Aldo Leopold) to "live without wild things."

Lately Abbey has drawn other fire. For at least some in the brave new Anthropocene world, Edward Abbey represents all that the baby-boomers' environmental movement got wrong—a loner in love with an illusory wilderness, a purist with a deaf ear and blind eye toward human suffering and injustice, a radical hypocrite unable to abide, or abide within, the world as it exists. (How I wish Abbey were here to provide this caricature himself! He'd do it so much better: "You see before you an affront and abomination, a romantic amid the rot, a passé poseur. While you calculate your ecosystem services to the sixth decimal point, I speak the quiet wild voice that whispers from your heart of hearts. Your youthful fling with me and my words embarrasses you, and now you must warn your children. But don't worry. They now exist in a state of constant hypnotic, electronic rapture. They will pay no attention to the cussed old lout wandering into town from the desert." C'mon writers . . . embrace your inner Abbey!)

There are fine ironies in all this. For both his "classic" and postmodern critics, Abbey is an ultimate environmentalist (despite his protestations on this point), a misanthrope in the Anthropocene. He is supposed to be standard-bearer for a movement, but the only standard he could bear was his own. He was held, by friend and foe alike, to be the voice of the sacred wild, but, as Wendell Berry so rightly comments (in "A Few Words in Defense of Edward Abbey"): "[Abbey is] a great irreverence of sacred cows."

When I stop regarding Abbey the writer and begin to review Abbey the conservationist, I can join in the postmortem assessment.

I wish Abbey had lived on and written more—much more—of home; of his home in Home, Pennsylvania (now at the heart of the Marcellus

Shale frack zone); of the semi-wild places that buffer—and extend—the big wild. I wish he had given us more on reconciling his anarchism and his communitarianism. I wish he had addressed at greater length the state of agriculture and the cities, joined in the conversation that Wes Jackson (among others) seeded: "If we don't save agriculture, we won't save wilderness."

Some of my favorite passages of Abbey's now are those in which he wrote against type: his rant on (among many other forms of American junk) "acid-injected tomatoes and hormone-polluted beef shipped from 3,000 miles away"; his call for "good fresh healthy food for all, . . . food that's fit to eat"; the "shiver of pleasure" he sensed—the tree's he meant, but more his, I think—when he planted a "young budding cottonwood," knowing that he himself would never see it reach maturity. I could make an argument that the most radical of all his essays is "Thus I Reply to René Dubos":

Who would deny the beauty as well as the utility of well-tended fields, close-cropped pastures, barns, farmhouses, stone walls, small dams, waterwheels, winding dirt roads lined with poplars, any and all things built with care by human hands, nourished and nurtured into fruitfulness by human love? Who would deny it? . . . I cannot imagine any conservationist so "pure" as to object to farming—by freeholders—in its traditional style.

The comforts of home and the vitality of the wild, all held within an honored Earth. He knew it, it's where we are now, and, since he can't do it himself, I will amplify those passages now. He once wrote to an interviewer that "if most Americans eventually decide that they want to surround our national parks with an industrial slum of strip mines, power plants, trailerhouse cities, there's not much that people like me can do about it except complain." Maybe not, Ed. But many of those who read you have been doing much more that complaining, have been hard at work buffering and sustaining the "protected" places by connecting them, conserving the lands and waters beyond their boundaries, revitalizing the degraded places (wild, rural, and urban), and challenging the cultural and economic forces that threaten them all, and all they contain.

• • •

I don't write often to my inspirations anymore, especially after they die. I am more likely to seek inspiration in the steady commitment of nearby and everyday friends, to acknowledge them by buying them a drink, and to toast them rather than eulogize them after their demise. Yet I still hear Ed's quiet wild voice. I always will. It's embedded. It still calls me to outrage and laughter and mischief but also to making the difference I can, where I can, while I may. And to make a difference, one needs many voices and many tools.

CHAPTER 5

Abbey's Secret

BEN A. MINTEER

IN MAY 1988 Edward Abbey went into southeastern Utah for a four-day horseback trip with a small "expedition" party. Accompanying him was his friend, outfitter and guide Ken Sleight (according to Abbey lore, Sleight was the model for the character Seldom Seen Smith in *The Monkey Wrench Gang*); Sleight's assistant, a young packer named Grant Johnson; and two others.

The journey was into the craggy backcountry of Grand Gulch, a winding series of slickrock canyons worn into the sandstone plateau of Cedar Mesa in Utah's San Juan County. It is, by all accounts, an extraordinary place, its arresting red rock beauty embroidered by bursts of archaeological richness. The Grand Gulch canyons contain a remarkable collection of Ancestral Pueblo cliff ruins and rock art, some of it long since rendered inaccessible by the erosive force of the desert winds.

Despite the company of his friend Sleight, despite the appealing remoteness of the place, and despite it being the desert Southwest (a place that was for Abbey "love at first sight"), it was in many ways just another job. Abbey was there on assignment for *Condé Nast Traveler*, which had commissioned him to write an essay for a special issue of the magazine, "The Glory of the West." The essay that emerged from Abbey's Grand Gulch trip carried an alluring air of mystery in its title: "The Secret of the Green Mask." Reading it today, a couple of things stand out.

One is the photographs: two large, black-and-white photos from the trip accompany the essay. Abbey appears in both. In the first, he's taking an afternoon siesta, lying on the valley floor on his back with arms outstretched, his straw hat strategically placed over his face to provide some shade. He's framed in the lower right of the photo, reclining to the right of a round cottonwood tree. Two packhorses stand at the left of the tree, one of them with its head partly in the branches, perhaps seeking shade or looking for something more interesting. The canyon walls fan upward in the background, appearing to move away from the tree at the center of the photograph and ending in a puff of white cloud and sky at the top of the photo. It's a nicely composed image, conveying at once the power of the personality—even at rest—and the beauty and resonance of place.

The next photo is even more striking. In this one Abbey is positioned on the left side of the image, sitting on a small rock bench and taking notes, with his back nearly pressed against the curved wall. The place is Turkey Pen Ruins, a sandstone alcove that curves upward to the top of the image and appears as an amphitheater of stone, framing a view of the canyon to the right of the photograph. Abbey's here a solitary figure looking out into the distance, into the vastness of the desert landscape.

• • •

The photos were the work of Mark Klett, another member of that Grand Gulch party in May 1988 and also on assignment for Condé Nast. The editor of *Traveler* had in fact paired the two men, thinking that it would be interesting to couple prominent writers and landscape photographers for the special issue on the West. (Full disclosure: Klett is a colleague of mine at Arizona State University and I've known him for a few years, although I only recently became aware of his Grand Gulch trip with Abbey. I asked him to sit down with me to talk a little about his recollections of the assignment, about Abbey, and about those photographs.)

Already by then an accomplished fine arts photographer known for his innovative "rephotography" of the western landscape, at the time of the trip Klett had read and admired *Desert Solitaire* and some of Abbey's other essays. But he had little sense of Abbey the person other than the familiar stories (often told by Abbey himself). Klett thought that the author's persona was a bit over the top, so when Condé Nast called and asked him if he "wanted to go on horseback trip into southern Utah with Edward Abbey," he agreed, but with slight trepidation. Abbey himself chose the location, selecting a place that was interesting and remote, yet not so secluded that attracting the attention of *Traveler* readers would pose any great concern.

Abbey's arrival at the Grand Gulch trailhead did little to dispel an

Kiva in Grand
Gulch (November
2003)

over-the-top reputation. Klett described the author's showy entrance in his red Eldorado convertible, a Cadillac cowboy riding high on the seatback, whooping loudly and wildly waving his hat. But Abbey soon set Klett at ease, and today the photographer has very fond memories of the trip.

Klett shot more than one hundred photographs on the Grand Gulch assignment, although only two ended up in the published article. I asked him about that Turkey Pen Ruins image, which Klett has put on exhibition at various venues over the years. A slight smile crossed his face. "It's my favorite photograph from the trip and from that period in my work. It really captures how I saw Abbey experiencing the place on that trip, gauging that experience, recording it."

Abbey's *Traveler* essay is a light piece, but a lively one (he may have been writing for Condé Nast but he was still Ed Abbey). For the most part he stays within the sunny conventions of the travel essay, though he can't resist taking a few jabs at old foes. Noting that cattle were banned from the canyon decades earlier, Abbey delights in the signs of a recovering landscape: the reappearance of wild plants, the stabilization of the stream banks, the return of deer to the canyons. And he expresses the hope that someday all of the public lands of the American West will be similarly regenerated once they, too, are no longer "infested with domestic live-stock." It's a vintage Abbey riff, though his punches were pulled more than usual (he was clearly on his best behavior for the Condé Nast crowd).

And then there is that mystery alluded to in the essay's title. It's one that Abbey the dramatist takes his sweet time in unveiling. But he eventually describes a haunting image encountered in the rocks, the Ancestral Pueblo "green mask" pictograph high up on the wall of Grand Gulch's Sheik's Canyon. Abbey's depiction of it is one of the essay's best passages:

> Most unusual, however, is the life-size floating head at the far end of the gallery, a yellow face with red hair (or headdress) and a green mask painted across the eyes. A troubling apparition, centuries old, spooky, queer, sinister—if I were the superstitious type I'd flee this place at once. But as comfortable modern rationalists, we simply turn our backs on the Green Mask, eat our lunches, and stare with pleasure at a scrim of light rain falling beyond the shelter of our amphitheater.

At the end of the essay Abbey struggles to capture the essence of "this quiet, secret, and secretive canyon." He quickly throws in the towel, however, and acknowledges that a four-day pack trip is nowhere near enough time to understand the place. To really understand it, Abbey writes, he'd have to come back and live in the canyons for a while, "perhaps a century or two, through all the transformations of the seasons and the years." Until then, he'd rather not discuss something he can't even name. If we really want to know more about the elusive essence of the canyon, then we should, Abbey suggests, "ask that head on the wall, the creature behind the Green Mask."

It's a circumspect and meditative Abbey, playing a game of metaphysical hide-and-seek that he started decades before in *Desert Solitaire*. An unsettling cipher, the green mask seems to signify to him the irreducible mystery and power of place, to be a sublime marker both of our presence and our evanescence. The true meaning of the desert landscape is in the end unknowable, beyond the measure of science, beyond the comprehension of even Abbey's vast poetic faculties.

• • •

There is another secret in the Grand Gulch essay, however, one that also turns on a key image from the trip. It's a small secret, but knowing it has the effect of knowing all good secrets. It makes you feel like you understand something a little more fully, maybe even that you've become privy to some deeper truth.

As Klett and I were talking about the Turkey Pen Ruins photo, he shared a surprising detail. "You can't tell, but he's not alone in that photo." Abbey was, in fact, sitting next to someone in the scene, the fourth member of the trip, a woman named Carole who is mentioned only in passing in the piece (she was apparently a friend of Sleight's, though that isn't entirely clear from the record of the trip). Klett didn't think the magazine would be interested in a duo in the photograph, and he didn't want to move them to get a solo shot of the author, so he found the perfect vantage point in which only Abbey is visible.

I looked even closer at the high-resolution print of the photo that Klett had brought with him. I tried to see the other figure in the picture, to see some sort of visual "tell"—perhaps a slight shadow, maybe something in Abbey's body language—suggesting that he was not really alone in the scene. Nothing. I still saw only Abbey.

Knowing this little secret about the photo, though, made me think differently about the image. And it reminded me that so much of the reception of the writer and his work has been swamped by that Abbey myth: the image of "Cactus Ed," the solitary, self-styled desert anarchist, zealous defender of the wilderness, someone who'd "rather kill a man than a snake." The power and beauty of Klett's photo of Abbey in the Grand Gulch ruins can reinforce this image (although it's far too tranquil a scene to evoke homicide): Abbey as the "lone voice crying the wilderness." But of course, that's only on the surface. Both the photo and Abbey's persona (another kind of "mask") are careful and deliberate aesthetic creations. If we forget that we risk taking both images of Abbey as the truth.

When that happens, Abbey's voice, his work, his environmental vision—all get hollowed out and distorted. He becomes the one-trick pony: the radical wilderness preservationist with little appetite for modern society but a definite taste for writing screeds against cattle ranching and urban sprawl ("Phoenix should never have been allowed to happen"). Abbey, it must be said, brought much of this on himself, especially when he let it rip (which he did often). But those who knew him—and those who read him more carefully—know that this Abbey was mostly a fiction, a mischievous invention.

The problem is that the image of Abbey as the anti-modern, misanthropic environmentalist can eclipse his more tempered thinking and writing, rendering the latter all but forgotten. But recall the philosophical punch line of *Desert Solitaire:* "Balance, that's the secret. Moderate extremism. The best of both worlds." Hardly the words of a radical primitivist. Or think of how Abbey similarly commends (in *Abbey's Road*) "a wholesome and reasonable balance between industrialism and agrarianism, between cities and small towns, between private property and public property." The desire to mix wild and civilized, natural beauty and pragmatic utility, animates some of Abbey's best and most mature work.

In Grand Gulch, Klett got to know this more moderate, three-dimensional man behind the brash rhetoric and the Cactus Ed caricature. Klett fittingly saw the fuller picture: "Here's a human guy, living a life, not taking himself too seriously. I liked that about him. If he'd really been a raging ideologue, an environmental extremist, well, it probably wouldn't have been a very good trip."

● ● ●

The Grand Gulch essay appeared in print in March 1989, the month and year of Abbey's death. It remains a little known piece and hasn't been reprinted. Track it down for the photos or to be reminded of the author's easy hand with the immersive travel essay. Or read it for a more poignant end, as a record of one last journey—exuberant, playful, earthy, and still searching—into the heart of Abbey's country.

PART 2

INDEPENDENT AUTHORS

The artist's job? To be a miracle worker: to make the blind see, the dull feel, the dead to live.

—EDWARD ABBEY, *A VOICE CRYING IN THE WILDERNESS* (1989)

Island in the Sky, Utah (April 2001)

CHAPTER 6

The View from Alaska

NANCY LORD

THOSE OF US of a certain age look back fondly on those formative books that matched the innocent and idealistic times in which they came to us. In my case, my well-worn paperback copy of *The Monkey Wrench Gang* seems to suffer from shrunken print size. But when I open and browse through it, I find underlined passages. On one early page, the single word "eco-raiders." Then a mention of Albuquerque, "surrounded by the bleak, black, slovenly wilderness that never would shape up. Where the lean and hungry coyote skulked, unwilling to extinct." A gorgeous paragraph describing river and sky. This litany: "River, rock, sun, blood, hunger, wings, joy." A quote from Hayduke: "Always pull up survey stakes." More about the land, the "holy country." A warning that must have seized me: "Somewhere in the depths of solitude, beyond wildness and freedom, lay the trap of madness."

Who was this person, this Nancy Lord who found something underline-worthy in each of those passages? I likely purchased my paperback in 1976 or 1977, when I was in my midtwenties and had already been living in Alaska for a few years, determined that it was and would remain my chosen and fiercely protected home place. I know I looked up to Edward Abbey, whose *Desert Solitaire* I'd already absorbed. I knew that he, like me, had grown up on the East Coast and fled west to find a larger and wilder land. Only I had gone farther, beyond the West that was already filling up, in the 1970s, with people, homes, roads, fences, dams. Still, I felt that kinship, that allegiance to the place that was home not because of ancestral ties but because it was *chosen*.

Desert Solitaire begins, "This is the most beautiful place on earth." Abbey meant the Utah canyonlands, the slickrock desert.

On my arrival in Alaska—specifically on finding myself among granite

65

peaks north of the Arctic Circle—I wrote this sentence in my journal: "This is the most beautiful place in the world." I'm sure I wasn't aping Abbey; I'm sure I didn't remember that he'd said the same thing. I was emoting genuinely, because I had discovered a land that matched my spirit. I lacked the language, then, to say what that meant for me, or even to begin to describe the beauty that lay before me. It would take more reading of Abbey—and of other writers who contemplated the natural world—to learn how to express that which is so unsayable. But I knew it; I felt it. I had found a home in the world.

Today I pull from my bookshelf a half dozen Abbey books, fiction and nonfiction, all of them marked by my young and impassioned person's pen and none of them reopened now for decades. I try to remember who I was when I bent over their small print and marked what was especially meaningful to me at the time.

My ink in *The Monkey Wrench Gang* suggests two things to me. One, I was learning how to be in the world, how to respond to what was beautiful and what was ugly, what to look for, how to see, how to think. And two, I was paying attention to language. I was learning that words could create a world, even one—the Southwest desert—that I knew nothing about. The words could be as lovely as the land. I find in my scribblings my beginnings as both citizen-conservationist and writer.

But this is not about me. I was only one among thousands, perhaps millions, of readers who were moved in some large or small way by reading Abbey's words. (The first paperback editions of *Desert Solitaire* and *The Monkey Wrench Gang* each sold half a million copies.) Abbey lives among the giants who have spoken truth to power and driven cultural change. Think of Thoreau's *Walden* and *Civil Disobedience*. John Muir. Aldo Leopold and his insistence on a land ethic. Rachel Carson's exposé of the chemical industry. Bill McKibben's *The End of Nature*. Every writer today, "environmental" or not, stands on the shoulders of this line of writers, each of whom spoke in words and ways that resonated with their particular times.

Abbey fit his time like his character Bonnie Abbzug fit her straw hats.

The Abbey era, in which—remember—a common bumper sticker advised "Question Authority," called for his irreverence. It demanded not earnest expressions of the harm we do to the planet but sarcasm, hyperbole, pretend fantasy, and pretension, a kind of anarchic extremism written in exclamation points. And laughter. We had to laugh (or we would cry.) *The Monkey Wrench Gang*, while describing an abused land, took readers on a wild ride that was anything but a "downer." Abbey himself called the book "a sort of comic extravaganza." Have fun with chainsaws and explosives! Imagine blowing up dams and power stations! Indulge your revenge fantasies! Hang out with crazy characters! That's the beauty of fiction, its ability to carry readers into an imaginary world they wouldn't exactly want to live in—but that leaves its indelible mark. Even as we laughed, we had to think serious thoughts. What if we, readers, did really honor those river canyons and roadless areas? What if we left some wild places alone? How far would we go to live our beliefs?

Abbey's genius (some of it, anyway) lay in presenting himself as a crusty redneck who had no truck with academics or pointed-headed pontificating, even as he injected all his work with a fine and learned intelligence. The image was beer-guzzling bad boy, breaker of rules, resistance fighter. The man was Fulbright scholar, Stegner creative writing fellow, owner of multiple philosophy degrees. The latter could seduce you with the former while carrying you into deep and creative inquiry. *The Monkey Wrench Gang* was constructed not out of thin air and theatrics but with grounding in a master's thesis concerned with anarchism and the morality of violence. Abbey's works are packed with references, direct and otherwise, to Nietzsche, Darwin, Thomas Wolfe, the Bible, as well as to the natural history he claimed to know so little about. ("I am not a naturalist. . . . I'm not even an amateur naturalist.") He wrote, he said, "in a deliberately provocative and outrageous manner because I like to startle people." He also knew the value of writing a story that people would want to read, one that would entertain.

I never met Abbey, although, in those years when I was reading so much of his work, I'd planned to. In the mid-1970s my local conservation group invited him to Homer, Alaska, to give a reading and speak about advocacy for western lands. At the last minute, he canceled because of conflicting commitments.

He did make it to Alaska on at least two other occasions, river trips in the southeast and in the Arctic. It's hard for me to know if the persona he created for the 1983 essay "Gather at the River" (in *Beyond the Wall*) represents the true man or is meant as more provocation, but he didn't seem to enjoy much about Alaska. He calls himself "the most sissified rugged outdoorsman in the West" and complains of the cold and mosquitoes—this while rafting the incredible Kongakut River in the Arctic National Wildlife Refuge among caribou, wolves, and true wildness. It is clear enough that the technically "desert" landscape in Alaska's Arctic was not the desert he loved and longed for. Alaska, he said, was "the last pork chop" for Americans; he meant that we would fight to gobble it up and leave nothing but scrap.

Earlier, before Alaska made it onto his map, he wrote in *Desert Solitaire* about being grateful for its existence, whether or not he ever went there: "We need the possibility of escape as surely as we need hope; without it the life of the cities would drive all men into crime or drugs or psychoanalysis."

Over several days I reread *The Monkey Wrench Gang*. I lingered with its loveliest landscapes, the lives of desert plants and red canyon rock, an extravagance of language, the jokes (Bonnie removing from a dynamite box her very valuable copy of *Desert Solipsism* along with her panties and Doc's dirty socks, Hayduke concerning himself with the ethics of leaving climbing aids in place, Hayduke as a "pyromantic"). I shot through the fast-paced dialogue, the wacky characters colliding with one another and the world. I wondered at all the details of construction equipment, explosives, power production: an impressive acquaintance, and not a little scary in our current terrified-by-terrorism age. And what the heck is apodictic rock? ("Apodictic": true, certain, incontestable because it has been demonstrated.) I stopped at a brief mention of oil shale development; who would have thought, back then and there, that tar sands extraction and fracking would become the horrors they are today all across our country and beyond? I thought, as the characters thought, about the damage done to the places we love, and of the needs and greeds of people, and of how any of us decide what a right and moral defensive action might be. I considered cyclic and linear theories of history, wavering and waffling along with Hayduke.

Killing people with dynamite is not good PR, Doc Sardis opines. I'm in his camp, and then some.

Spoiler alert—no one dies in *The Monkey Wrench Gang*. Abbey was careful to distinguish between violence against property and violence toward people. He may or may not have anticipated that others would embrace his novel as a guidebook for disabling bulldozers and spiking trees, for what became known as ecoterrorism. Hayduke-inspired tactics were literalized by some, which was not good PR, certainly not for a conservation movement hoping to build its constituency and drive political change.

To be sure, rereading *The Monkey Wrench Gang* for its fortieth birthday, I often felt uncomfortable. (Isn't that a primary purpose of art, to shake us from our comfortable moorings?) I didn't so much rejoice at the antics of the gang of four as feel embarrassed by their vigilantism, based as it is in self-righteous indignation. They are of course comic characters, cartoons, not representational people, but I was sometimes less amused than critical and weary of them. Perhaps the problem isn't with them but with me; I'm simply too weary altogether, facing global-scale environmental threats that no one with a wrench can even dream of stopping.

My discomfort extends, in our sensitive age, to Abbey's portrayals of the sexes and Native Americans. How annoying I now find Bonnie, with her sexiness at every turn, her endangering stupidity, her narcissism. And how often do I need to read about men drinking and peeing, dangling or thrusting their penises and throwing their beer cans around? Ghost of Ed Abbey, forgive me if I now find that tiresome. And cringe I did at the degrading, racist comments made by members of the gang about Native Americans. Their efforts to frame innocent people for their monkey wrenching are offensive and unrepented. But, as I say, we live in a different time now, one less tolerant of that kind of silliness, more apt to be repulsed than entertained by suggestions of sexism, racism, violence of all kinds. And I've become a grouchy old woman.

How many writers today would take the risks Abbey took in portraying so agreeably such characters and behaviors? Not many, I bet. Ed Abbey was a singular fellow, and we're not likely to see his kind of provocateur again.

Abbey died—tragically young—the same year that Bill McKibben brought "popular" attention to global warming for the first time. We can only wonder what a man so concerned with global overpopulation, industrialization, and nuclear war would make of the earth in 2015, and whether his good humor would still temper his outrage.

Alaska is far from Abbey's Southwest, but the threats he and his characters anguished over are now writ large in our pork-chop North. The largest open-pit gold and copper mine has been proposed in the watershed of the world's largest salmon runs. A gigantic coal mine for export to Asia is poised to dig through another salmon river. The massive Susitna dam is again under study. The current governor is all about "roads to resources." And, of course, oil and gas exploration and production continue apace, extending now even into treacherous offshore Arctic waters. Greenhouse gases from all the world's fossil fuel burning and deforestation are melting Arctic sea ice at an unprecedented rate, and that same carbon overload is acidifying our oceans. The stakes are very high in this last place that still has free-running rivers, ancient forests, herds of caribou, landscapes to get lost in.

Abbey lives with us here. The man who didn't love Alaska and who wrote in "Gather the River" that "the most attractive feature of Alaska is its small, insignificant human population, thanks to the miserable climate" continues to test and inspire us. Our population, not so small and inconsequential now, might actually stand up to rapacious corporate interests. Our Native American peoples are among the staunchest defenders of land and sea and what they provide, nutritionally and spiritually. So are fishermen. And mothers concerned about clean air, clean water, and clean food.

The last word should come from the rebel himself. It's an Abbey quote that's circled widely in Alaska over the years, appearing in conservation newsletters and on bulletin boards. A tenet in the lives of today's activists, it's advice that reminds us always of why we do the hard, painfully slow work: "It is not enough to fight for the land; it is even more important to enjoy it. While you can. While it's still here. So get out there and hunt and fish and mess around with your friends, ramble out yonder and explore the forests, encounter the grizz, climb the mountains, bag the peaks, run the rivers, breathe deep of that yet sweet and lucid air, sit quietly for a while and contemplate the precious stillness, the lovely, mysterious and awesome space."

CHAPTER 7

A Meditation on Two Works by Ed Abbey

GLENN VANSTRUM

DON'T LOOK AT me, Your Honor. I'm not blowing up Glen Canyon Dam. I ain't gonna sink no nuke-you-lar aircraft carrier. Nope. Not me, Sir.

I'm old and tired. I write my annual checks to Planned Parenthood, to Sierra Club, to Ocean Conservancy, to the National Resource Defense Council. I boo when, in the name of all-powerful commerce, mindless concrete-laying road builders succeed in obliterating yet another thousand acres of wilderness. I cheer when some brave soul stymies the forces of development. But I don't pour Karo syrup down gas tanks of D-9 caterpillars, or pull up survey stakes for oil pipelines, or attach plastique to mining bridges.

I'd like to, but I don't.

Every now and then, though, a "damp, drizzly November in my soul" (thank you, Melville) grinds me down. Even the ocean, my usual spiritual savoir, fails me. The only cure is to gas up and sneak off to Abbey country.

It's eight hours to Zion from my house in San Diego, and even with that most un-macho of cars, a Prius, traveling there means burning at least eight gallons of gas. It's another six hours across Utah to Moab, Arches, Canyonlands, and the stark beauty of the Four Corners. I don't go often. I don't go in the summer—too hot for a California surfer who grew up in Minnesota. I prefer the cold, like my familiar East Pacific, chilled by currents sweeping south from the Gulf of Alaska.

One winter I found myself unrolling a down bag on the slickrock under Delicate Arch, the better to stare for hours at the unfolding of a lunar eclipse. Damn, but it was frigid. The hot beauty of that Japanese lantern moon made up for it, though. Pretty much.

Another time I pitched a tent at the bottom of Bryce Canyon and woke up beneath six inches of snow. Crystalline perfection dusted every hoodoo in the park. Not Abbey's summer desert, but winter desert and still bitchin'.

There was that long wade up the Virgin River Narrows in Zion. A warm day, that one, in September. Cool down in the canyon, though. One has to ignore the posted warning about flash floods and plow ahead. "Abandon all hope ye who enter here" is the sign's approximate gist. Several miles in, a spooked mule deer headed downriver trotted past me, so close I could have touched his sleek, cougar-evading haunches.

There was getting lost in a slot canyon somewhere outside Blanding, losing my way back up and out, unable to find my entrance rope, despairing, kettledrums of thunder blaring—fortissimo, not pianissimo—and fear of a flash flood browning my pants. Sorry, TMI, as the kids say.

Yeah, every now and then I feel the need to imbibe something dangerous, something anarchistic, something flammable. If I can't make it to the desert, I go for the next best thing.

Desert Solitaire. The Monkey Wrench Gang. Or maybe *Hayduke Lives* or *Fool's Progress* (I like a book that opens with the hero shooting his refrigerator). They're all good.

I read Abbey, and, for God's sake, I feel better.

• • •

It's hard to forget the "Ah ha!" moment one gets upon reading *The Monkey Wrench Gang* for the first time. The four main characters—Doc Sarvis, Seldom Seen Smith, Bonnie Abbzug, and George Washington Hayduke—leap off the page and gobsmack the brain. Their actions—for character is best revealed through action—ring bright, bells of freedom sounding so bold, so wrong, so right, so revolutionary, so far-fetched, and so believable you can get tinnitus for a month just from a quick skim. The book is the kind of fantasy that makes you say, "If only . . ."

If only the relentless forces of development could be stopped by half-crazy, lovable eco-activists.

If only September 11, 2001, hadn't give ecoterrorism a bad name.

If only the Keystone pipeline could be halted by pouring sand and Mrs. Butterworth's syrup down the fuel intake lines of a few Allis-Chalmers HD-41s.

Abbey was a renegade, of course, a hard-drinking cirrhotic with too many wives and too many kids to be a proper poster boy for

Zion Canyon, Utah
(June 1995)

environmentalism. His books, however, remain an inspiration. We'll never know how much his "rednecks for wilderness" writing affected people like Dave Foreman, Paul Watson, and Judi Bari. We can guess how tree spiking and other acts of ecotage grew from his work, how it might have helped catalyze groups such as Earth First!, Earth Liberation Front, and the Sea Shepherd Society, but we'll never be sure.

Twenty-five years after Abbey's death and unembalmed burial in the desert, forty years after the publication of *The Monkey Wrench Gang*, and forty-five years after the publication of *Desert Solitaire* (his non-fiction masterpiece), we still do not know the man Edward Abbey. Nor should we care about our ignorance. Cranky curmudgeon that he was, he wouldn't give a damn whether or not we praise, vilify, anoint, or desecrate his memory.

Hell, he's dead.

We can and do know his work, though, for his writing is very much alive, very much real, and very much cogent to the present day. His books shine with the luminescent hue of a handful of raw diamonds studding the dull red of a slickrock landscape.

Aided by a fellowship at Stanford with Wallace Stegner in creative writing, birthplace to such luminaries as Ken Kesey, Wendell Berry, and Tobias Wolff, Abbey learned to shape words into a saber dance. Over the years the man honed his verbal tools to samurai-sword sharpness, whetting his crusty, eloquent, and profane voice on a life spent in the wilderness he loved.

Start with lists. Nobody makes them like Abbey. It's hard to pin down exactly what seems so evocative about his long juxtapositions of striking verbs and nouns, but he is a master at it. His rant from *Desert Solitaire* on getting people to walk in national parks, the tirade ending with pouring piss from a boot, makes a wonderful example.

There's the bit from *The Monkey Wrench Gang* where Bonnie allows a suspicious park official to look inside Doc's station wagon. In one perfect sentence, Abbey manages to arouse a panoply of appetites, from hunger, to sex, to artistic inspiration. Kippered herring, sweet bikini panties, a first edition book, and foul socks never fit together so well.

Then there's Abbey's varied cast of sinners, criminals, drunkards, heroes, and villains. A misanthrope through and through, he nevertheless pays kind and loving attention to character development, most especially with his *Monkey Wrench Gang* desperados. The book opens with a chapter on each (the four sections entitled "Origins"). Far from rough notes on personality traits, these portraits use language dabbed with thick-brushed primary colors, often accompanied by action, to paint the character, and, more importantly, the motivations, of our fledgling saboteurs.

The good doctor appears full formed from the outset, nonchalantly setting ablaze a Phoenix billboard. The menacing Hayduke shows up next, guzzling beer, armed to the teeth, and half crazy from his sojourn with the Montagnards in the Vietnam War.

The river-rafting desert rat, Seldom Seen Smith, arrives after Hayduke, along with descriptions of his three wives. Did I forget to say Abbey's writing is often sexist, horny, and expressive of unrepentant fondness for the female body? The author is not one to stand up for gun control, rights of women, or any other form of political correctness (that oft-used synonym for liberalism). In truth, he would fit in with a lot of red state heartland types, if only he didn't love wilderness so much.

One might conjecture Abbey's somewhat fractured relationships with women made it hard for him to shape his female characters. His portrayal of Bonnie Abbzug might be derided by some, but for me, at least, she bursts to life fully formed. OK, she's hot. She's a dancer. She can't help it. I knew several women like her, women I met in Salt Lake one summer many decades ago, all Jack Mormons, all members of the University of Utah dance department, all pot-smoking, lovely, and environmentally conscious. Bonnie is the real deal. Trust me on that.

Vivid characterizations abound in Abbey's other works as well. No writer could do better than he does with his sketch of Viviano, the Basque cowboy in *Desert Solitaire*, the wild man who dashes on horseback down muddy cliffs, between boulders, and over rocks with "complete indifference to life and limb, the vulnerability of the flesh."

Master sentences—a term coined by Brooks Landon, writing professor at the University of Iowa—abound in Abbey's work. These winding beauties of syntactical perfection alternate with short punches to the verbal groin. But make no mistake: Abbey the outlaw, the anarchist, the iconoclast, did not hew to Strunk and White principles. He cast aside conventions of subject-verb-object whenever it pleased him.

At the heart of Abbey's voice lies contrast, stark contrast between the intellectual and the profane. In *The Monkey Wrench Gang*, violent acts of sabotage alternate with melodic prose praising nature. Four-letter Anglo-Saxon verbiage mixes freely with precise cultural and scientific jargon. Paranoid thoughts and nightmares of capture and imprisonment alternate with fearless ecosabotage madness. Rough smells and scenes abut profound philosophical meditation.

From *Desert Solitaire*, as the author and companions carry out the dead man at Grandview Point, a clueless tourist who died from thirst after getting lost, you get moments where in one sentence there is wonderful dialogue about what a heavy, bloated son of a bitch the corpse is followed by a soliloquy on how natural, normal, and good it is for people to die, all the better to make room for the young and vital.

Standard Abbey fare is an expletive followed by a literary zinger, often in French or Latin, as when the four saboteurs in *The Monkey Wrench Gang* confer after Hayduke, free rappelling his jeep by winch down a cliff and hiding under an overhang, makes a miraculous escape from six armed pursuers. After a typical Hayduke barrage of four-letter words, out comes the pronouncement of "deus ex machina," from the lovely lips of Miss Abbzug.

Writing about music (like dancing about architecture) is another skill Ed Abbey utilizes in abundance. A wannabe concert pianist myself, I'm always on the lookout for a writer with a melodic ear.

In *Desert Solitaire*, Abbey describes how after almost dying while exploring a slot canyon, he started bellowing Beethoven's "Ode to Joy." Having been in similar situations, I'd be singing in ecstasy, too. His discussion of the unearthly music from a den of coyotes, in the same book, is another example of his talent for writing about music.

One of the final chapters in *Desert Solitaire* takes Abbey into the forbidding realm of the Maze, a world of tortured paths, twisting tracks, and box canyons. Not a place for wimps, city slickers, or the faint of heart. Yet, along the way, the author rhapsodizes:

In the desert I am reminded of something quite different—the bleak, thin-textured work of men like Berg, Schoenberg, Ernst Krenek, Webern and the American, Elliott Carter. Quite by accident, no doubt, although both Schoenberg and Krenek lived part of their lives in the Southwest, their music comes closer than any other I know to representing the apartness, the otherness, the strangeness of the desert.

There are a lot of nature writers out there, but few so cultured that they understand the bizarre twelve-tone works of Schoenberg and his peers. Only Abbey gets how their strange music forms a metaphor for the austere beauty—and downright eeriness—of the desert.

• • •

Isolated linguistic feats, of course, mean nothing unless they pertain to the whole. A graduate of the University of New Mexico philosophy department, Abbey had plenty of hidden ice submerged beneath the berg of his literary chops. His master's thesis asked "to what extent is the current association between anarchism and violence warranted?" and "in so far as the association is a valid one, what arguments have the anarchists presented, explicitly or implicitly, to justify the use of violence?"

Anarchism, the political philosophy that promotes stateless societies and, in general, holds the state to be evil, clearly attracted Abbey, appealing to his rebellious, freedom-loving nature. Unlike modern-day Tea Partiers, though, to him "the state" was a composite of both corporate industry and government. He knew monolithic, faceless entities were responsible for the desecration of the desert he so loved, and the constant debate in his mind was how best to combat such powerful enemies.

You can feel these questions burgling beneath the fine writing, the verbal flourishes, the all-pervading humor, the bits of scintillating prose, and the ribald gestures. What we've got, especially in *Desert Solitaire* and *The Monkey Wrench Gang*, are two books that carry more weight than Hanging Rock. Arguably, it is this profundity of theme that ought to keep Abbey's work alive long after his death, even as the writing of other master wordsmiths (Thomas Pynchon and Jim Harrison come to mind) may fade. Scholars have, justly, compared his work with Aldo Leopold's *Sand County Almanac* and Rachel Carson's *Silent Spring*. This is not due to his brilliant verbosity but to the leathery strength of his convictions.

Desert Solitaire, beyond its disguise as a primer on the natural history of Arches National Park, is a meditation on the crimes and misdemeanors of anthropocentrism, on the inconsequence and malignancy of overpopulated humanity, and on the overriding worth and sustaining soul of the desert in particular and wild nature in general.

Summarizes Abbey therein: "I am not an atheist, but an earthiest."

The Monkey Wrench Gang is a fictional response to this meditation, a fantasy how-to novel, a thinly veiled blueprint for a possible violent response to mindless, nature-strangling growth.

One can only wonder what Abbey's response to climate change might be, Abbey, the author who, in numerous diatribes, curses the automobile roundly and praises the value of getting off one's fat ass and walking. As each year of global weirdness progresses, as each cataclysmic storm from Katrina to Sandy punches yet another city with yet another knockout blow, more and more people will read his books. Or ought to read his books. And they will realize just how prescient Abbey was. And they will stew. And they will get pissed off.

If one were to pick a geographic focal point for Abbey's angst and anger, the root cause for the inner conflict pitting the man of letters against the violent anarchist, it would have to be the damming of Glen Canyon. The section in *Desert Solitaire* portraying his rafting/camping trip down the canyon, just before completion of the dam, just before the flooding and permanent destruction of this wild and mysterious place, is as poignant and wonderful a piece of nature writing as ever was penned.

The constant references in *The Monkey Wrench Gang* to the destruction of the cursed dam lead nowhere, a dream too far-fetched even for fiction. Renting houseboats, loading them with explosives, and blowing the concrete behemoth to smithereens is only discussed by the heroes, never attempted. Still, if the author had a utopian vision, the magical resurrection of the lost canyon would, to my read, be it.

Abbey himself no doubt burned a few billboards and pulled up his share of surveyor's stakes, but, in the end, pacifism and writing won the internal battle with his violent tendencies. Even though he lived his anarchistic, radical, alcoholic life a bit too far in the past to know everything we know at present, he still understood the big picture.

I do not believe he would be surprised to find many scientists now opine that humans are well on their way to causing the sixth mass extinction. Today there are seven billion people on the planet, a billion more than when Ed died. Each one of those seven billion wants three square meals, a roof, and a car. All will suck water from failing aquifers, burn firewood and gasoline, kill animals and uproot plants to eat, and, in general, follow the cruel dictates of the second law of thermodynamics. The plague of humanity has not—as yet—resolved itself. Abbey, I think, could see all this coming.

If one sits down, opens a can of beer, and muses at length about it, as I'm sure Ed did on more than one occasion, it ought to be clear that even with all the damage humans cause today, have caused in the past, and will cause in the future, our Earth will shrug its Himalayan shoulders and carry on. Countless trillions of microbes and insects will thrive no matter what we humans do. Various reptiles, mammals, and birds will handle whatever we throw at them. When our species becomes extinct—as it will, like all other species—something else will take its place. Crows, dolphins, rats, or, yes, maybe cockroaches will triumph.

Abbey, in meditating on the benefit of the death of the man at Grandview Point, came close to the bitter truth that, just as the demise of an older individual makes way for youth, so the extinction of a species, on a grander scale, cracks open ecologic niches for new life. If we take things even further, the sun will, in due time, blaze into its own death cycle, engulfing the rocks orbiting around it with supernova energy. Gamma, alpha, and beta rays will fry our humble globe into a radioactive cinder.

Yup, it's gonna happen. Humanity will be no more than a hiccup of cosmic history, molecular debris floating in a vacuum amid the far-flung jetsam of space. Abbey's books will be gone someday, just like my books and yours. All the works of Shakespeare and Beethoven, too. Gone. Atomized.

What does facing all this leave us with? Nihilism? Anarchy? Mass suicide?

I think not. In the end, there remains but one thing granting us hope and allowing us to carry on in a temporary world: love. Love for the waves cascading over our beaches, love for the beauty of a mysterious slot canyon, love for one other.

Beneath all of Abbey's works flows the hidden current of this river of emotion. If he didn't feel enamored, he never would have written so eloquently about the desert's wonders, about the joys of female companionship, about the pleasures of hiking with a buddy deep into the perilous Maze. Actions reveal character much more clearly than words, and Abbey's deeds—the writing in his books—show love triumphs over violence.

Damnation and hellfire, those of us left here alive can still have a blast during the short time allotted us. We are all blessed with the opportunity to stride, cycle, swim, hike, surf, mountain climb, and hobble our way all over this wondrous blue-green sphere, with its teeming oceans, rivers, forests, canyons, and glaciers, with its wildlife—naked apes included—and yes, with its deserts. And if certain individuals and organizations want to hasten our planet's inevitable demise, we should do everything we can to prevent them from succeeding.

There really is no excuse. Like Abbey, we should all be earthiests.

PART 3

FRIENDS, ACQUAINTANCES, AND COLLEAGUES

It is not enough to understand the natural world; the point is to defend and preserve it.

—EDWARD ABBEY, *A VOICE CRYING IN THE WILDERNESS* (1989)

Owachomo Bridge, Utah (April 2001)

CHAPTER 8

Abbey's Road

EDWARD HOAGLAND

EDWARD ABBEY, WHO died in March 1989, at sixty-two, seemed, at his best, like the nonpareil "nature writer" of recent decades. It was a term he came to detest, a term used to pigeonhole and marginalize some of the more intriguing American writers alive, writers who are dealing with matters central to us, yet it can be a ticket to oblivion in the review media. Joyce Carol Oates, for instance, in a slapdash though interesting essay called "Against Nature," speaks of nature writers' "painfully limited sense of responses. . . . REVERENCE, AWE, PIETY, MYSTICAL ONENESS." She must have never read Mr. Abbey; yet it was characteristic of him that for an hour or two, he might have agreed.

He wrote with exceptional exactitude and an uncommonly honest and logical understanding of causes and consequences, but he also loved argument, churlishness, and exaggeration. Personally, he was a labyrinth of anger and generosity, shy but arresting because of his mixture of hillbilly with cowboy qualities, and even when silent, he appeared bigger than life. He had hitchhiked west from Appalachia for the first time at seventeen, for what became an immediate love match, and, I'm sure, slept out more nights under the stars than all of his current competition combined. He was uneven, self-indulgent as a writer, and sometimes scanted his talent by working too fast. But he had about him an authenticity that springs from the page and is beloved by a rising generation of readers who have enabled his early collection of rambles, *Desert Solitaire* (1968), to run through eighteen printings in mass-market paperback, and his fine comic novel, *The Monkey Wrench Gang* (1975), to sell half a million copies. Both books, indeed, have inspired a new eco-guerrilla environmental organization called Earth First!, whose other patron saint is Ned Ludd (from whom the Luddites took their name), though it's perhaps no more radical than John Muir's Sierra Club appeared to be in 1892, when that group was formed.

Like many good writers, Abbey dreamed of producing "The Fat Masterpiece," as he called the "nuvvie" he had worked on for the last dozen years of his life, which was supposed to boil everything down to a thousand pages. When edited in half, it came out in 1988 as *The Fool's Progress*, an autobiographical yarn that lunges cross-country several times, full of apt descriptions and antic fun—*Ginger Man* stuff—though not with the coherence or poignancy he had hoped for. A couple of his other novels hold up fairly well too: *Black Sun* and *The Brave Cowboy*, which came out in movie form starring Kirk Douglas and Walter Matthau in 1962 (*Lonely Are the Brave*) and brought Abbey a munificent $7,500.

I do think he wrote masterpieces, but they were more slender: the essays in *Desert Solitaire* and an equivalent sampler that you might put together from subsequent collections like *Down the River, Beyond the Wall*, and *The Journey Home*. His rarest strength was in being concise, because he really knew what he thought and cared for. He loved the desert—"red mountains like mangled iron"—liked people in smallish clusters, and didn't mince words in saying that industrial rapine, glitz malls, and tract sprawl were an abomination heralding devastating events. While writing as handsomely as others do, he never lost sight of the fact that much of Creation is rapidly being destroyed. "Growth for the sake of growth is the ideology of the cancer cell," he wrote. And he adopted for a motto Walt Whitman's line "Resist much, obey little." Another was Thoreau's summary of *Walden*: "If I repent of anything it is very likely to be my good behavior. What demon possessed me that I have behaved so well?"

Abbey traveled less than some writers do, but it is not necessary to go dithering around our suffering planet, visiting the Amazon, Indonesia, Bhutan, and East Africa. The crisis is plain in anyone's neck of the woods, and the exoticism of globe-trotting may only blur one's vision. Nor do we need to become mystical transcendentalists and commune with God. (*One Life at a Time, Please* is another of Abbey's titles. On his hundreds of camping trips he tended to observe and enjoy the wilds rather than submerge his soul.) What is needed is honesty, a pair of eyes, and a further dollop of fortitude to spit the truth out, not genuflecting to "Emersonian" optimism, or journalistic traditions of staying deadpan, or the saccharine pressures of magazine editors who want their readers to feel good.

Emerson would be roaring with heartbreak and Thoreau would be raging with grief in these 1990s. *Where were you when the world burned? Get mad, for a change, for heaven's sake!* I believe they would say to milder colleagues.

Abbey didn't sell to the big book clubs or reach best-sellerdom or collect major prizes. When, at sixty, he was offered a smallish one by the American Academy of Arts and Letters, he rejected it with a fanfare of rhetoric, probably because it had come too late. Warhorse that he was, he did not find a ready market in mainstream publications of any stripe and was relegated through most of his career by the publicity arm of publishing to the death trap of "naturalist" stuff. So the success, wholly word of mouth, of *The Monkey Wrench Gang* in paperback pleased him more than anything else, and he delighted in telling friends who the real-life counterparts were for its characters, Seldom Seen Smith, Bonnie Abbzug, and George Washington Hayduke. They, too, had torn down billboards, yanked up survey stakes, poured sand into bulldozer gas tanks, and sabotaged "certain monstrosities" in fragilely scenic regions that shouldn't need freelance protection in the first place, as "Seldom Seen" says, still taciturn now, when you call him up.

Abbzug speaks of how Abbey in real life would go through three (used) cars a year, bouncing across the Sonoran desert on his pleasure jaunts, peeling the plates off of each as it died. And when they got fooling, he would laugh till he had to come up for air, then laugh some more, even once when they'd broken down a great many miles from water and thought they were doomed, with only a bottle of wine to live on. Most good writers are walkers, but Abbey was something different, ranging the Southwest afoot or river running with somewhat the scope of John Muir in the High Sierras. It was the building of Hetch Hetchy Dam in Yosemite National Park (now thought to have been unnecessary for San Francisco's water needs) that finally embittered Muir, and the unfinished business of "monkey wrenching" in the *The Monkey Wrench Gang* is to blow up Glen Canyon Dam, a structure that, before Abbey's eyes, had drowned a whole stretch of the Colorado River's most pristine, precious canyons.

Robinson Jeffers, another regionalist of fluctuating popularity, who made of the close examination of his home country at Big Sur in California a prism to look at the rest of the world, concluded in several poems that mankind had turned into "a sick microbe," a "deformed ape," a "botched experiment that has run wild and ought to be stopped." In "The Broken

Balance" (1929) he spoke for Abbey's anger as well:

> The beautiful places killed like rabbits to make a city,
> The spreading fungus, the slime-threats
> And spores . . . I remember the farther
> Future, and the last man dying
> Without succession under the confident eyes of the stars.

"Let's keep things the way they were," Abbey liked to say. Yet he was a bold, complex man who had had five wives and five children by the end of his life; and although he spilled too much energy into feuds with his allies and friends, he was often a jubilant writer, a regular gleeman, not just a threnodist, and he wanted to be remembered as a writer of "that letter which is never finished"—literature—such as *Desert Solitaire* is.

We corresponded occasionally for twenty years, wanting to go for a lengthy sail on the Sea of Cortez or go camping somewhere in the hundred-mile Air Force gunnery range, which, for its isolation, eventually became another favorite redoubt of his. I hoped we could drift down the Yukon River together and compile a dual diary. ("Is that dual or *duel?*" he asked once.) He had lived in Hoboken, New Jersey, for a couple of years while unhappily married, with the "Vampire State Building" on the skyline—also in Scotland and Italy—and responded to Manhattan's incomparably gaudy parade of faces as a cosmopolitan, though marked, himself, as an outlander by his uncut grayish beard, slow speech, earnest eyes, red-dog-road shuffle, raw height and built, and jean jacket or shabby brown tweed. On his way home to Oracle, Arizona, he'd usually stop in the Alleghenies, after conferring in New York City with editors, to visit his mother, Mildred, a Woman's Christian Temperance Union veteran, and his father, Paul Revere Abbey, a registered Socialist and old Wobbly organizer, who'd met Eugene V. Debs in his youth and has toured Cuba and still cuts hickory fence posts in the woods for a living.

Abbey died of internal bleeding from a circulatory disorder, with a few weeks' notice of how sick he was. Two days before the event, he decided to leave the hospital, wishing to die in the desert, and at sunup had himself disconnected from the tubes and machinery. His wife, Clarke, and three friends drove him out of town as far as his condition allowed. They built a campfire for him to look at, until, feeling death at hand, he crawled into his sleeping bag with Clarke. But by noon, finding he was still alive and possibly better, he asked to be taken home and placed on a mattress on the floor of his writing cabin. There he said his gentle good-byes.

His written instructions were that he should be "transported in the bed of a pickup truck" deep into the desert and buried anonymously, wrapped in his sleeping bag, in a beautiful spot where his grave would never be found, with "lots of rocks" piled on top to keep the coyotes off. Abbey of course loved coyotes (and, for that matter, buzzards) and had played the flute to answer their howls during the many years he had earned his living watching for fires from government towers on the Grand Canyon's North Rim, on Aztec Peak in Tonto National Forest, and in Glacier National Park, before he finally won tenure as a "Fool Professor" at the University of Arizona. His friend who was the model for G. W. Hayduke in *The Monkey Wrench Gang* was squatting beside him on the floor as his life ebbed away—"Hayduke," under a real-life name, is a legend in his own right in parts of the West, a contemporary mountain man who returned to Tucson as to a "calving ground" several years ago when he wanted to have children—and the last smile that crossed Abbey's face was when "Hayduke" told him where he would be put.

The place is, inevitably, a location where mountain lions, antelope, bighorn sheep, deer, and javelinas leave tracks, where owls, poorwills, and coyotes hoot, rattlesnakes crawl, and cacomistles scratch, with a range of stiff terrain overhead and greasewood, rabbit-bush, ocotillo, and noble old cactuses about. First seven, then ten buzzards gathered while the grave was being dug; but, as he had wished, it was a rocky spot. "Hayduke" jumped into the hole to be sure it felt OK before laying Abbey in, and afterward, in a kind of reprise of the antic spirit that animates *The Monkey Wrench Gang* (and that should make anybody but a developer laugh out loud), went around heaping up false rock piles at ideal grave sites throughout the Southwest, because this last peaceful act of outlawry on Abbey's part was the gesture of legend, and there will be seekers for years.

The stuff of legend: like Thoreau's serene passage from life muttering the words "moose" and "Indian," and Muir's thousand-mile walks to Georgia, or in the Sierras, "the Range of Light." Can he be compared to them? Muir, after all, bullied the Catskills naturalist John Burroughs from sheer orneriness, as Abbey, the controversialist, regularly blistered his colleagues with vitriol through the mails, and Thoreau—a stark individual in his own way—orated vehemently on behalf of the reviled "terrorist" John Brown. (That Thoreau of witticisms such as what a pearl was: "the hardened tear of a disease clam, murdered in its old age.") A magazine published Abbey's last account of a trip by horseback through Utah's slickrock canyons, and it's got a hop like a knuckleball's on it, unmistakably Abbey, as briny with personality as his heyday essays. Nor had twenty years changed him. Thoreau, by contrast, in a swift incandescent burst of work, vaulted from the relatively conventional *Week on the Concord and Merrimack Rivers* to the vision of *Walden,* but soon fell back into dutiful natural science. And Muir went from being a lone-wolf botanist and geologist to a passionate advocate, skillfully lobbying Teddy Roosevelt and William Howard Taft on behalf of Yosemite National Park, until, late in life, when he was finished with localism, he wandered rather disconsolately to Africa, Asia, and South America in celebrity guise.

Abbey was consistent but, unlike Thoreau, was not self-contained; some compulsive agenda unknown to him blunted his efforts to surpass himself. And his ambitions were confined to truth telling, rhapsody, and the lambasting of villains. As an essayist he did not aspire to the grandeur or versatility, or try hard to turn into a man of letters either—his novels can seem flat or foreshortened next to Peter Matthiessen's, for example, and his literary pronouncements were scattershot, bilious, or cursory. Like most conservationists, he was a political radical but a social conservative, going so far as to aver the old-fashioned idea that there are two sexes, not simply one, which expressed with customary crowing, abrasive overstatement, offended people. (Yet he wrote in a love letter to a woman friend after a breakup, "If you ever need me in any way I will cross continents and oceans to help you," a sentiment that even his favorite bête noire, Gloria Steinem, might have appreciated.) Speaking of various sins of omission of his personal life, he would sometimes describe himself as a coward—as being a neglectful father to his sons and a passive witness to his second wife's death by cancer, in particular.

There's a saying that life gets better once you have outlived the bastards, which would certainly be true except that as you do, you are also outliving your friends. I miss him. Sitting in silence in restaurants as our twinned melancholy groped for expression, or talking with him of hoodoo stone-pillars and red-rock canyons, I've seldom felt closer to anybody. Honesty is a key to essay writing; not just "a room of one's own" but a view of one's own. The lack of it sinks more talented people into chatterbox hackwork than anything else. And Abbey aspired to speak for himself in all honesty—X: His Mark—and died telling friends he had done what he could and was ready. He didn't buzz off to Antarctica or the Galapagos Islands, yet no one will ever wonder what he really saw as the world burned. He said it; didn't sweeten it or blink at it or water it down or hope the web of catastrophes might just go away. He felt homesick for the desert when he went to Alaska, and turned back, yet if you travel much there, it is Abbey's words you will see tacked on the wall again and again in remote homestead cabins in the Brooks Range or in offices in Juneau, because he had already written of greed, of human brutality and howling despair, better than writers who write books on Alaska.

Last year a paean to Abbey's work in *National Review* finished with a quote from a passage in Faulkner: "Oleh, Chief. Grandfather." To which we can add Amen. But instead let's close with a bit of Ed Abbey, from a minor book called *Appalachian Wilderness* (1970), which foretold why he chose that lost grave where he lies:

> How strange and wonderful is our home, our earth, with its swirling vaporous atmosphere, its flowing and frozen liquids, its trembling plants, its creeping crawling, climbing creatures, the croaking things with wings that hang on rocks and soar through fog, the furry grass, the scaly seas . . . how utterly rich and wild. . . . Yet some among us have the nerve, the insolence, the brass, the gall to whine about the limitations of our earthbound fate and yearn for some more perfect world beyond the sky. We are none of us good enough for the world we have.

CHAPTER 9

Desert Solitaire Revisited

DOUG PEACOCK

WHEN *DESERT SOLITAIRE* hit the bookstores in 1968, the world was introduced to a writer who was at once eloquent, angry, poetic, crude, and funny
as hell. Edward Abbey wrote precise prose that raced like a jackrabbit, and
he spoke with a voice that stung with the pungency of garlic. Abbey was
a fierce defender of wilderness, the enemy of injustice, and champion of
the voiceless and powerless of the world. Along his cantankerous path, Ed
slaughtered as many sacred cows as he could. Accordingly, *Desert Solitaire*
was received with both exuberant praise and caustic scorn.

Clearly, *Desert Solitaire* belongs on a separate shelf from most "nature"
books. It advocates civil disobedience and empowers many readers to
action, even to change the course of their lives. Forty years ago, my best
friend from Michigan pored over the book, passed it on to me, then
took up residence defending the high desert. A woman in Oregon read
it, packed up, and moved to southeastern Utah where she took a job as
a national park ranger, busting archeological thieves for looting Indian
burial grounds. She's still out there.

The publication of *Desert Solitaire* and the emergence of the militant
western conservation movement in America was at least synchronous and
arguably no coincidence. The radical environmental group Earth First!
was a direct descendant of Abbey's writings. Throughout the 1970s and
1980s, more lives changed in response to Ed's challenge; conservationists
and new crops of activists pledged allegiance to the rights of wild animals,
plants, and rocks. Abbey lives on today as the ethical compass, the tribal
muse, and sacred rage inspiring those who steer the helm of the more
visionary and wide-reaching of contemporary wilderness preservation

efforts, such as the Wildlands Project or America's Round River Conservation Studies.

Because of this influence, Abbey was stamped with various labels, wrongly tagged as a misanthrope (Ed was a man fueled by love and joy), eco-anarchist, and called the patron saint of American radical environmentalism. Such confining representations miss the considerable artistry of his writing and nowhere is this literary legacy better illustrated than in *Desert Solitaire*. The range of this book runs from tight lyrical passages of desert beauty to parables of nuclear war, from ribald, politically incorrect rants to paradoxical hints of a post-apocalyptic world, all wrapped in contradiction and served up with a self-deprecating belly laugh. The more you ask from this book, the more you reap.

Current biographies of Abbey sometimes state he was born in Home, Pennsylvania, and died in Oracle, Arizona. Neither is true. Ed simply liked the names (he got his mail in Oracle). Although Abbey would be accused of never letting a few unimportant facts get in the way of a good story, he was in fact after a larger truth. "This is not primarily a book about the desert," Abbey wrote in his introduction to the original edition of *Desert Solitaire*. "Since you cannot get the desert into a book any more than a fisherman can haul up the sea in his nets, I have tried to create a world of words in which the desert figures as more as a medium than as material. Not imitation but evocation has been the goal."

Thus Abbey listens to spadefoot toads singing from their summer rain-filled potholes and finds an alternative view to traditional biology: "Why do they sing?" Ed asks. Is it the poison in the amphibian's skin that permits such bold toad singing amid choruses of prowling coyote yips? No, they sing from joy, he writes. "Has joy any survival value in the operations of evolution? I suspect that it does; I suspect that the morose and fearful are doomed to quick extinction. Where there is no joy there can be no courage; and without courage all other virtues are useless."

The popular reception of *Desert Solitaire* mildly irritated Ed Abbey. Like other novelists who prefer to be remembered for their fiction, Ed considered his desert masterpiece an unexpected, unintentional love child. The commercial success of this classic especially surprised him. "After [writing] that book," he said, "I've never had to work an honest day in my life."

It might appear that Edward Abbey stood by every word he wrote in *Desert Solitaire*, but that was not the case. He lived to doggedly regret the passages on desert composers: "I'd do anything," he told me back in the

Monument Valley, in the heart of Abbey country (May 1998)

1970s, "to take back those pages on music [Berg, Webern, etc.]." Ed went on to prefer Mozart or the late quartets of Beethoven, "Good ol' Ludwig," he wrote, "old courage-giver, hero of Western man."

With his magical, sensual evocation of the desert, fierce defense of wilderness, and irreverent attacks on conventions of every angle of the political spectrum, Abbey has been compared favorably to his heroes and fellow conservationists: Henry David Thoreau, Aldo Leopold, and John Muir. But *Desert Solitaire* stands apart from the works of these great men in that it is a thoroughly modern classic; it carries us beyond the end of the twentieth century and into the perilous topography of today's world. Abbey tells us right off that the pristine landscape of *Desert Solitaire* "is already gone or going under fast." The cloud on his horizon is "Progress." The bulldozers of corporate development scrape away at the wilderness and "Industrial Tourism" invades our national parks.

And there is more: The terrible beasts stalking the edges of our human world today—nuclear warfare, even global warming—are already taking shape in the landscape of *Desert Solitaire*. In "Rocks," Abbey tells a story of a murderous love triangle wrapped in atomic treachery and the rapaciousness for uranium mines. At the end of the tale, a child experiences a beautiful hallucination of the living Earth, then dies of massive overexposure to radiation—from atomic rays or rays from the sun, a parable of apocalyptic war or approaching climate change? Abbey provides no easy answers, but this much is evident: Just as we grasp our absolute need for the wild beauty of the world, we are losing it. And it is children who will pay the price.

Ed is clear what drives this madness: human greed exemplified by too many people living too high on the hog. Abbey foretells the collapse of industrial civilization, warning us that we must reduce our ecological footprint before catastrophe does it for us. He fears a world, as he put it, "completely urbanized, completely industrialized, ever more crowded environment. For my own part I would rather take my chances in a thermonuclear war than live in such a world."

Time and wind will bury the polluted cities of the Southwest, he warns, "growth for the sake of growth is a cancerous madness," he said, and human population will be dramatically reduced by the consequences of our self-destructive industrial technology. Out of this wasteland, the boldest of survivors will wander a new wilderness and perhaps get it right the second time: "Feet on earth. Knock on wood. Touch stone. Good luck to all," Abbey's "bedrock of animal faith."

Edward Abbey is not alone in these views, just significantly ahead of his time. James Lovelock, famed contemporary global warming critic and originator of the Gaia hypothesis, predicts that in the next thirty years rising oceans will displace a billion hungry refugees, worldwide desertification will draw the Sahara north into Europe, and Berlin will be as hot as Baghdad. By the end of the century, Lovelock predicts, the human world will be torn apart by famine and disease, starving Asians who cannot grow their own food migrating into Siberia and precipitating nuclear war between Russia and China, all factors combining to kill off 6 billion of the world's 6.6 billion human beings. The plants and creatures of our lovely planet will suffer the sixth great extinction, the most severe yet and entirely human caused. Human civilization, Lovelock fears, would collapse.

Abbey, on the other hand, doesn't allow us to settle into our easy chairs of hard numbers and precise prediction; yet he firmly plants the warning seeds of industrial ruination and the fate of the earth in the cryptogamic soil of *Desert Solitaire*. Instead, his polemic alternates with poetics and contentious humor. Ed used contradictory argument as an art form. He wanted to speak the truth, "especially unpopular truth." Truth that offends the "traditional, the mythic, the sentimental."

What we are left with is a book like no other. Ed's own introduction is among the very best in American letters. *Desert Solitaire* is prophetic, a classic of a nature book and a hoot to read. Ed's central message proclaims the paramount importance of wilderness and the necessity of the fight against the destruction of wild places, just as we would defend our own home from an armed intruder. Many of us thought that someone, maybe several writers, would come along and fill those big lecherous, toothy shoes Ed left behind. But, for whatever reason, they didn't. I believe Abbey's masterpiece is the most important book yet written in the considerable library of conservation literature.

Edward Abbey died as he had lived, with great dignity, fierce in his love of life, thinking of the wild desert and of his children. I shudder yet with the memory: his death was the bravest I've attended. To live in the joy of each day, experience the sorrow, and, yes, to fight, to rage: Wilderness, he said, is the only thing worth saving.

On his very last solo camping trip to our most inviolate of desert places, the Cabeza Prieta wildlands of Arizona, Abbey scratched out his last notes in his field notebook around a tiny campfire:

Smog in the valley between here and the Growler Range. Fucking Phoenix. Fucking LA. Fucking techno-industrial culture. You know what? I wish Doug Peacock would appear, looking for me.

Well, Ed, I say to the smoke, I'm on my way. We all are.

CHAPTER 10

Abbey Following His Own Truth

JACK LOEFFLER

AS I WRITE these opening lines, I reflect back twenty-five years when four of us carried our fallen comrade, Edward Abbey, to his grave in a distant desert hinterland. The night before we buried him, we camped well apart, giving each other space to ruminate on our respective loss. Tom recalled that in the night, a band of coyotes came into our camp and sang their wild chorus (a song of farewell?), then left us to our silence. That was Ed's last campsite above ground.

Ed was a dear friend to many of us. No one can claim Ed all to himself or herself. Ed was big enough to go around. Indeed, twenty-five years after his death, he remains larger than life and is still growing. Every week or two or three, Ed shows up in my dreams looking not a day older than his sixty-two years of allotted life on this planet Earth. And in my dreams we continue the conversation that we have shared now for many decades. Never does he say, "I told you so," even though he reminded me to "Follow the truth no matter where it leads" on many occasions when we camped or hiked our seemingly endless trail that sadly come to an end on March 14, 1989.

In retrospect, Ed could see as far and wide as anyone I have ever known. He needed mountaintops to let time and space pass through his highly honed mind. He was happy to head into the wind, hike upstream to glimpse what was coming. And he did.

On the first day of 1983 by current reckoning, Ed and I returned from a camping trip in the Superstition Mountains. By then, he knew that his time on the planet was limited by the malaise that would finally kill him. We had talked about this nightly as we sat looking into our campfire. There was nothing maudlin in our conversation, just a righteous pissed-offed-ness that old age was not in Ed's future, ever tempered by Ed's wry sense of humor. When we got back to his homeland west of Tucson, I pulled out my tape recorder and we spent the afternoon recording Ed's words and thoughts for posterity. Right off the bat, Ed said, "I think human beings have made a nightmare out of their collective history. Seems to me that the last five thousand years have been pretty awful—cruelty, slavery, torture, religious fanaticism, ideological fanaticism, the old serfdom of agriculture and the new serfdom of industrialism. I think humankind probably made a big mistake when we gave up the hunting and gathering way of life for agriculture. Ever since then the majority of us have led the lives of slaves and dependents. I look forward to the time the industrial system collapses and we all go back to chasing wild cattle and buffalo on horseback.

"I think that the human race has become a plague on this Earth. There are far too many of us making demands on one defenseless little planet. Human beings have as much right to be here as any other animal, but we have abused that right by allowing our numbers to grow so great and our appetites to become so gross that we are plundering the Earth and destroying most other forms of life, threatening our own survival by greed and stupidity and this insane mania for quantitative growth, for perpetual expansion, the desire for domination over Nature and our fellow humans.

"The wilderness is vanishing. Next to go will be the last primitive tribes, the traditional cultures that still survive in places like the Far North and the African and South American tropics. And if the whole planet becomes industrialized, technologized, urbanized, that would be almost the worst disaster that can befall the planet and human beings. I think it would lead to the ultimate techno-tyranny that some of our better science fiction writers have prophesied.

"I think by virtue of reason, common sense, the evidence of our five good bodily senses and daily experience, we can imagine a better way to live, with fairly simple solutions. Not easy—but simple. Beginning here in America—we should set the example. We have set the example for pillaging the plant and we should set the example for preserving life, including human life. First, most important, reduce human numbers, gradually, by normal attrition, letting senile old farts like you and me die off. Reduce the human population to a reasonable number, a self-sustaining number—for the United States something like one hundred million, or even fifty million should be plenty. And then, second, simplify our needs and demands, so that we're not preying to excess on other forms of life—plant life and animal life—by developing new attitudes, a natural reverence for all forms of life.

"I consider myself an absolute egalitarian. I think that all human beings are essentially equal, deserve equal regard and consideration. Certainly everyone differs in ability. Some people are bigger, stronger; some are smarter; some are more clever with their hands; others are more clever with their brains. There's an infinite variation in talent and ability and intelligence among individual humans, but I think that all, except the most depraved, violently, criminally insane—generals and dictators—are of equal value. There's another basis for this kind of egalitarianism. Just by virtue of being alive, we deserve to be respected as individuals. Furthermore, that respect for the value of each human being should be extended to each living thing on the planet, to our fellow creatures, beginning with our pet dogs and cats and horses. Humans find it easy to love them. We can and must learn to love the wild animals, the mountain lions and the rattlesnakes and the coyotes, the buffalo and the elephants. And developing that way, extend our ability to love to include plant life. A tree, a shrub, a blade of grass deserve respect and sympathy as fellow living things.

"I think you can even go beyond that to respect the rocks, the air, the water. Because each is part of a whole—each part dependent on the other parts. If only for our own self-respect and survival, we can learn to love the world around us—go beyond the human and love the nonhuman. Instead of trying to dominate, subjugate, enslave it, as we've been doing for the last five thousand years, learn to live in some sort of harmony with it. Use what we must use; all living creatures have to feed on other living creatures. But do it at a reasonable level so that other things can survive. I guess Albert Schweitzer was right when he said, 'We must learn reverence for all forms of life,' even those we have to hunt, kill, and eat. Especially those. . . . We've got to teach our children sympathy for life and all living things. That begins as an individual, personal responsibility—develop this love for life in ourselves, try to pass it on to our children, try to spread it beyond the family as far as we can by whatever means are available. Teachers, writers, artists, scientists, performers, politicians have the primary obligation. A good politician is one with the ability to lead people toward this attitude. It's hard to think of any such."

This is the model by which Ed tried his best to live his life. In order for him to feel a sense of balance within himself, he had to interrupt his writing time at his manual typewriter, and his time as a husband and householder, to spend time in the wilderness, periods of time long enough for the spirit of the wild to seep into his soul. It was while camping that his sense of egalitarianism evolved from political to reverential proportions.

Ed was a lifelong anarchist who believed in self-governance, or governance from within small communities. He regarded anarchism as democracy developed to its highest level. Egalitarianism lies at the heart of anarchism, and Ed was able to extend his sense of anarchism far beyond just the human realm to include all life and beyond. He loved the natural world with an intensity so profound that he inflamed that early cadre of environmentalists who read his classic book of essays, *Desert Solitaire*. Through his great talent as a writer, he melded anarchism and environmentalism.

Ed once told me that he regarded the Tao Te Ching as "the best little book ever written." His professor, Archie Bahm of the philosophy department at the University of New Mexico, had penned an interpretation of this Chinese treatise attributed to Lao Tzu that he titled *Nature and Intelligence*. Bahm's interpretation is essentially for Western eyes and in that respect is well done. It had to have influenced Ed Abbey as he worked toward a master's degree in philosophy. His master's thesis is entitled "Anarchism and the Morality of Violence" and focuses on five thinkers: Pierre-Joseph Proudhon, George Sorel, William Godwin, Mikhail Bakunin, and Pyotr Kropotkin.

After Ed's death, Archie Bahm told me that Ed had wanted to write a history of anarchist thought for his master's thesis. Bahm and department chair, Herbert Spencer, thought this too ambitious a project and limited Ed to a more modest kernel. Years later, Ed gave me a copy of George Woodcock's *Anarchism*, which he regarded as adequate, competently written. Bahm later told me that in his opinion, Abbey had lived his anarchist philosophy completely, that indeed he was far better prepared to give voice to anarchist thought than anyone else in his generation. Thus, Archie Bahm came to realize that academic anarchism is greatly superseded by the real McCoy.

One of the main themes of our ongoing conversation involved defense of the natural world. I asked this of Ed, "When it becomes apparent that we're not gaining fast enough in the wake of big business and political maneuvering, what steps do you think are justifiable in trying to turn the tide that seems to lead, literally, to a dead end, not just for our species, but the whole planet?"

Ed replied, "I suppose if political means fail us—public organization and public pressure—if those don't do what has to be done, then we'll be driven to more extreme defensive measures in defending our Earth. Here in the United States, I can see a lot more acts of civil disobedience beginning to occur as the bulldozers and the drilling rigs attempt to move into the wilderness and into the back country and the farmlands and the seashores and other precious places. And if civil disobedience is not enough, I imagine there will be sabotage, violence against machinery, property. These are desperate measures. If they become widespread, it could be that the battle has already been lost. I don't know what would happen beyond that. Such resistance might stimulate some sort of police state reaction, repression, a real military-industrial dictatorship in this country.

"But still, personally, I feel that when other means fail, we are morally justified—not merely justified, but morally obligated—to defend that which we love by whatever means are available. Just as, if my family, my children were attacked, I wouldn't hesitate to use violence to defend them. By the same principle, if land that I love is being violated, raped, plundered, murdered, and all political means to save it have failed, I personally feel that sabotage is morally justifiable. At least if it does any good, if it'll help. If it will only help you to feel good . . ."

I responded, "I would hazard that some would call acts of physical sabotage 'terrorism.'"

To which Ed replied, "The distinction is quite clear and simple. Sabotage is an act of force or violence against material objects, machinery, in which life is not endangered, or should not be. Terrorism, on the other hand, is violence against living things—human beings and other living things. That kind of terrorism is generally practiced by governments against their own peoples. . . . Our government committed great acts of terrorism against the people of Vietnam. That's what terrorism means—violence and the threat of violence against human beings and other forms of life. Which is radically different from sabotage, a much more limited form of conflict. I'd go so far as to say that a bulldozer tearing up a hillside, ripping out trees for a logging operation or a strip mine is committing terrorism—violence against life."

I asked Ed what he thought to be the American Southwest's biggest enemy.

He replied, "Oh, the same old thing—expansion, development, commercial greed, industrial growth. That kind of growth that has become a pathological condition in our society. That insatiable demand for more and more; the urge to dominate and consume and destroy. The rangelands overgrazed and the hills being strip-mined and the rivers being dammed and the farmlands eroded and the air, soil, and water being poisoned in the usual, various ways—just the endless speeding up of this process and the expansion of its territory. The whole West is being destroyed by this corporate greed. Not to mention the rest of the world. . . .

"But where, how did the disease begin? It really does seem to me like a kind of cancer, a tumor on human society. I would say it began when we gave up the traditional hunting and gathering way of life and made the terrible mistake of settling down to agriculture. Somebody said that the plough may have done more damage to human life on the planet than the sword. I'd be inclined to agree.

"Then agriculture was followed by industrialism, which began only about two hundred years ago, as a new way of looking at the world by a few European philosophers and scientists a century earlier. They discovered the means, the ability to achieve mastery over nature. And here we come back to human nature again. Once we discover we have the ability to push things around, or to push other people around, most humans do not have the self-control to refrain from using such power. 'Power corrupts,' as some wise man once said. 'And absolute power corrupts absolutely' [Lord Acton]. Science and technology give us absolute power over the rest of life, including human life. And power not only corrupts; it attracts the worst elements of the human herd. Power attracts the worst men and corrupts the best."

Edward Abbey was committed to the defense of the natural landscape of the American Southwest. At one point, his agent Don Congden had advised him to write about what he loved. Thus Ed wrote *Desert Solitaire*, one of the most enduring classics in southwestern literature. Ed was an avid reader his whole life long. He told me that he regarded William Shakespeare as a toady, a sycophant, an author whose greatest hero was Caliban with nary a Spartacus in his oeuvre. In his own literature, his greatest hero in my opinion was Jack Burns, who first appeared riding his horse into Albuquerque from the Northwest, occasionally having to cut barbed-wire fence to get to Albuquerque to save his friend from bondage in jail. Burns was the hero of his third novel, *The Brave Cowboy*, which was to become the great feature film *Lonely Are the Brave*. Jack Burns was loosely modeled after his friend Ralph Newcomb, who appeared in the flesh as Ed's river-running mate in *Desert Solitaire*.

Jack Burns rode through three more of Ed's novels: *The Monkey Wrench Gang, Good News*, and *Hayduke Lives!* It wasn't until *Hayduke Lives!* that Jack Burns was revealed to be both the Lone Ranger and the father of George Washington Hayduke. It was in this novel that one of the good guys shot and killed one of the bad guys. Indeed, Jack Burns himself shot and killed one of those Earth-plunderers, who was both terrorizing the landscape and was about to shoot Hayduke. Thus Burns both saved the life of his son and helped stop the razing of the land. He defended what he loved, no holds barred. That was Ed's final statement on the subject. He wrote the first draft of *Hayduke Lives!* and died a week or so later. He himself had wanted to die a hero's death, but by then he was too weak. One can rarely foresee the actual circumstances of one's death.

He said this to me back in 1983: "I look forward to the day when somebody with a terminal disease (such as life) is going to strap a load of TNT around his waist and go down onto the bowels of the Glen Canyon Dam and blow that ugly thing to smithereens. That would be a good way to go.

"I think that one should live honorably and die honorably. One's death should mean something. One should try to have a good death, just as one tries to have a good life. And if it's necessary to die fighting, then that's what we should do. If we're lucky, we can die peacefully. But few of us will ever live in such a world."

At one point, Ed told me that he was a pantheist. At another point, he called himself a "naturist." He believed in the flow of Nature, and therein lay his spiritual consciousness. He recognized his kinship to this living planet and all its components be they living or inert. He wanted to be regarded as a writer, an artist. When he wrote, his head sweated profusely, as though his sweat glands were trying to temper the fires in his mind. He wrote with passion.

Ed was a true friend, as true a friend as I'll ever have. We hiked, we ran rivers, we camped, we talked, we minded each other's backs—we tried to peer into the mystery of existence, listen to its song. We shared a deep and abiding love and deep reverence for this planet Earth and its denizens.

In Ed's own words: "I regard the invention of monotheism and the otherworldly God as a great setback for human life. Maybe even worse than the invention of agriculture. Once we took the gods out of Nature, out of the hills and forests around us and made all those little gods into one great god up in the sky, somewhere in outer space, why, about then, human beings, particularly Europeans, began to focus our attention on transcendental values, a transcendental deity, which led to a corresponding contempt for Nature and the world that feeds and supports us. From that point of view, I think that the Indians and most traditional cultures have a much wiser world view, in that they invested every aspect of the world around them—all of Nature, animal life, plant life, the landscape itself—with gods, with deity. In other words, everything was divine in some way or another. Pantheism probably led to a much wiser way of life, [making populations] more capable of surviving over long periods of time. . . .

"Call me a pantheist. If there is such a thing as divinity, and the holiness is all, then it must exist in everything, and not simply be localized in one supernatural figure beyond time and space. Either everything is divine, or nothing is. All partake of the universal divinity—the scorpion and the packrat, the June bug and the pismire, and even human beings. All or nothing, now or never, here and now."

Ed clearly understood that if humankind is going to survive the massive extinction of species that we have initiated and are daily invigorating, we are going to have to undergo a massive shift in both cultural attitude and cultural practice worldwide. When Ed died twenty-five years ago, the human population of the planet was six billion. Today it is over seven billion and rising. We are extracting ever more resources from a planet with but finite resources, and in so doing, we are leaving an enormous swath of devastation. Most of us do not love the planet as we should. Most of us are so caught up in our paltry quest for economic growth that our sensibilities have calloused over. Today, we as a species are among many species that live at the edge of oblivion.

Edward Abbey realized that we have to view reality through many windows, that techno-tyranny and economic overindulgence are blindsiding us. Ed loved science as a process of human consciousness, but he rued the overabundance of misapplication of science and also how we are collectively becoming bereft of other means of perception. Ed took his cue from the flow of Nature. With his insightful mind, he peered into many avenues of existence. Because of his endless curiosity and strong will, he concluded that no single path is the one true path. He understood that the human species is but one of millions, billions of species that have thrived on this planet. Nature itself is an ever-shifting panoply of myriad manifestations of which we are but a tiny part. He lived simply but was no stranger to complexity. He loved his life.

"There will always be something worth fighting for and something worth fighting against. That's the drama of the human condition. That's what makes life so interesting, and so entertaining, and so full of laughs— the fighting, the struggling, the friction. I don't really want to live in a peaceful utopia. From a personal point of view, the world we live in is just fine with me. Because there are so many things to laugh at and laugh about, so many things to admire and love, and so many things to despise. It's an ideal world for a writer, for anybody whose emotions are alive, for anybody who wants something to think about and talk about."

CHAPTER 11

On the Edge with Edward Abbey, Charles Ives, and the Outlaws

CHARLES BOWDEN

THE SUMMER FINALLY came when I decided to give composer Charles Ives a second chance. I was huddled along the border near the Sonora/ Arizona line in the extreme northern range of violet-crowned humming-birds and the farthest southern reach of the Border Patrol. The place is famous as a migration route of human beings and the drugs human beings need to face the dread of life. Edward Abbey was always touting Ives to me, and for years my efforts at listening had found nothing but noise. Ives himself hardly dissuaded me by saying, "in 'thinking up' music I usually have some kind of brass band with wings on it in back of my mind."

I thought I'd see if Ed was still wrong.

The area around me had fallen quiet as the new standing army of gun-men filtered into the empty ground. Choppers chuffed overhead and when I'd take a walk looking at birds, agents rolled by in their big war wag-ons. There had been no sign of the poor—the little empty tins of chili or fish, the dropped jackets, shirts, and pants, the small fires made to warm the hands—for at least three years. And then one morning I found some cast-off clothing circling a small, spent fire, empty cans, a worn shoe left behind. It had a feeling like hearing that first crane in the sky.

I remember a piece Ed put in his book *One Life at a Time, Please* back in 1988. The history comes bubbling up as I stare at the migrant camp along the creek. I quoted the stuff on illegal immigration in a review at the time and hell boiled over because people resented what Ed had written. He told me later he regretted the remarks because they were hurtful.

Like so many things he wrote, the piece begins with a roar. And then gets louder.

107

In the American Southwest, where I happen to live, only sixty miles north of the Mexican border, the subject of illegal aliens is a touchy one. Even the terminology is dangerous: the old word wetback is now considered a racist insult by all good liberals; and the perfectly correct terms illegal alien and illegal immigrant can set off charges of xenophobia, elitism, fascism, and the ever-popular genocide against anyone careless enough to use them. The only acceptable euphemism, it now appears, is something called undocumented worker.

Mexican American friends called me up and asked how I could quote anything so mean. I was putting out a magazine and people made noises about picketing it.

Ed was my friend, and I never picked friends because they agreed with me or were useful to me. For me, friendship, like love, lacks a motive. And often, there are rough edges, just as the ground that matters most to me can rake me with bad storms.

Sometimes when I wander along the creek where I stumble on the cold fire of migrants struggling north on foot, I bump into a couple that ride on an ATV complete with rifle and shotgun and strap pistols on their hips. They are armed in part because lions hunt here. And in part because of the Mexicans. Once the man waved a rusty can he discovered and warned me of the danger of illegals in the area.

I go armed with binoculars and a bird book.

Ives blasts in my head, and I can hear Ed's soft voice chastising me about my lack of understanding of this great American music. I can hear him telling me that he wants to stop every Mexican at the line, give him a gun and ammunition and send him home to fix his country. I can hear people complaining about him, though I was struck how after he died he changed and seemed to have a helluva lot more friends than he managed when alive and somehow the rough edges of his ideas and nature seemed sanded smooth and made safe.

Charles Ives says, "Stand up and take your dissonance like a man."

I have never had an Abbey problem. I have had an Abbey wound. Since he died, there has been a hole in my life, and this hole has surprised me because I think I have been around more than my share of dying and killing and did not expect his death to be more than a passing pain for me.

People sometimes look me up and want to interview me about Ed. They always had two questions it seems. Where do we find the next Ed

Abbey? And what should we do now that he is gone and can't tell us what to do?

I always tell them the same thing: we don't need a new Ed Abbey, the old one is pretty damn serviceable and besides, I want to live in a world where no one reads Ed Abbey.

I have spent decades helping illegal people break the law by driving them around checkpoints, giving them food, money, and water, giving them work when they had no work permits. I have always paid them the going rate for a U.S. citizen. I have also spent decades decrying the growing population in this country as murder of the land. And I have written and said in speeches that illegal immigration drives down wages for American citizens. I have some rough edges of my own.

About a year and a half ago I was close to stone broke and looking at birds along the creek when a Central American came out of the brush. He was dirty and confused and had gone three days without food. I fed him, cleaned him up, got him outfitted—new phone, limitless thirty-day call card, clothes, daypack—and ran him around the Border Patrol checkpoint. I also gave him a hundred or two hundred bucks from my dwindling reserves. I did this even though I am against all immigration, not simply illegal, and when I am truly sober want to cut the population of the United States down to about a hundred million maximum. And yes, while I was neglecting my bird watching and helping propel this illegal human being into the guts of the republic, I could hear Ed's voice in my head—and my God for such a bellicose guy he had a soft voice— chastising me and asking how a grizzly bear or a beleaguered wolf might feel about my decision.

I remember writing an article about an outlaw financial guy and Ed asking me how I could possibly spend time around such a man? And I remember Ed telling people when I was killing myself creating and putting out a publication that he wished I'd quit spending time on that "silly magazine."

This is the guy I miss.

Just as I miss the Central American I put up and helped avoid the agents on the line. I think if I'd ignored the illegal or Ed Abbey I'd be killing the part of me that can taste life and help life. Things are not as simple as the authorities like to make out. I remember reading a review of one of Ed's books where the critic said he was basically a fraud, that no one could know as much about classical music as Ed did and still be such a profane, woman-chasing, hard-drinking, irritable, redneck rascal.

Yes, he could.

I live in an open wound called the border. There is no easy solution. Ed's notion is sending illegals home with muskets is a quip for the barroom. In a six-year period in Mexico (2006–2012), 130,000 people or more were murdered and another 27,000 vanished into the night. Deportation, with or without guns, would explode Mexico, just as the timely shipment by the United States of gang kids raised here is causing slaughter in Guatemala, El Salvador, and Honduras.

Here, Ed, pour us another drink.

There are now over three hundred million Americans murdering the nation. There are over 112 million Mexicans living on ground devoured by centuries of abuse. There are at least ten million Mexicans living in the shadows here and, if they are sent home, they will rip the entrails out of their country. There is a big wall now on the border, one that impedes game, costs billions, and does nothing beneficial. There is a standing army of twenty thousand agents, and the boys say we cannot be safe unless we pump this up to forty-six thousand agents, lest the lesser breeds and drugs make it into our lives. There are drones in the sky and also spy cameras in planes, which, it turns out, watched and mapped out over thirty murders in Ciudad Juarez, Mexico, as a kind of test frolic (Craig Timberg, "New Surveillance Technology Can Track Everyone in an Area for Several Hours at a Time," *Washington Post*, February 5, 2014, http://www.washington post.com/business/technology/new-surveillance-technology-can-track-everyone-in-an-area-for-several-hours-at-a-time/2014/02/05/82f1556e-876f-11e3-a5bd-844629433ba3_story.html).

I can't turn my back on the poor and I can't speak up for a police state. And yes, I believe in the right to bear arms but not in the polished boots crowding my life.

Lock them out, Mexico explodes and more people flee north. Send them back and Mexico explodes. Let the corporate state keep ambling along and everything dies. Call the cops and we get the growing police state on the line. Look into the eyes of a frightened girl in the desert trying to reach her people in some small town in America and all the clever words fall into the dust.

What of it? say the documented liberals; ours is a rich and generous nation, we have room for all, let them come. And let them stay, say the conservatives; a large, cheap, frightened, docile, surplus labor force is exactly what the economy needs. Put some fear into the unions: tighten discipline, spur productivity, whip up the competition for jobs. The conservatives love their cheap labor; the liberals love their cheap cause. (Neither group, you will notice, ever invites the immigrants to move into their homes. Not into their homes!)

She says she is bipolar. For years, she lived in what politicians love to call the heartland, their code for where whites dominate. She left Mexico as a small child. Then came her teens, drugs, trouble. She bounced in and out of mental health facilities and finally had a scrape of some sort and they found out she was illegal and tossed her back. Now she works as a prostitute in a border city. When things get too out of control, she checks into an asylum where she can detox or recover from a beating by a customer.

Her smile is infectious. She is in the kitchen chopping vegetables for 120 lunatics, addicts, killers, lap dancers, and other destroyed human beings. And she is in love with an inmate of the asylum, a guy so addled he can only make visits to reality. He has never been the same since a gang member almost beat him to death. I knew the gang guy—he was a killer before he keeled over with a heart attack. I remember over lunch how he told me, with a voice so soft it reminded me of Ed, of killing, of running drugs across by paying the Border Patrol. He never mentioned beating the girl's boyfriend into a kind of dementia, but I am sure there had been too many for him keep them all in mind. He was the perfect example of what Ed wanted to keep out of the country. I took him to lunch.

She is mentally ill, has had serious problems all of her life—she beat up her grandmother, for example—is an American in all but law. And the solution was to boot her into a country as foreign to her as to Edward Abbey and now she hooks and does drugs. And loves a broken man in the asylum.

I know a man from Los Angeles. He was in a gang. He had a house, a wife, children, but he threw it away in crime, went to prison, and then was deported because he'd been born in Mexico. The heroin took over then. He got gangrene and lost some fingers. Now he is clean and he works in the asylum where the woman chops vegetables. He is in charge of the drugs for the patients.

For years, he would not leave the asylum. He was afraid the streets would whisper heroin in his ear. Now through a fluke of the Internet, he has established contact with his daughter—for years she had thought him dead. He wants to return to Los Angeles for visits and try to heal the wounds he created. He is built like a tank and he is a man on a mission. This time from God, he says.

I am in a café, the girl has just finished high school. She is illegal. She has worked for years in the fields and now wishes to go to college. She is a Dreamer, a person with goals but a legal question mark. She wants to be a nurse because she saw nurses take care of her brother as he fought cancer. Her other brother was deported, and she cannot see him because she lacks the papers to cross and come back. Her mother cleans for a guy in the big house outside of town, and when the Border Patrol raided the giant agribusiness the guy owns, the Mexican woman hid in the bushes outside the house. The whole family worked in the fields for years, where they could earn eighty cents for each ten-gallon bucket of green chiles. The onions, she tells me, were the worst because you had to crawl on your knees to top the plants.

A family of coatimundis forages slowly in front of me. Wild turkeys move through the yellow grass and a few rose-throated becards nest here on the far north rim of their world. The nearby refuge catches shots of lions on its hidden camera. Or a line of men tired and dirty moving north to the cities of the United States. There is a place along the dirt road when someone leans a pole in such a way as to signal to the driver that the cache of drugs is off in the trees. A local girl goes down for driving a load. She's twenty, lives at home, and has never touched drugs. The family is short of money. She earns $8.08 an hour at Walmart but can't get more than thirty hours a week.

None of this matters in Ed's logical arguments against legal and illegal immigration, a piece commissioned by the *New York Times* and then spiked when the gods of the op-ed felt the heat coming off the page rather than the comforting tut-tut-tut they sought. The piece that I have found rollicking for years has no people. It is an argument without a heart. Just as the people coming north are messy and full of faults and virtues.

The position in Ed's piece is clear. We are overcrowded. Our numbers now murder our native ground. We cannot afford to take on more unless we hate all the other living things that live around us. The poor and vicious nations of the world must help themselves because everyone cannot move here. If the people of the earth are to escape squalor, they must embrace population control and create societies of social justice. And we should look out for ourselves, bring our armies home and guard the line.

I can see him smiling as he knocks down other positions like ten pins with the force of his argument.

But I want him to meet the girl hooking in that border town, the girl waitressing in small-town America and dreaming of being a nurse, the gang guy now marooned across the line who wants to return to save others from the hell he helped create and the hell that burned his own life to ash. And I want all those who wish to help the girl and her dream of nursing to think of the group of coatis, females and young, wandering a little patch of creek in a dying landscape. The creek itself shrinks a bit each year and most of the time is dependent on effluent from a sewage plant upstream to keep up its bold look of a little water in a desert.

If you live on the line and see the murder of dreams up close you must consider some facts beyond logic. The millions here are not going home. The new steel barrier and police state destroys American freedom as illegals scrub our dirty floors off in the shadows. And the time is past that the world can be kept at bay by a wall.

I am sitting outside a bar drinking.

The man at the table rails against illegals, says anyone could shut the border down with troops. I point up at the sky, tell him the climate is getting warmer, ask him how high a wall must be to keep out the pollution of China and what army can stop the new dragon's tongue licking the sky with carbon as the rivers die around us.

He gets angry.

I drink.

I remember the girl in the cheap café who wants to be a nurse. Her other dream is to see Disneyland.

I tell her that now that she is semilegal with her Dreamer status, she can go visit the Magic Kingdom.

She looks at me sternly.

No, first nursing school. Then Disneyland.

Helping her solves nothing.

But I cannot say no to someone who wants to do the right thing.

Just as I cannot say yes to more guns and walls and prisons when the problem is poor people feeling doom.

And I can't think of a logical position that will help anyone now. The human numbers are launched—people drown off Lampedusa seeking Italy, they drown trying to reach Australia from Asia, they die crossing deserts into the United States, they wander as vagabonds within China or rot in prison-style dorms that flank factories. And things playing out in nature—the melt of the ice, rise of temperatures, failure of the rains, death of the trees, decline of the rivers, mutilation of the species—cannot be walled off, and I have found no refuge or wilderness that can escape these forces.

Therefore—let us close our national borders to any further mass immigration, legal or illegal, from any source, as does every other nation on earth. The means are available, it's a simple technical-military problem. Even our Pentagon should be able to handle it. We've got an army somewhere on this planet, let's bring our soldiers home and station them where they can be of some actual and immediate benefit to the taxpayers who support them.

About the time I met Ed I became crazed over Mexicans crossing the southwest deserts, dying, and these deaths being of little note. So with a friend, one night long ago I crossed illegally in the western deserts and walked forty-five miles in one night. We lost track of the Mexicans and we lost track of our own minds. We got out around 9:00 a.m. in the blazing heat and our bodies were ruins. And so I learned about that hunger driving people north. When I questioned a Border Patrol agent then about the hard march through the June desert people were making, he said simply "born walking."

I am crazed about cranes. I snap alert when I hear them overhead, I go visit their winter haunts, they float through my dreams. Sandhill cranes have been tracing routes over North America for millions of years while the rivers have come and gone and marshes spread and then gone dry. The lesser sandhills fly all the way to Siberia, the larger sandhills go to northern tier of the United States or the Arctic, the wing beat slow, a measured thing against eternity. And Ives's first piano sonata drums against my skull, a noise that becomes notes and then somehow becomes beauty with warring chords banging against each other, old hymns erupting and vanishing again, the thing slows, my God the wing beats seem frozen in the winter sky oh so blue and the light aching to become spring and hard low notes clang in the Ives sonata, the thing flows but halts and then leaps, marches then ambles, Walt Whitman is at the piano, a nation pouring through his fingers, only old Walt, that gay blade, seems out of his head on meth and the cranes land, they come down out of the sky like parachutes and feed in groups of three, the mother, the father, the young, usually one young because the first hatched does away with those who follow, there is so little food, the season in the north so short, the migration beyond our imagination, the flight of cranes so long that the Japanese thought their birds must vanish into heaven and take messages to those Shinto gods they knew before transistors stormed the temples and toppled ancient ways, the wing beats, Ives, that drunk on the stool at the bar who drones on and on and then suddenly says something brilliant and you backtrack, listen again, and realize the drunk was never droning but clearly you were dozing and missed the wonder, and sandhills winter down Mexico way and summer in Siberia and ignore all the lines, the churches also I think and my God Ed you were on to something with this Ives stuff, an insurance man in Connecticut who had his ears forever changed when two brass bands met at a small town intersection when he was a kid and the roar of each never abated but somehow made a new whole, and Ives walks down a street and a hymn flows out of a Sunday door of the chapel and the cranes beat overhead, I am sure the cranes slowly beat overhead and paid no never mind to the preacher or the choir or the band, and there is a knock at the door, and this is not heaven's door, no, this is my door and a poor face looks at me with hunger eyes and my God there is no room in the house and I look past the face at a battered land, the ground on fire, the streams boiling, the sky black with dread, birds falling dead from the heavens and I should say no, I should say there is no room at the inn—there's a story about all this I think—and I read that seventy percent of the earth's biomass is now devoured by my kind or my beasts and enough is enough, my God call the army and bring them home to form a wall for fire and hate on the beloved line, the slow wing beat, that penetrating guttural call of the cranes that easily carries a half mile and in the trees I see a half dozen immature bald eagles, America the Beautiful, and on the brown stubble of the bunked corn here and there are the big wings of a crane taken down by a coyote and now two ravens feed on the scraps and life is hard, it is written, not by Charles Ives, maybe it was that Charlie Darwin guy? or was it Charlie Parker? anyway life is hard, law of the jungle they say, not dog eat dog but coyotes eat crane, slow wing beat wandering through time, but that face is at the door, that poor hungry face.

Actually the face is in the room.

Let me tell you a story.

She is a young woman, not quite twenty. She has no money. She has no country.

She has a child. She has a husband being destroyed by diabetes. She has no job. This is all her fault. I will explain.

Her husband's sister in Mexico was married to a guy who ran a used car lot. They came and said, "Pay us extortion." Somehow he failed to meet their standards and was murdered. So the woman with children and now no husband went to work in a bar to feed her family. One day, the federal police came and demanded the cellphones of everyone in the bar and then left. A few minutes later, the killers came through the door and slaughtered everyone. Except the woman. She survived because all the bodies fell on her. She crawled out and struggled to the door and the federal police were there, and she thought I am dead, but then suddenly some city police came and she fled during the confusion of authorities. But a gunman came to her father's house seeking her, and when he did not help they murdered him. That is when she fled across the border with her four children, her mother, her sick brother and his wife and child, because they had it in their heads they would all be killed. They asked for asylum—the case is still pending and Christ may have returned to Earth before my government can decide such a case. Asylum seekers go into limbo. That is where we store our justice system. I can hear Ives now, he is shredding a hymn, "Bringing in the Sheaves," the young woman is mopping a floor, the call came this morning, there is no money, there is no work, there is no place to flee to, there is . . . and she cleans the house, lunch will be served shortly. I can't fit this into a sensible story. Go back, she dies. The child, well, they don't spare the women and children. Not my problem. Fix your own country.

There is a knock at the door and it is not heaven's door and I open it and there is face, a poor face, a hungry face, a frightened face.

Long ago, I read an essay called "Lifeboat Ethics" by Garrett Hardin, a great essay by a great person. And he said that this moment I face at the door would come and if I let the person into the lifeboat, it would sink and everyone would die.

There is a knock at the door, a face is there, poor, frightened, and hungry.

I say come in.

The slow wing beats are overhead, the cranes are heading to heaven,

I know it, I look up and beg them to take me with them into the endless music of time. Ives is banging away at that damn piano, he's playing the refrain from Beethoven's Fifth Symphony, he's got a thing about it. He never really composed after age forty, something happened, maybe he was consumed and lived content with the ashes of his hungers. His last symphony never boomed out until about fifteen years after his death.

My God, Charles Ives is good, far more tasty licks than Charlie Darwin playing those old bones. Ed, you were right. We gotta get Ives into the lifeboat.

And the woman knocking at the door who needs work and if she goes home to that country that birthed her, the one south of here, well, they'll kill her man and her child. Move over Ed, she's climbing aboard.

Especially the neighbors.

Ah yes. But what about those hungry hundreds of millions, those anxious billions, yearning toward the United States from every dark and desperate corner of the world? Shall we simply ignore them? Reject them? Is such a course possible?

"Poverty," said Samuel Johnson, "is the great enemy of human happiness. It certainly destroys liberty, makes some virtues impracticable, and all virtues extremely difficult."

You can say that again, Sam.

The nation state is over. But so is the tribe. We cannot keep the problems at bay with our spears. We cannot build walls high enough to keep out the demons we have unleashed.

There was a time years back, in that golden glow when our notions of free trade were rising over Mexico, when the millions had yet to flee north and the deserts were not cluttered with the bones of failed dreams, back then I drove with a friend to Parral, Chihuahua, the city where Pancho Villa was murdered in 1923. We found a guy riding an old bicycle with a one-string guitar strapped to his back. He pulled over and played his one song, "My Life is Nothing," the line repeating in a drone.

Music lingers in my mind, sometimes people sing, sometimes other bloods. The door is open, a summer breeze rustles the cottonwoods, the ash, the sycamores along the creek. I have Ives pounding away at his piano, I am standing at a high table writing and then amid the clatter of the sonata I hear the quiet and watch a full grown bobcat stroll past

Chihuahuan Desert near Las Cruces, New Mexico (April 1997)

the French doors ten feet away as if nothing exists on the planet save his beauty, his fur, and the purr of his song.

Then, there is the time a coatimundi, hair still wet from the creek, does the same thing. And the voices I hear—this some years back—and I break off my work, go out front and find twenty exhausted men sprawled under mesquites. They are thirsty, they are hungry. I tell them the Border Patrol checkpoint is maybe eight hundred yards up the dirt lane. They nod and shrug and laugh. I turn on the hose, they drink. I point to the cases of soup I keep outside in an alcove for the wayfarer. They help themselves. Then they melt back into the land. Their walk has thirty or forty miles more before they are safe from the agents and can pile into vans and ride the night highways into the heart of the heart of the heart of the country.

None of this is an answer but all of this is at least the question. I was told as a child about that fatal line between the quick and the dead, but now I think my mentors had it wrong. The agents up the road, the ones that glare and ask me if I am a citizen of the right place, they may be the dead. The men and women and children clawing through walls and hard ground and dying now and again on their journey, they may be the quick, like the bobcat at the door, the wet coati at the door, the poor and hungry and frightened face at the door. Maybe nobody gets out of here alive, but some at least get to live.

Robert Frost, yes, "something there is that doesn't love a wall," Molly Bloom, yes, "as a girl where I was a Flower of the mountain yes when I put the rose in my hair like the Andalusian girls used or shall I wear a red yes and how he kissed me under the Moorish wall and I thought well as well him as another and then I asked him with my eyes to ask again yes and then he asked me would I yes to say yes my mountain flower and first I put my arms around him yes and drew him down to me so he could feel my breasts all perfume yes and his heart was going like mad and yes I said yes I will Yes," and Edward Abbey, yes, with his goddamn Charles Ives, his hard questions about people and human numbers and our fangs on the throat of the natural world and his cranky comments and his love of life itself. His spiked op-ed on immigration is not going to go away until we face his questions.

I would like to live long enough so that no one read Edward Abbey because we had ended our murderous ways, abandoned the dangerous gods of the military and of the industrial and corporate, left Wall Street as roadkill by a country lane, yes, yes, leave all those killers behind, grab a flagon, dance around the Maypole with the bear, the orca, the louse, and the diamondback rattlesnake of our desires. I want Ed unread because Ed finally won and we love the ground and still make time for Saturday night and hell we'll spend our time drinking and romping and leave behind the lonely of *Desert Solitaire*.

Clearly, the nation is overpopulated, and by my count it was overpopulated the day I was born, though I am glad an exception was made in my case. And given the numbers of people and the shortages of everything else—my God, we are even running out of sharks—there is no easy way to the future. Besides, there is talk of a warming trend. And yes, I have my moments when I agree with his noble sentiment: "I am a humanist, I'd rather kill a man than a snake." But I can't escape my skin or my heart.

My head agrees with Ed, but I survey a world made desolate by thinking overwhelming feeling. The killing fields of the twentieth century were designed by ideas. And I think logical solutions are beyond us now for two reasons. Solutions are too final to be possible and logic is too vicious to be sustained.

If we truly wish to help them we must stop meddling in their domestic troubles and permit them to carry out the social, political, and moral revolution which is both necessary and inevitable.

Or if we must meddle, as we have always done, let us meddle for a change in a constructive way. Stop every campesino at our southern border, give him a handgun, a good rifle, and a case of ammunition, and send him home. He will know what to do with our gifts and good wishes. The people know who their enemies are.

Down the lane the refuge closes on Monday and Tuesday. The staff says this lets the beasts and thickets rest. But of course this is a ruse for humans to have some time off. Out on the ground there is no rest. And out on the ground there is no refuge.

In our cities, we have slowly succumbed to gated communities, and these signal the death of the cities, as some members retreat into their new castle keeps and pretend what happens beyond the gates will not reach them. The twentieth century featured a series of human convulsions—wars and revolutions—that mocked such ideas and massacred those who believed them.

Out on the land we created national parks and monuments, wildlife refuges, swatches of wilderness, all as bulwarks against ourselves. I have spent much of my life supporting such efforts and thinking that somehow these bunkers against our murderous rage would keep other life forms alive until our gluttony had passed. This seemed logical. And now I must face the fact that this was wrong. The sanctuaries have become internment camps where other creatures do time until they are crushed by our numbers or by the poisons of our habits. No refuge is large enough to either sustain itself or keep the new forces at bay. The skies change, the forests shrink, our numbers grow. And the heat comes on.

We are a people of walls. The Massachusetts Bay Colony was not simply to be a City upon a Hill but also a gated community. When many fled the regime of the Puritan divines, Governor John Winthrop lamented "there was about liberty of removing for outward advantages, and all ways were sought for an open door to get out at; but it is to be feared many crept out at a broken wall. For such as come together into a wilderness, where are nothing but wild beasts and beastlike men." Then as now, walls were thrown up under the assumption that they would offer security to those within, and then as now they were overwhelmed by traffic in and out. And as the gospel song goes, the walls come tumblin' down.

The wall now rising on the Mexican border is a comfort to police agents and small children, the only two groups that might see it as a solution to overpopulation, resource limits, poverty, and global warming. It will buy some votes for politicians, it will create some misery for migrating humans and wildlife. But it will not alter the future. Nor will turning the poor back at the border with some guns and ammo stave off the storm. For some years, the numbers coming north have fallen thanks to the collapse of the U.S. economy. This is small comfort for those who dread the poor and brown and disheveled. At the same time, the number of agents has exploded, the wall has grown, drones hum in the sky, and yet the flow of drugs has not skipped a beat and every kilo arrives on time.

What I am saying is simple. Edward Abbey had a point when he wrote about putting the army on the line and keeping the hordes at bay. I never really agreed with him, but it was a logical argument. Now, the time is past for such a solution. We either help those struggling beyond our borders or they will explode or they will flee here. We either stop the production of lethal gases and materials here and beyond our borders or the modern industrial state will kill us all. We can't live in the past unless we wish to miss the future. The gated communities will be the new cemeteries, the knock is at the door and to not hear it will not make us safe.

I am standing in a valley that was once the last wolf run in the region. The border begins just over the pass. Government hunters slaughtered the last litter of wolves here in the early fifties—the bitch fled into Mexico. Illegal migrants course up the valley—that hidden camera sometimes captures them marching through and also the sauntering of lions. There are turkeys here, birds restored after the slaughter of settlement. Just over the ridges is the U.S. Army intelligence center, part of the secret network of my nation that I am told protects me and yet paws through the last remnants of privacy seeking enemies that might lurk in metadata. I stand here on a cold winter day and watch two drones all but silently pass over. Now they keep watch for the enemies.

There is no future in this. I am watching my government build our tombs while the noise of the new world being born grows louder and louder.

They're coming, coming now to carry me home. Ain't no refuge big enough, ain't no wall high enough.

Every time I walk the line I think of Joe Louis's saying of an opponent, "He can run but he can't hide." Every time I walk the line I hear Louis Armstrong's shredding the walls of American song with the opening notes of "West End Blues." Every time I walk the line I hear Ed speaking softly and wondering what has come to pass as the troops of the empire storm past and guard the parapets of a new jackboot face of America.

The gray hawks cry, this is the edge of their range, everything slops over here.

Charlie Ives snaps, "Music is one of the many ways that God has of beating in on man."

Amen, Charlie.

I want the wolf back at the door. But I can't ignore the others that show up any more than I can ignore the weather. And time has passed when this is even a choice. Everything I need and love is now an outlaw.

Christ, there is that knocking at the door.

Time to open and stare tomorrow in the face.

It won't be easy and it won't be pretty but it will come. And I am tired of people saying they demand a solution. They are lying. What they demand is that nothing change in their lives, that when sky goes black from smokestacks someone whip up a witches brew of nuclear magic, that when the rivers go dry someone suck salt from seawater and ship the pure flow to their house. Sometimes I think one shouldn't touch on these matters—limited resources, too many people, a murdered natural world, the glances of lingering beasts as they stagger past to extinction—without firing up some of Ives's brass bands so everyone can be of good cheer and we will all say easy solutions cannot be part of the package.

I don't know a bird or a beast or plant or a hungry face moving through the hard ground toward a dream of a job demanding easy solutions.

Edward Abbey was not of one mind himself. Nor was he in the market for easy answers. Like a lot of cantankerous souls, he knew life was far too good to simply be a matter of tossing out opinions. He scribbled in his journal a kind of vade mecum, a guide for us as we stagger on with our lusts, dreams, bad habits, and loves. I'll be a sport and give him the last word:

My loyalties will not be bound by national borders, or confined in time by one nation's history, or limited in the spiritual dimension by one language or culture. I pledge my allegiance to the damned human race, and my everlasting love to the green hills of Earth, and my intimations of glory to the singing stars, to the very end of time and space.

CHAPTER 12

The Age of Abbey

JOHN A. MURRAY

The struggle toward the summits itself suffices to fill a man's heart.

—ALBERT CAMUS, *THE MYTH OF SISYPHUS*
(INSCRIPTION ON THE MEMORIAL IN LOURMARIN)

1

I MET EDWARD ABBEY over lunch in March 1988, during the author's final book tour through the West. Also present at the Mercury Café that day were two other scholars from the University of Denver. My graduate advisor, Ed Twining, arranged the gathering. The "permanent associate professor," as he referred to himself, was a longtime friend of Abbey's. He had known two of Abbey's five wives. He often spoke in positive terms of Renee Downing, the teenage muse who, after a two-year courtship, married the forty-seven-year-old Abbey in 1974. The young woman inspired the middle-period works that found such an enthusiastic audience with other members of the baby boomer generation. Professor Twining compared the influence of Renee upon Abbey to that of Juan Hamilton, the twenty-seven-year-old New Mexico sculptor, upon the eighty-six-year-old Georgia O'Keeffe (1887–1986). Hamilton's Zen-based approach fostered a creative burst in the artist as she neared the century mark (1973–1986). The same dynamic of transcendent catalysis animated the twelve-year union between Charles Dickens (forty-five) and the Haymarket actress Ellen Ternan (eighteen), which yielded *A Tale of Two Cities* (Lucie was based on Ternan) and *Great Expectations* (Estella was based on Ternan).

The extraordinary books of Edward Abbey's late forties and early fifties, during what Twining refers to as "the Renee period," include *The Monkey Wrench Gang* (which sold 270,000 copies in its first three years and was film-optioned by Dennis Hopper), *The Journey Home*, and

Abbey's Road. Twining, who resembled Abbey if the author had had a handlebar mustache and a barrel chest, was known across campus as the most independent member of the department. A graduate of the University of Connecticut and a Korean War veteran, Twining served on committees only if compelled to by the graduate school dean, who was another English professor (Harvard-educated Thoreau biographer Robert Richardson). As soon as the grades were turned in, Twining jumped in the car and headed for the Canyon Country. He and his wife resided in a beige brick-and-stucco storybook home (2339 South Adams) near campus, where Edward Abbey stayed when visiting Denver. When Twining died in 2009, his widow, Mary Beth, requested donations be made in her late husband's name to the Southern Utah Wilderness Alliance.

Also present was Douglas Wilson, who taught at the University of Denver (DU) for thirty-five years, until passing in 2008. The department chair evoked a Santa Fe Trail boss in his calm bearing and cowboy-like appearance (bolo ties and neck bandanas). Wilson, the father of four daughters, grew up on a ranch at the headwaters of the Cimarron River in New Mexico. The son of a Protestant minister, he was educated at Williams, Oxford, and Harvard. He completed his dissertation on Wordsworth, whose raison d'être was the Lake Country, under Walter Jackson Bate, whose biographies of Keats (1964) and Samuel Johnson (1978) received Pulitzer awards. Wilson's last book, *The Romantic Dream: Wordsworth and the Poetics of the Unconscious* (1993), explored the relationship between psychoanalysis and the literature of nature. His terrace-style manor (2551 East Flora), with the six cottonwoods in the front yard (one for each family-member), was the location of a memorable department party for Edward Abbey and Renee in November 1979 (the two separated after the *Abbey's Road* tour). Wilson's wife, Diana, a Cervantes scholar, was also a professor in the department. I had the pleasure of taking her Renaissance humanism seminar. The course provided valuable insights into Abbey's intellectual origins, as his thinking and sensibility were deeply rooted in that epoch's free-spirited writings. Her husband's Wordsworth seminar proved just as enlightening with respect to Abbey's literary heritage on nature.

Wilson, who directed my thesis (a history of sacred space in Western culture), was a fan of Abbey's books. He loved analyzing the relationship between Abbey and the original nature rebels—the English romantic poets. On both subjects the avuncular, white-haired scholar was blessed with great understanding and knowledge. He and I once fished some beaver ponds in

Park County I had discovered in 1978 while guiding elk hunters for Jerry Risner, a first sergeant in my marine reserve unit who was also an outfitter (and whose son Henry, serving in the Tenth Mountain Division, was killed in action during the invasion of Iraq on August 18, 2004). Wilson spent much of the angling trip describing his visits to Wordsworth's cottage and the rugged Cumbrian mountains of what our British counterparts refer to as Wordsworth Country. Such locations as Windermere, Esthwaite Water, and Grizedale Forest, all in the Lake District National Park above the Irish Sea, were recalled. Our discussion ranged into the complex literary relationships between Abbey, Thoreau, and Wordsworth. Like me, Wilson was familiar with Abbey's oeuvre and was eager to have an enlightening conversation with him.

2

I could sense that the author of *Desert Solitaire* and the holder of two philosophy degrees from the University of New Mexico regarded the least senior person at the table (I was thirty-four at the time) with a mixture of amusement and curiosity. A year before I had sent Abbey a copy of my fourth book, *Wildlife in Peril: The Endangered Mammals of Colorado*, with a foreword by James B. Ruch, the director of the Division of Wildlife. Abbey had responded by mail. In that way our correspondence began. Abbey embraced the thesis of my book, namely that all six endangered species be returned to the state. The list included *Canis lupus* (which, in 1995, was restored to Yellowstone, as the book urged, and has since made its way back via the Red Desert) and *Ursus arctos* (which is repopulating the Wind River Range and will presumably make the same crossing). Abbey was among the first to support my proposal that a national park be established at the Navajo River headwaters, anchored by the 77,000-acre Banded Peak ranch, in order to protect grizzly habitat in the southern Rockies. He provided validation and encouragement that were helpful to me at the time. I later offered the same support to emerging authors as the director of a graduate professional writing program and as the editor of nineteen nature collections, many of which featured unknown young writers (including several, such as Emma Brown at the *Washington Post*, who went on to successful national careers).

On that afternoon I brought the bard of the Southwest another gift—a peer-reviewed tract I had published the previous month in *Western American Literature*, then edited by Thomas J. Lyon at Utah State University. The article was entitled "The Hill Beyond the City: Elements of the Jeremiad in Edward Abbey's 'Down the River with Henry Thoreau.'" Without looking at it, Abbey expressed his gratitude, folded the pages, and put them aside. Wilson then handed Abbey his present—the Fawn Brodie edition (1963) of Sir Richard Francis Burton's *The City of the Saints, and Across the Rocky Mountains to California* (1861), with the Brigham Young interview. Abbey was surprised and thanked him. He said he had read Burton's *Pilgrimage to El-Medinah and Mecca* (1855) and the *Arabian Nights* translation (1885) while working as a fire lookout in Arizona.

Abbey was striking in person. In *Abbey's Road* ("In Defense of the Redneck" [1979]) he describes himself in characteristically self-deprecating terms: "dark-complected, lug-eared, beetle-browed." I will add that the author was tall, lanky, angular, brown haired, and gray bearded. He smiled more often than frowned. His dark umber eyes, set under a prominent bony arch, sparkled with mischief and vitality, and his voice was deep and resonant, with a rural twang. His well-featured, Romanesque face alternately evoked that of a medieval English lord or a celebrated highwayman. In looking at him from a distance of several feet, I recalled what the Denver-based frontier photographer William Henry Jackson wrote of General Custer, who once sat for Jackson's camera, in his memoir *Time Exposure* (1940): "The children loved him, the ladies adored him, and all men envied him." Throughout our time together, Abbey was congenial and engaging, although he certainly understood by then that he had little time left. As with most readers, I was not aware of the health situation until after his passing. Abbey did not discuss his travails in public (in 1982, a Santa Fe doctor had given him six months to live). His widow later informed me, in a 1996 phone conversation, that he wanted people's respect and not their pity. It was also, more fundamentally, part of his nature to accentuate the positive. As he observed in "Anna Creek" (1979): "When the situation is hopeless there is nothing to worry about."

The only indication of illness that day with Abbey, other than his somewhat gaunt appearance and Spartan fare (a bowl of soup), was a respiratory ailment, which he attributed to Denver's smog. He also mentioned a dream from the night before, as the salads arrived, that, in retrospect, had a symbolic resonance to it. In the dream he was back in war-torn Europe, looking for a clinic. He encountered some other soldiers. They informed him the medics were four miles back. He searched in vain, awakening in a cold sweat before dawn. In the context of our conversation, the dream seemed an enigmatic and inconsequential event. Abbey dismissed it as the result of "too much cough syrup." After his death, it seemed less a cryptic augury and more a clarifying lens.

I asked him if he remembered a backcountry meeting in Canyonlands National Park in March 1975. I was hiking in Big Spring Canyon over spring break with two international students from the University of Missouri (one from Bourges, France, the other from Prague) I'd met at the Squaw Flat campground. Our destination was Druid Arch. We stopped and conversed with a stranger on the trail. I recognized him from media photographs but said nothing, sensing that he, like me, valued his privacy. Abbey smiled and said: "I do remember. I advised you to take the left fork at the cairn, because the right fork led off into the rocks." I thanked him, thirteen years later, for his advice, as the right fork had appeared more traveled. He said later the same week he had hiked the White Rim trail and was treated to a blizzard.

As the soup and sandwiches arrived, Abbey spoke not of such matters as my article or his speech ("A Writer's Credo") at Denver's Trinity United Methodist Church (1820 Broadway) on the same trip that was attended by several hundred people, including myself and my father. Rather, he discussed the tenth anniversary of the 1978 protest at the Rocky Flats plutonium trigger facility and the subsequent trial of the protesters, led by the writer Allen Ginsberg (1926–1997). Their tent on the railroad tracks and the Jefferson County trial had inspired Abbey's essay "Of Protest" in *Down the River* (1982). The defendants included Daniel Ellsberg, associated then as now with the Pentagon Papers and the antecedent of such figures as Edward Snowden.

Their attorneys raised a novel defense. Abbey describes the strategy in his essay: "They pleaded not guilty [to trespassing] using as their defense an old Colorado 'choice-of-evils' statute that allows the intentional commission of an illegal act when the purpose of such act is to prevent a greater harm or a greater crime. For example, the law allows you to violate speed limits when your purpose is to save a life, or to escape imminent danger." In the end, each defendant was fined and received a suspended six-month sentence. One individual declined to pay the fine. He served three months before sympathetic associates pooled their resources and obtained his release.

To Abbey (who assured us he took time off from the trial to tour the Coors brewery) the political drama, which started a national conversation on nuclear weapons, was a "condensed metaphor" of the American experience. He supported, as did Ginsberg, the concept, based in the New Testament and Thoreau's civil disobedience writings, that, as he phrased it, "speaking truth to power is a beautiful thing." Although I did not know it in March 1988, my father, who worked as a special assistant to the director at the EPA National Enforcement Investigation Office in Denver, was coordinating, with his counterparts at the FBI, the federal raid of the Rockwell Rocky Flats facility that would occur fourteen months later. This operation confirmed violations of state and federal health laws and led to the plant being decommissioned. Since 2000, the 6,400-acre tract has been managed as a national wildlife refuge.

In this discussion of Ginsberg and the protest, Abbey surprised two of his three hosts by announcing that he revered Ginsberg's masterpiece *Howl* (1956). He described the iconic poem, according to my journal notes, as "a brutally honest critique of our nemesis, Fate." I was the only person at the table who shared that view, not common in academia at the time, or who knew Ginsberg. I had become acquainted with the son of Louis, a Newark high school teacher, and Naomi, a radical socialist, in Boulder during his Jack Kerouac School of Disembodied Poetics period (1974–1976) and then again in the post–Rocky Flats Naropa phase (1983–1986). I shared some insights, as Abbey had lapsed into silence and seemed preoccupied, perhaps, knowing what I do now, with some aspect of his illness. The Beat poet, immortalized in *The Dharma Bums* (1958), lived across the street from me on "the Hill" during the mid-1970s. His roommate at the time, with the mercurial Peter Orlovsky temporarily out of the picture, was the movement's longtime spiritual advisor, William S. Burroughs. The pair resided in an incense-scented residence filled with books by Blake and Whitman, framed prints by Ginsberg (he joked, "I have the largest collection of Ginsberg's in the world!"), and musical instruments. These included the harmonium he used in public readings.

Ginsberg and I met at a block party, which are common in Boulder and particularly in the neighborhood adjacent to the Hill. Our initial conversation led to his recounting his Parisian years of exile during the conservative 1950s, when intellectuals and dissenters were being blacklisted, persecuted, and imprisoned in the United States. It was during this expatriate phase, living with William Burroughs at the Beat Hotel (a Francois

Villon–like lodging above a bar), that Ginsberg wrote his prophetic meditation on being and nonbeing, *Kaddish*. That work, together with the earlier *Howl* so admired by Edward Abbey, secured his reputation as one of the most persuasive advocates for change in midcentury America.

At one point Ginsberg described an encounter with *his* hero, Albert Camus (1913–1960), known for *The Myth of Sisyphus* (1943) and *The Plague* (1947), as well as for an essay on Oscar Wilde ("The Artist in Prison" [1952]). Abbey altered his demeanor and evinced much closer interest when the laureate's name was mentioned. It is helpful to recall that the author of "Emerson" and "Theory of Anarchy" (both 1988) held an advanced degree in philosophy. Abbey quotes Camus in chapter 11 of *The Fool's Progress* ("There is no pain . . . which cannot be surmounted by scorn") and makes reference to *The Stranger* (1942) in the preceding chapter.[1] In his youth Camus had studied Tolstoy and the anarchist movement (Abbey's thesis was on anarchy), served in the Resistance, and supported the Hungarian revolt against communism. Abbey was drawn to the philosopher for the same reason Ginsberg was—his independence. Camus was born and educated in Algeria. He remained a citizen of the Mediterranean, a North African at a distance from Europe. From the beginning, Camus was, in the tradition of Descartes and Rousseau, a rebel outsider similar to those about whom he wrote in the abstract. In 1952 Camus startled his adopted continent by breaking with Sartre over Stalinism. Sartre (who rejected the Nobel Prize with the statement "a writer should refuse to allow himself to be transformed into an institution") has since been surpassed in the popular culture by his muse Simone de Beauvoir, who produced the founding text of feminism, *The Second Sex* (1949). Her little known essay "Pyrrhus and Cineas," written during the Nazi occupation, is one of the lost gems of the twentieth century. Camus has entered the humanist pantheon of Voltaire and Hugo.

According to Ginsberg, the encounter occurred at a signing for *Exile and the Kingdom* (1957). Camus had a dry, sardonic North African sense of humor, as opposed to a lighthearted southern European sense of humor (*Don Quixote*) or a more formal northern European sense of humor (Goethe's Italian journals). He smiled when Ginsberg gave him a copy of *Howl* and referred to Camus as a "hip dude." Ginsberg explained, in broken French, that the term was untranslatable. Camus, familiar with the phrase, said, in the form of an inverted compliment: "Pour un Americain, vous n'est pas stupide" (For an American, you are not stupid). Ginsberg turned to the woman standing beside him, with whom Camus had been exchanging glances, and asked, "What did he just say?" Camus laughed. The philosopher understood English from his translation of Faulkner's *Requiem for a Nun* (1956) and from the U.S. tour (1946–1947), during which he began his lifelong association with the at the time nineteen-year-old *Vogue* intern Patricia Blake (in 1957 she was dining with the author in Paris when he learned, through a radio broadcast heard by a waiter, that he had received the Nobel prize in literature).

On a regular basis, a colorful assemblage of partygoers gathered at Ginsberg's residence, from what remained of the underground Beats (for example, Carolyn Cassady, a DU graduate and the artist-widow of Kerouac's friend Neal Cassady) to those occasionally featured in the pages of *Time*. In May 1976 Bob Dylan (who I did not meet), in town on the Rolling Thunder tour and looking for an off-the-grid place to relax with trusted comrades, spent the night. On another occasion in 1974 John Lennon, after a marathon recording session with Elton John ("Lucy in the Sky with Diamonds") at the Caribou Ranch studio in Nederland, arrived in a cab so intoxicated that he required the assistance of the cabbie and a neighbor (me) to make it to the courtyard, where he promptly became ill, much to the horror of two coeds who didn't recognize who he was. Ginsberg's friendship with the musician had begun a decade earlier, on the eve of the band's first American appearance (1964). That was the occasion, in a Manhattan hotel room, when the poet soon to be crowned "King of May" in Prague and the chief disciple of Woody Guthrie introduced the quartet to cannabis. Ginsberg was later in the studio for the satellite broadcast of "All You Need Is Love" (1967).

Ironically, as I related to Abbey, my first piece to be published in a book was a Lennon memorial (*Denver Post*, December 15, 1980) that Yoko Ono selected, together with contributions by President Carter and others, for *A Tribute to John Lennon*. The volume was published in London a year after his murder by a deranged individual, the royalties from which were donated to John and Yoko's charitable organization, the Spirit Foundation. I will always be grateful to Lennon's widow, because that marked the beginning of my literary career. For the decade prior I had only published in magazines and newspapers. With that work in hand, I could inform editors I had been published in a book, and the contracts started appearing in the mail.

Abbey, who was no fan of popular music, stated that he preferred

Aaron Copland to Dylan or Lennon. He pointed out that Wendell Berry's first book written after completing the Guggenheim year in France was a heroic poem about President Kennedy (*November Twenty Six Nineteen Hundred and Sixty Four* [1964]). He compared the process of getting a first book published to a forest, in which a tree falls and seedlings rise to occupy the space filled with light. Professor Wilson reminded him that Copland had incorporated "Bonaparte's Retreat," as rendered by a blue-grass fiddler, into the theme of "Rodeo" (1942). Acknowledgment was duly made.

I concluded by recalling the day the three of us (Ginsberg, Burroughs, and myself) went for a picnic in Sunshine Canyon. Ginsberg described his trip to Point Barrow, Alaska, as a deckhand on the *Pendleton*. Burroughs, the *éminence grise* of the local counterculture, did most of the talking. (I might say that the best photograph of Burroughs I ever saw, that captured his unique combination of the ordinary and bizarre, was Robert Mapplethorpe's 1981 studio portrait of Burroughs with a pellet rifle.) The author of *The Yage Letters* (1963) spoke of such wonders from his Mexican exile period (1950–1952) as the 853-foot Basaseachic Falls (Cascada de Basaseachic) in the heart of what he referred to as the "Tarahumara peyote country," a region (southwest Chihuahua) now under the demonic reign of the Sinaloan drug cartel.

At that point Abbey, who seemed to have regained his equanimity, sat back in a more relaxed posture and described a backpacking trip through the Barranca del Cobre with Renee ten years earlier. His voice modulated when he spoke of his fourth wife. I had the impression—as one man reading another—that a part of him still cared for her, or perhaps fondly recalled the productive literary period she symbolized, even though he had been happily married for six years to Clarke, with whom he was raising two children. Clarke impressed me, in several phone conversations after his death, as a strong, life-affirming spirit in whose presence the author had found peace, stability, and love. A trogon sighting marked the high point of the expedition. Abbey added that the subtropical bird, like the thick-billed parrot, was not frequently seen in the Arizona canyons anymore. He had been amazed by the Tarahumara and the condition of their feet, as they wore no shoes and ran considerable distances. He spoke fondly of the fireflies, which reminded him of his boyhood. The bioluminescent insects were "like something out of Castaneda." Wilson asked what he thought of Castaneda. Abbey said the creator of the Don

Juan series was "given to the occult, but without Poe's spark" and was a "low-watt bulb on a high-watt bulb shelf."

Abbey turned to his cause célèbre (the greater canyon country). He observed that a long association with a natural landscape was a predicate for writing about it, and expressed disdain for those members of the guild (John McPhee and Barry Lopez were cited) who visited a location for a brief time and then attempted to write an authoritative piece about it. He preferred writers—he mentioned John Haines of Alaska and Wendell Berry of Kentucky—who put down permanent roots and wrote about an area based upon a substantial period of interaction. My early research—which would culminate in the three books I published with Oxford University Press in the early 1990s on the Caribbean, Africa, and Alaska, as well as a fourth volume on the Pacific basin with Sierra Club Books (1994)—indicated that the opposite could also be true. I shared that observation and offered a defense of McPhee and Lopez.

Quite often, I had found, the best writing about a region came from authors whose experiences appeared to be the most superficial. I cited Mark Twain's *Innocents Abroad* (1869). With its vivid passages capturing the charm of Europe and the Holy Lands, the book had remained in print for more than a hundred years. In deference to company, I also made reference to Abbey's "Gather at the River" in *Beyond the Wall* (1984), which narrates a trip through the "arctic desert" and pays homage to the bard of the Far North, John Haines (a year later in Alaska I would have the same conversation with Haines, who agreed with Abbey). It all came down in the end, I believed, to natural talent and acuity of vision. Both varied from individual to individual, as in our guest's case.

"Well 'Murray's Paradox' is all well and good," observed Abbey, who enjoyed a discussion with someone who disagreed with him, "but to produce something they can roll into the vault with the rest of the antiques you need more than that." To counter my thesis, he raised the example of Thoreau. Abbey could quote the master from memory, as he did that day, from *Walden*: "Be rather the Mungo Park, the Lewis and Clark and Frobisher of your own streams and oceans; explore your own higher latitudes" and "It is not worth the while to go round the world to count the cats in Zanzibar." He cited Emerson, who called travel "a fool's paradise" and wrote of the traveler who "carries ruins to ruins." Abbey observed that people often travel in pursuit of an illusion they are progressing, when, throughout their wanderings, they remain fixed in one place. The irony, he observed, is that those who stay in one location sometimes experience the most growth. With a smile, he referred to that as "Abbey's paradox."

Wilson chose that moment to interrupt. He had the impeccable instincts of a scholar who had navigated all the stations at Oxford and Harvard. He asked Abbey about his experiences at Yale (Abbey withdrew from the doctoral program in 1953 after two weeks) and Stanford (he studied for part of one year, 1957–1958, in the writing program). The comic shift drew a chuckle, as Abbey described "the Rhadamanthine" Wallace Stegner as having "the most distinguished bags under his eyes." The only Stegner book he had read was the Powell biography (1954). The fiction was "unreadable." He said his arrangement with the University of Arizona, in which he taught each spring, was "the best that could be expected for a ridge runner like myself." He added that he felt guilty about teaching young writers, because "they are taking money from poor kids to train them for careers that don't exist." In retrospect, the choice to teach may have been related to the need for comprehensive health insurance. Abbey, turning the conversation back to the canyon country, then spoke of his favorite western book (the Powell journals).

One could sense the man's passion and commitment to the open spaces and public domain. Having lived in the humanized landscapes of Europe twice (as soldier and student) for three years, Abbey did not want to see the West Europeanized. He spoke of his concerns regarding the "insidious" privatization of public land. He bemoaned escalating land-use fees, the ever-increasing number of locked gates, concessionaires "usurping" the public domain, and the (now forgotten) Sagebrush Rebellion. He said the party of Lincoln had "about as much appreciation for the public lands as there is honey in the venom sack of a Gila monster" and joked that "they want to make 'Puttin' on the Ritz' the national anthem." Much of his commentary echoed, in tone and substance, the statements he makes in the "Polemic" chapter of *Desert Solitaire*.

After spending time with him, I could see that Abbey the person was, like Abbey the author, an alert and well-read citizen of the twentieth century who was quick to perceive the heart of any matter, however recondite. If genius can attain no higher felicity than the ability to perceive the natural comedy of a situation and to dissipate the prejudice that connects an affirmative embrace of the journey, or reasoned dissent, with vice, then Abbey was a regular source of merriment. I enjoyed his strongly held convictions, interesting anecdotes, funny comments ("Reagan should have been president of the Tampico, Illinois, chamber of commerce"), truthful observations, and illuminating comments about contemporary literature.

His views, as a Lockean rationalist, on the religious subtext of Annie Dillard's *Pilgrim at Tinker Creek* (1975) echoed what he had written in *Abbey's Road* (1979). He joked that Dillard was "Jane Fonda's twin sister kidnapped at birth and raised by theology professors." His views regarding Barry Lopez's works were similarly frank. Abbey's perspectives were summarized in a letter he sent me in 1987, which was published in *Orion* in 2006: "It's wrong . . . to adopt the lofty stance, the wise man's tone, and do nothing more. . . . I despise the role of guru, or leader, or remote philosopher, earning easy money . . . while the 'troops' actually stand before the bulldozers. . . . How far can you go in objectivity, in temporizing, in fence-straddling before it becomes plain moral cowardice?" He considered Lopez a "chronic depressive" and an "irritating scold." He joked that the author had "missed his calling" and should have been "writer-in-residence at the Trinity Site." His observations vis-à-vis Terry Tempest Williams focused, in the same candid spirit, on the deficiencies of her minimalist prose ("you can't put an opera into a cameo locket"), her "Mayan pyramid of the self," and the environmental record of the family business. Abbey stated, in response to a question from Douglas Wilson, that his favorite female nature writer was Josephine Johnson, a Pulitzer recipient (*Now in November* [1935]), whose 1969 book *The Inland Island*, about her Ohio farm, he had reviewed for the *New York Times*. He enjoyed Johnson's "unpretentious Mid-western delights." When asked about his favorite female nature poet by Professor Twining, Abbey said there were "actually two—Maxine Kumin and Linda Hogan" (ten years later I interviewed Hogan, then a University of Colorado writing professor, at her mountain home for the *Bloomsbury Review*).

All this put me in a complex position, as I knew the three nature writers mentioned. I had corresponded with Lopez, and later, as a professor, hosted him at my home for a gathering with the eighteen graduate students in my nature-writing seminar. (The course served as the basis for the textbook that appeared the next year. The work provided instructive examples from nature writers, including Lopez. It remains in print two decades later, published by the University of New Mexico Press). As an editor, I published Lopez in books eleven times over fourteen years, dedicated a book to him, and interviewed him for the *Bloomsbury Review*. Similarly, I published Williams seven times in books and dedicated a book on the national parks of the Painted Desert to her. Dillard presented an especially delicate problem. She was a confrere of another DU professor, Robert Richardson, to whom I dedicated the nature-writing textbook I edited. Annie and Bob ultimately married and taught at Wesleyan. While there, she arranged for me to appear as the guest prose writer, along with the Pulitzer recipient Robert Creeley (a Black Mountain poet friend of Abbey's from the sixties), at the Oklahoma Arts Institute.

Because of these professional relationships, I maintained an attentive but respectful silence. Abbey kept looking at me to comment and join in, but I just smiled and nodded. His contempt for the "croaking frogs and ladder-climbing lizards," "cormorants and conger eels," and "globe-trotting trust funders" of the literary world had at that point become quite bilious. Finally, in an effort to change the atmosphere, I jotted down an equation I had presented in a paper at the 1987 MLA convention in San Francisco. I told Abbey that I believed the potential force of repulsion, as measured in conflict levels, between two guild competitors equaled a constant (G) times the collective product of the two careers, measured in books, divided by the square of the competitive distance between them, measured in awards and cumulative sales, so that $F = G(m_1 \times m_2)/D^2$. Abbey asked what the value of the constant was. I told him that, like Faraday, I would have to await a Maxwell to give mathematical form to the intuition. Abbey smiled and put the napkin in his pocket, even as Twining reached for it and had his hand swatted away. Abbey asked, "Do any of you hillbillies know what Plato inscribed over the door of the Academy?" Wilson replied, "Let no man enter here who does not know geometry." The table erupted in laughter.

Even then, in 1988, I was aware that Abbey had refused to speak to Larry McMurtry for several years because he had referred to Abbey as a "nature writer" in a review. The quarrel over taxonomy was settled when the Texas writer bought Abbey a steak dinner. Wallace Stegner, who taught both (Abbey in 1957, McMurtry in 1960), once told me he thought the "rodeo dustup" was amusing. The dispute was reminiscent of the 1960s feud between Ansel Adams and David Brower. I questioned Brower (thirty-three first ascents in the high Sierras!) about this matter in a 1990 *Bloomsbury Review* interview. He described it as a territorial battle (leadership of the movement) that had manifested itself as a Sierra Club budget dispute. After establishing Friends of the Earth, Brower became the subject of John McPhee's *Encounters with the Archdruid* (1971).

McPhee made dismissive reference to Edward Abbey, referring to him as the "angry author of *Desert Solitaire*," which started another feud. Abbey later recommended Brower to Jimmy Carter for a cabinet position (in a 1976 letter) and in 1984 informally nominated Brower for a Nobel Peace Prize (preface to *The Best of Edward Abbey*). Ansel Adams presented a discussion of the Brower matter in his autobiography (1985).

When unleashed in private, Abbey's wrath was something to behold. I leave it to posterity to decide whether Abbey's antipathy for certain individuals and groups, especially toward the end of his career (see the immigration essays), was in part a projection of his inner pain, given the breakdown of his central organs (pancreas, liver, and esophagus) and physical suffering, which, to his credit, he endured with courage and grace. Abbey, who at that point was a tenured professor, had a global knowledge of the humanities and social sciences. He could make reference to Marcel Proust ("Fire Lookout: Numa Ridge" [1977]), recall a line from Goethe in the original German ("Wovon man nicht spraechlien Kann, darueber muss man schweigen" [Of that which man cannot speak, he should remain silent], "Episodes and Visions" [1968]), or quote the diaries of Paul Klee ("Desert Images" [1984]), but he was also a mortal human being and subject to the universal dynamics of human nature.

The only living writer Abbey treated with deference that day was Hunter S. Thompson (1937–2005). He spoke of the Aspen resident effusively, and in terms similar to those in *Abbey's Road* (1979): "Among journalists I have but one hero, and that is Dr. Hunter S. Thompson. I honor him because he reports the simple facts, in plain language, of what he sees around him. . . . Dr. Thompson's problem is how to equal, without merely imitating, the scholarly precision of *Fear and Loathing in Las Vegas*. He is really much more than a journalist. Not a journalist at all, but one who sees—a seer." In a 1977 interview with James Hepworth (in *Resist Much, Obey Little: Remembering Ed Abbey* [1989]), Abbey stated with similar enthusiasm: "I'm a Hunter S. Thompson freak."

Abbey brought up Daniel Defoe's *A Journal of the Plague Year* (1722) as the source for Thompson's technique, much to the approval of Wilson. The department chair had, the previous quarter, directed a seminar meeting for the ailing and elderly Professor Hyman Datz, our eighteenth-century expert, on the relationship between Defoe's book and *The Plague* of Camus. Twining smiled and reminded everyone the outbreak had occurred when Defoe was five years old. Abbey shrugged his shoulders, said "So what," and noted that "The Dead Man at Grandview Point" in *Desert Solitaire* had been based on his brother's account. He said the only thing that mattered was "the text itself." He observed that Defoe's early venture into new journalism, *The Storm* (1704), anticipated the plague book. Abbey was far more acquainted with the major and minor works of Western literature than many realize (even offering a passing critique of Henry James in "Back of Beyond"). He had a natural dislike of televisions, radios, and telephones, which he considered useless distractions. He regularly kept his phone unplugged, much to the consternation of relatives, colleagues, and friends. Apparently, based on what we observed that day, he spent considerable time reading (a subject upon which Thoreau devoted an entire chapter in *Walden*).

As dessert arrived, and Abbey concluded with his praise of Thompson, I recalled some of my experiences with the founder of gonzo journalism. I met Thompson in the winter of 1984, at the Hotel Jerome in Aspen, while working as a delivery driver along the I-70 corridor for a Boulder-based bakery. This was during my wilderness period, after I lost the 1982 election as the Democratic candidate for House District 25 in Jefferson County. Upon learning this, Abbey insisted that I elaborate upon the topic. (Neither professor was aware of this experience. Their knowledge about me was limited to the narrow academic context.) This was the same quixotic campaign, in a traditionally Republican district, that had been endorsed by the *Denver Post* and *Rocky Mountain News*, the teacher's union, the AFL-CIO, the Colorado Open Space Council (an environmental consortium), NOW, and Governor Richard Lamm. After the delegates nominated me at the convention (my sole elective experience had been student body president at UCD), the Republicans directed the county clerk, also a Republican, to declare me improperly registered and remove my name from the ballot. A party lawyer, Charles Flett, filed suit. In a hearing before a county judge (a Republican), we prevailed. This was followed by an IRS audit (a Reagan appointee at the helm of the agency) that confirmed I was a law-abiding citizen.

Abbey clapped his hands and exclaimed, "The Republicans never let us down!"

After three public debates, and two months of campaigning, I was defeated, the vote going straight down party lines, by the incumbent Frank DeFillipo, a mining executive and chairman of the State Affairs Committee who had a considerable war chest (a gift from beer magnate

Joe Coors), as compared to the few hundred dollars I raised by selling my Guild guitar. The high point was meeting Jack Swigert at the third debates. Jack was the Republican nominee for the Sixth District. We dined at the county fairgrounds before the debates began. As we shook hands, I told him he was one of my heroes. Over the fried chicken and mashed potato dinner he described the lunar voyage, which became the subject of a Ron Howard film (*Apollo* 13 [1995]), in which he was portrayed (by Kevin Bacon) as a playboy. In truth, the former astronaut, like Andy Warhol and Joseph Cornell, lived with his mother. While eating dessert, Jack developed a nosebleed. I gave him my napkin, but it was a gusher. His aide rushed him to Swedish Hospital, where they performed a cauterization and determined the cause, a tumor in his right nasal passage. Jack won the election but died two days after Christmas.

Abbey interrupted to say that Tom Wolfe's *The Right Stuff* (1979), about the early astronauts, was the only book "of merit" the author had produced. He expressed distaste for the *Bonfire of the Vanities* (1987). Wilson recalled that Wolfe held a Yale doctorate in American studies. Abbey shuddered and grimaced, and we chuckled.

My opponent was a member of what the Denver papers termed the "House Crazies." President Reagan named the other members of DeFillipo's group to federal office. Anne Gorsuch became the administrator of the EPA. My father served as the assistant administrator for policy under her at the national headquarters in Washington. My mother was among the Washington women Nancy Reagan called upon for events such as the April 19, 1982, Queen Beatrice reception, at which she heard the president refer to the First Lady affectionately as "Mommy." Bob Burford, who Anne married, became director of the Bureau of Land Management. James Watt, their associate at a conservative Denver legal foundation, was appointed secretary of the interior, much to the consternation of Edward Abbey, David Brower, Ansel Adams, and other environmental leaders. DeFillipo subsequently worked as the legislative liaison for Denver mayor Federico Peña, the former House minority leader who had provided me with the records necessary to factually engage DeFillipo in the debates even though Peña understood that my opponent, with his business acumen and political connections, would be useful in building Denver International Airport and constructing Coors Field.

Abbey said DeFillipo reminded him of "a saying we had in Indiana County," namely that "a cow is good in the field but must be kept out of the garden." He stated the man "probably knew how to drill a straight shaft through the side of a mountain" but then used the same "focused mentality" to "create havoc" in the state house and that "all the lead in Galena couldn't hold him down" in that pursuit.

Everyone laughed. I proceeded with my recollections of Thompson, which took us into coffee. I might emphasize that one of the keys to understanding Abbey in the 1970s and 1980s is his literary relationship with Thompson. The cross-fertilization, as with many intellectuals—Voltaire and Swift, Washington Irving and Sir Walter Scott, Richard Dana and Melville, Hugo and Tolstoy, Tolstoy and Gandhi—was important to both, but especially to Abbey. A limited portion of what I related is included here, taken from my 1983–1986 journals, for the benefit of those studying the western literary landscape in the age of Abbey.

When I walked into the place known locally as the J-Bar in November 1984, Thompson was pursuing one of the activities he most enjoyed—holding court at a public tavern. He was entertaining a table of skiers with his exploits as a *Rolling Stone* correspondent in Grenada in December 1983, during what he referred to as "Ray-Gun's" war. His comments regarding the president, who had recovered after being shot by Denver resident John Hinkley in 1981, were amusing. I jotted them down on my delivery clipboard. "He's like an iguana on a feeding frenzy. Everybody knows the only thing he's good at is backgammon. He calls his dog 'Lucky' for god's sake. What kind of a human being—I say it again—what kind of a human being does a thing like that? His entire life has been devoted to undoing *everything-that-is-good-and-decent-in-this-country*" (now pounding the table with his free hand, the other holding the Rocky Mountain version of a mint julep [cannabis], which, following a state referendum, was finally legalized thirty years later).

From there he went into a riff on Senator McGovern, who could be "chemically reconstituted" and "with a proper retrofitting" run for the office again. The Democratic field Thompson compared to a "flock of courthouse pigeons." The front-runner "was about as exciting as a piece of mail addressed to occupant." He then addressed the largest male at the table. "Let me ask you a question. You look like a reasonable person. Would you rather have your toenails forcefully torn out or spend a week at the beach with the ex-husband of Jane Wyman [former wife of Reagan]?" The man, who was wearing a red Nebraska Cornhuskers wool beanie and had several empty beers in front of him, began to speak and then paused. "Just as I thought," Thompson said. "I will grant him this much, though. That Bel Air smile could cheer up a baby funeral."

The doctor was wearing a sheriff's badge, as he often did after running for that position in 1970 in Pitkin County on a unique platform (first, change the name of Aspen to Fat City, second, sod the city streets at once, and third, prosecute all dishonest drug dealers). His campaign symbol, a clenched fist holding a peyote button, also had no precedent. Like Gore Vidal (Congress, 1960), James Michener (Congress, 1962), and Norman Mailer (New York City mayor, 1969), Thompson ran for office in a campaign that, partly by design, had a beneficial effect on his book sales. He learned, as was seen in his Nixon ruminations, and as I discovered in my 1982 campaign, that the best education about America, other than to serve in the enlisted ranks, is to run for office.

Amber-tinted shooting glasses kept the world at a distance, and his skin had a peculiar extraterrestrial cast. His face was strongly featured and well engraved with laugh lines, but even his wives and girlfriends would have conceded that Hunter was not blessed with Edward Abbey's good looks. In the harshness of daylight, Thompson evoked the working-class folk—from seasoned copper miners to circus carnies to Raymond Carver-esque retail clerks—gathered in Richard Avedon's portfolio *Into the West* (1985). In the muted light of a tavern, he resembled one of those Roman emperors who battled invaders and insurrections. After finishing with the former California governor, Hunter returned to Grenada, describing a Caribbean insect bite on his leg "the size of a tropical fruit" and the surprising side effects of a prescription medication if taken "in nonstandard dosages." He then suggested that "someone, somewhere" should obtain the number of the Eighty-Second Airborne general commanding the operation and publish it in a newspaper as the number for a "female looking for love."

I cleared my throat and interrupted the proceedings. He graciously signed the paperback copy of *The Great Shark Hunt* (1979) I had carried around town in hopes of meeting him. He returned the book and asked about the bloodstains on my down vest. I explained they were the result of a state-record mule deer taken on my day off while guiding hunters and shared the picture I carried in my wallet. He passed it around and asked which outfitter I worked for. I told him I had been fortunate enough to work for Ray Lyons, president of the state outfitter's association, at his Brush Creek camp. "Ah, the old bomber pilot who killed that homicidal bear!" exclaimed Thompson, referring to both Ray's service in World War II

John Murray with his state-record mule deer—photograph shown to Hunter S. Thompson

as a B-17 pilot and a 1971 incident in the Never Summer Range. On that basis, I was invited to visit his residence on the lower Woody Creek road ("just look for the American flags") whenever I was in town and to make use of the shooting range and reloading facility. I appreciated the gesture, having served as a marine rifleman in the 1970s and worked my way through college as a gun salesman at Gart Brothers in Denver. My customers had often been police officers obtaining Colt Diamondbacks for ankle holsters and short-barrel Remington 870s for silent alarm calls. They were always eager to share their adventures, some of which appeared in my later writings (as in *Another Country* [2002]).

Over the next several years, before I commenced graduate studies in 1986 and lost touch with him as his journey entered new waters, several funny things happened. He was often in San Francisco during that period, communing with West Coast friends like the artist Russ Chatham (my 2003 *Bloomsbury Review* interview with Chatham can be read online), but his base remained in Aspen. The merry prankster once led me up Snowmass Creek in search of psychedelic mushrooms to "spice up a birthday pizza" for a "special friend" (a local official). Hunter confided that he sought the picturesque valley "like a wounded snapping turtle" whenever he was sick of the world. He said it was his version "of a psychiatrist's couch." He avoided Capitol Creek because "Judy Collins and her llama trekkers have taken over the place." He said the drainage reminded him of why he came to the Rockies in the first place. It was on this expedition that he suggested we "jump the fence" and pursue the outlaw life, raiding estates "from Snowmass to Scottsdale," after which we could "decamp to Amsterdam" and reside among "mad drinkers and men of strange arts" (a common peroration).

"Where would our headquarters be?" I asked, recalling the film *Butch Cassidy and the Sundance Kid* (1969) we had just been discussing.

"Not in the desert, if that's what you're thinking. That's Bat Country."

"What about Ranching Country?"

"Gunnison? Are you serious? We'd stand out like a couple of Martians. Uniformed paratroopers would hustle us away to one of their tribunals. We'd have to face the succubus without benefit of counsel trained in their arcane sporting regulations. It would be like that one Star Trek episode. You remember . . ."

"Yeah. He was always on trial."

"Of course. He was Captain Kirk."

He then launched into his adventures with Cota, a "teenage wildman" he met in Cuzco who was in possession of a map, obtained in a card game, showing the location where a conquistador had buried "a solid gold human skull from Machu Picchu." Cota and his companion "copiously" chewed "narcotic coca leaves" as they hiked to the ruins and dreamed of a "peasant uprising," funded by the skull, which would resurrect the heyday of the Incas. The two never found the artifact, but made lighthearted plans for a revolution that would yield an Andean utopia of "drug commune musicians, screaming poets, local freaks." Eventually "a philosopher-king like Louis Rukeyser" (Princeton-educated PBS Wall Street commentator, 1970–2002) would emerge, and Hunter would travel there annually to escape Aspen, which had become a "decompression chamber of over-the-hill baseball players and faded beauty queens."

Edward Abbey broke in to say that "after the coming insurrection" any person who owned a trophy home in Aspen—he compared them to "a scourge of tent caterpillars"—would be sent to the reeducation center on the Sioux Reservation, which brought a round of chuckles. I continued. On another occasion, after putting an indignant garter snake in John

Denver's mailbox, we drove past Ashcroft in his Willy's jeep (the "Nova Express"), with the pirate flag mounted on the antenna, and made it half-way up Castle Peak (14,265 feet), in a quest for "revelations." A coughing seizure in Montezuma Basin (12,400 feet), which he attributed to radioactive dust from the high-altitude mines, brought him to his senses. We descended through serpentine curves to the valley floor listening to Warren Zevon (who had recently "received sniper training" at the compound) sing "Roland the Headless Thompson Gunner" and "I'll Sleep When I'm Dead" on a mixtape.

The last time I saw Thompson in Aspen, at the Ajax bar on the ground floor of Little Nell's, the author was in a subdued and thoughtful frame of mind, at least at first. It was past the dinner hour and a blizzard was in progress. After completing my deliveries I had started north. The truck hit a snow berm on the icy stretch out by the airport and spun around. In the time it takes to read these words I was proceeding north backward in the southbound lane at thirty miles an hour. After bringing the vehicle to a stop by colliding with the snow berm on the west side of the road, I returned to town. The laws of physics had pointed me in that direction. I would wait for State Route 82, the deadliest thoroughfare in Colorado, to be plowed and salted.

I parked in an alley space belonging to a restaurateur who was in southeast Asia for the month visiting relatives. During the 1980s Thompson's adopted community was filled with businessmen and women who had fled Vietnam after the collapse of the U.S.-supported regime in 1975. Many had made fortunes in drug trafficking. All have since disappeared back into the world. I knew the rig would be safe there and that the police, who I had befriended with free baked goods, would ignore it. I was glad the orders had been delivered (the nine-stop route started in Breckenridge). To be honest, I was glad to have any kind of work. Jobs were scarce in the prolonged 1979 recession (unemployment in 1982 reached 10.8 percent, the highest, to this day, since the 1930s). This was particularly true for an ex-marine with a humanities degree who had recently lost an election. During this "malaise" period, as President Carter phrased it in a July 1979 national address, both Edward Abbey and Hunter S. Thompson were insulated from the widespread ordeal, as they had been during the 1973–1975 oil crisis, by their affluence. In his journals during that decade Edward Abbey periodically commented on his worldly state: "MWG contract signed. A movie option 'probable' . . . I'm embarrassed by this sudden wealth" (October 5, 1974). This was not the case for many writers. I headed for a familiar retreat.

When I entered the place, the author of *Fear and Loathing on the Campaign Trail* waved me over to his booth, where he was sitting alone watching the news on the television across the room. I shook off the snow and sat down. He squinted through his glasses, studied my face, and said: "The road gods have brought him back."

"Yup."

He asked if I was going to drive back "over the mountain" (the Continental Divide) later that night. I told him I would stay with friends and return to Boulder the next day. We listened to the conversations around us and looked out the window at the snow falling. It was a peaceful scene. Hunter joked: "Everyone else is dead. We're the only survivors. The whole valley was frozen in situ. Greatest disaster in state history." He paused, watching the snow, and continued: "All caused by a seventh grader in Carbondale trying to make home brew, who is now frozen himself." The waitress came. I ordered hot chocolate. We spoke of inconsequential matters. Suddenly he turned in a different direction. I anticipated that something interesting was about to happen and reached for the notepad. I also activated the microcassette recorder I routinely kept in my shirt pocket on trips to Aspen.

"When the end of the world comes, get your nautical charts and set a course for those islands off the coast of eastern Canada."

"Why?"

"They live on strands of kelp and barnacle tea and cod intestines and live forever. The only news they get arrives via the Gulf Stream. I flew over that territory once on my way to Iceland with a bag of hash in my briefcase, a week before the Derby, and had my binoculars out. I undertook an aerial study. It's all in my files. Someday I'll write about it. It was night and you could see every porch light from six miles up."

"Didn't Mark Twain . . . ?" I began to reference his observation on the end of the world ("Go to Cincinnati because everything happens there a hundred years later"), but let the statement complete itself.

"He did, but I don't care. The world is my piñata now. Look at them," he said, nodding toward a trio at another table. "Even female tarantulas set them up that way. The males fight to the death and the winner is eaten by the *fee-mail*."

"And yet they keep trying."

"So do horseshoe crabs. All these bar tabs to feed the ravens at the city dump in the morning. There is only one thing that can save the human race, and that is freak power. That and the pimps of New Orleans. Be sure to write that down. That will be my next book. 'The Pimps of New Orleans.' If I were president I would make them all generals and admirals. Whatever they were wearing, that would be the new uniform. Most of them can drop a moving target with a sidearm while driving a car. One I know has fishing boat experience. Another flies model airplanes as a hobby. In short, they are qualified to lead the next invasion. And they know how to keep the troops happy. What more could you ask for? Are you getting this down?"

"Trying to." Like many people, and especially public figures, Thompson comported himself differently in private than in public. When in media view he tried to meet expectations, murmuring incoherently, behaving erratically, and appearing to be caught between worlds. In private he was lucid and controlled but spoke rapidly. Thompson was a nonlinear thinker. He moved at lightning speed through spontaneous and unpredictable intellectual vamps. One had to listen to every word to appreciate the unique vitality and scope of his agile mind. Edward Abbey possessed the same gift, though in a different way, which strengthened his discourse as well.

The waitress brought the hot chocolate. Thompson composed his face into a grave expression. He stated that he had neglected to share "a news bulletin from the city desk." He reported that her fiancé was having a party at their condominium with "those United stewardesses stranded by the storm."

The young woman evinced no reaction. I assured her he was joking.

"That's kind of you. I only wish I was," Thompson said. "The last thing he said from the balcony, where they were smoking that Temecula Tumbleweed, was 'Whatever you do, don't tell my girlfriend.' I sat here for two hours reflecting on the matter. The head of my security detail"—motioning toward me—"said I shouldn't interfere. I decided I had no choice. After all, my—"

"You know," she said, with an amused smile, "when I started here they told me about you."

"They? Who is 'they'? Is General Zuazua up to his usual tricks? Am I going to have to summon the helicopter gunships? Is there no one on this steam-powered riverboat"—now addressing the nearby tables—"who knows that I can hit every single high note on *Let It Bleed*, and that my mission is to train squires, wrestle giants, avoid the bitter chalice, and write sonnets to the memory of the pride and the glory that was once *Lou-ee-vole, Kin-tuck-eh?*"

She winked at him and returned to the kitchen. Thompson chuckled and said, "She'll be in my next book."

"You mean the one about New Orleans?"

"No," he said, moderating his voice. "This is another project I call 'The Feast of Depravity.'"

After I stopped laughing, he said, "Someday she'll have a face like Jackie Gleason, but right now she's like a Christmas tree with the star on top. Next week I'll give her the standard appetizer—a box of homeless kittens. It works every time."

"In what way?"

"They find it irresistible. Those plaintive cries could melt any glacier in Switzerland. I can see it now. A wedding ceremony on Easter Island. Honeymoon in a penthouse suite atop the Wells Fargo Bank in Mexico City. They'll make a movie about it one day starring Willie Nelson and the latest roadhouse singer to claw her way out of the Ozarks and call it 'Drunk and *Dee*-lighted.'" He paused, looked at me pensively, and said, "Let me give you a piece of advice. You're still a young man. When I was your age I was still in a Louisiana prison. You have the open road ahead of you. Put this in the 'Portable Thompson.' They will overlook everything if you can make them laugh so hard they . . ."

"What?"

"I don't know. Let me think. OK, I give up. But let me say this. Before Independence Pass opens next spring, a certain passing comet will be doing the Bourbon Street shuffle with a knight commander of the Royal Order of the Phoenix."

After a moment, fitting another Marlboro into his cigarette holder, he asked, "Did you hear that?"

I indicated with body language that I hadn't heard anything.

"The boiler room's about to explode!" He shouted to the entire room: "RUN FOR YOUR LIVES! THE RELATIVES ARE HERE!"

People looked at him, some indulgently and others in bewilderment.

I asked if he could recommend a mechanic to replace a rear brake light assembly. He whispered, "Speak of the devil." His gaze drifted to my left. I followed his eyes. A municipal functionary was approaching, en route to another table. Hunter's nickname for him was "Frederick de Claw." As he passed, the author of *Generation of Swine* coughed into his hand and said "douche bag" at the same time (a formulaic ritual). The man turned. Hunter pointed to me and said, "Please excuse my physician and confidential advisor. I will speak with him later."

The Monday Night Football pregame began. Frank Gifford, O. J. Simpson, and Don Meredith previewed the teams. Thompson chuckled and said that Frank Gifford looked "like a barge captain on the Intracoastal Waterway." He then asked, "Have you ever noticed how the rows of seats in a football stadium resemble the circles of hell?" I made a literary reference. He said, "You're the only person I ever knew who once made his living on the back of a horse and can locate Dante in the right century." The commercials came on. Knowing of his fondness for the Western Slope, I told him about the day I drove a herd of horses fresh off the truck from winter range thirteen miles up the South Fork Canyon to Doc Geesamen's fishing and hunting resort in the Flattops Wilderness. The climax involved a sidehill park in the White River National Forest, several hundred sheep, a pair of sheepherders from Alberta, and a pack of dogs trying to herd both horses and sheep.

He finished his orange juice and said, "I still think those two Canadians are buried under the aspens in Rio Blanco County. Frankly, I don't know how you live with yourself. You killed so many fine men on the way to becoming a crackerjack delivery driver." After a moment, he suggested a garage near the interstate that could make the repair and "might even work a trade for whatever it is you are *really* delivering from Boulder." The reference was a running joke. He continued: "You should get rid of that busted-up rig. Here's what you need. Write this down. A crow-black '53 Ford. Gangster whitewalls, two-bladed spinning hubs, high-rise polished chrome bumpers, and one of those clear death knobs with a skull embedded in it locked down on the steering wheel."

"Anything else?"

"The dancers from the ZZ Top video in the backseat."

"What about the front seat?"

"Of course not. That's reserved for the hitchhiker. There's always a hitchhiker in the MTV videos. The only hitchhiker in a swimsuit I ever picked up was on U.S. 89 north of Jackson Hole. I was driving a Volkswagen painted like an Easter egg with warped brass valve guides and a blown cylinder head gasket that was burning a quart of oil every two hundred miles. I was on a holy mission to see Hemingway's grave in Ketchum. Every bridge behind me was *on fire*. She had just kayaked the rapids and needed a lift to her jeep. I looked up at the sky, which was filled with the light of three suns, and said 'Thank you, God!'"

Once I stopped laughing, he continued: "*Life* magazine can say what they want about the sixties. I was there when Jerry Garcia shot up a drover dart of China White and danced across the Fillmore stage with the ghost of Hank Williams. Even Bob Weir had to get out of the way. But nothing compared to the Commander Cody concert at the Hollywood Bowl. Nothing." I tried to picture the Lost Planet Airmen. "Trust me," he said. "You had to be there. Rockabilly. I should write an article. What was your best concert from the sixties?"

"To be honest, the closest I got was Johnny Winter at the Ludlow Garage in 1970."

"See? I rest my case. A year after Woodstock. The candle still burned."

We watched the game. The second quarter concluded. I took note of the subsiding storm and rose to leave. He produced an olive and purple rock and said, "Here. You might need this in your travels." I thanked him and asked what it was. He said the angular fragment was a "thunder flint." He had traded "half the contents of a Coleman cooler" for the desert stone at a roadside stand in the Zuni Mountains, which "is the only corner of the sandbox where Edward Abbey hasn't played." It was a choice between the phaser-like object and a deer-hide drum that could "summon the dead from outer space." The seller, a tribal magician in red basketball shoes, said if the energized shard was pointed in the direction of an evil entity the troublesome nuisance would explode like a "cedar struck by lightning." I asked if it worked. He said, "Well, look what happened to Nixon." I told him I didn't have anything to give him in return. He said, "Type up your notes someday. Show them what I was *really* like. They'll be shocked to learn about those time travelers dressed as leprechauns on St. Patrick's Day. And if you ever make it back to the Midwest, pull the stinger off one of those Republicans and bring it to me in a jar."

Several times during the recounting, Edward Abbey demonstrated he was capable of producing a hearty, room-filling laugh.

The last time I spoke with Thompson was on May 14, 2000. He and War-ren Zevon were leading a state capitol rally in Denver to free Lisl Auman. The event illustrates the essence of the man, who served as co-pharaoh in the American West during the age of Abbey. His battle for the young woman's freedom was his final large-scale undertaking. Three years earlier Auman had been handcuffed in a police cruiser when Mattheus Jaehnig, who she had met earlier that day, shot and killed Denver police officer Bruce VanderJaght. The officer, who was one of my former DU students (winter quarter, 1987), rushed into a tactical situation near my apartment—the sirens on Hampden interrupted my afternoon reading—without a ballistic vest before the SWAT team arrived. Bruce's first priority was to protect the children, potential hostages, at the school playground. He gave chase. Gunfire was exchanged. Bruce was killed at close range. Jaehnig, wounded and out of ammunition, then committed suicide with Bruce's weapon. Despite having been locked in a Crown Victoria at the time, Auman, who had earlier been under the control of the armed, meth-addled skinhead, was convicted of murder and sentenced to life in prison. After eight years she was released, following a national lobbying effort by Hunter. A documentary film chronicled his crusade to liberate her (*Free Lisl: Fear and Loathing in Denver* [2006]).

The slain officer had been enrolled in a core curriculum class. I arranged for him to register as an independent study, partly out of semper fidelis— he was a fellow marine NCO working for campus security—but primarily because he was already a capable writer. I also believed, from what he related about his schedule, that he could use more time with his wife. Having known Bruce, an exemplary human being, I believe he would have agreed with Hunter that Auman, whose mundane attempt to move morphed into allegations of petty burglary (a boom box) and a wild chase with a stranger, was as much a victim as he was and did not deserve a life sentence. I'm grateful the chief justices concurred. In a coincidence familiar to city dwellers, Jaehnig resided with his German-speaking parents in a colonial-style residence (3535 East Monroe) near the DU campus. The substantial home, in one of Denver's finest neighborhoods, sold in May 2014 for $1.6 million. I had seen him at that home more than once while riding my bicycle to the Buchtel post office. He was hard to miss with the shaved head.

During the rally Hunter, with characteristic aplomb, demonstrated his courtly side in defending Auman. Some said it was his finest moment, after relentlessly exposing the venal, flawed Nixon ("a man who could shake your hand and stab you in the back at the same time"). His campaign evoked Bob Dylan's efforts vis-à-vis Rueben "Hurricane" Carter (1975), Lennon and Ginsberg's 1971 Michigan concert for John Sinclair (sentenced to ten years for two joints), and Edward Abbey's solidarity with Ginsberg in the Rocky Flats trial (1978). Afterward, as we dined at Tashi's now-defunct Japanese restaurant on East Colfax, Hunter mentioned a work-in-progress about Auman entitled "Carnival of Betrayal." He compared it to *The Shawshank Redemption* (a 1994 Oscar-nominated film based on a Stephen King novella). He asked what I knew about social contract theory, in terms of his project. I recommended an essay by John Locke, who synthesized Roman law, Aristotle, and the biblical covenants, and suggested that his (Hunter's) appeal to reason, mercy, and common sense was something the officer, who left behind a young daughter, may have endorsed. Hunter inquired about him. I related my experiences and impressions. At the time of his death, Bruce was also pursuing a doctoral degree in psychology at the University of Colorado Health Science Center. I believe that Edward Abbey, who traveled eight hundred miles to Denver to support Allen Ginsberg, would have joined the effort to release Auman, had he been alive.

It is fitting that the honorary Kentucky colonel's final book *Kingdom of Fear* (2003) was, in part, a post-9/11 commentary on the passing of those freedoms that, for both the author and his fellow political insurgent Edward Abbey, were synonymous with the American century. In deference to the author of *Desert Solitaire*, Thompson included a quotation from Edward Abbey as an epigraph in the book: "I know my own nation best. That's why I despise it the most. And I know and love my own people too, the swine. I'm a patriot. A dangerous man." In the concluding essay Thompson stated that "the most disastrous day in American history was November 7, 2000. That was when the *takeover* happened" (his emphasis). He was referring to the contested election, and subsequent court ruling, that installed the defeated candidate, in terms of the popular vote, as president. In his thirteenth work the Air Force veteran (1955–1958), cofounder of the Fourth Amendment Foundation, and former candidate for sheriff asserted the democratic verities one last time, as the nation was transformed, much as Eisenhower had warned in his 1961 farewell address, into a national security state and then, as Hunter foresaw in the Patriot Act (2001), into a national surveillance state. Thirty-three years earlier, Edward Abbey had anticipated these developments in *Desert Solitaire* ("The Heat of Noon"): "Divert attention from deep conflicts within the society by engaging in foreign wars; make support of these wars a test of loyalty, thereby exposing and isolating potential opposition to the new order."

Thompson observed in *Kingdom of Fear* that he could not have chronicled the 1960s counterculture had it not been for his friendship with Allen Ginsberg, who accompanied him to the Hell's Angels interviews, and Jack Kerouac, who he met through Ginsberg. Both taught him that it was acceptable to document the carpe diem realm of heretics and pariahs at the margins of society toward which he gravitated. Without this influence, Thompson might have remained an irreverent but essentially mainstream political and sports journalist. The same might be said of Thompson's effect during the 1970s upon Edward Abbey. Because of Thompson's innovations, Abbey—a conventional western writer in the novelist/naturalist tradition of John Steinbeck and A. B. Guthrie through the 1960s—became increasingly liberated and emboldened as the decade progressed. Abbey studied and learned from each new book or *Rolling Stone* article published by the best-selling anarchist, who transformed literature and inspired three Hollywood movies. Evidence of Abbey's symbiosis with Thompson can be seen in the October 24, 1974, letter that the forty-seven-year-old sent (from Wolf Hole, Arizona) to *Rolling Stone* that concluded: "Also, more Doktor [*sic*] Hunter Thompson for chrissake! Why the fuck do you think we subscribe to your bleeding rag anyhow. For Christ's Sake?"

Unlike Edward Abbey, who was raised in a stable family in rural Pennsylvania, Thompson was born to a hardscrabble urban existence in Louisville. His mother, who became a heavy drinker following the death of Thompson's father, worked in a library to support the children. Thompson developed a sense of humor as a defense mechanism to deal with her presence. Ginsberg, raised by a schizophrenic mother, adopted similar coping skills. Notably, the word "fear" appears in four of Thompson's book titles (the titles adapted Kierkegaard's 1843 *Fear and Trembling*, the seminal text of existentialism). In a 1974 essay, Thompson referred to that decade as "The Age of Fear." One always had the sense that he wore a comic mask to conceal a tragic sensibility. It was not by coincidence that he died in the week after Valentine's Day, which can serve as a reminder of betrayal and human weakness as well as of affirmation and union. Behind the daring chronicler of the Hell's Angels, the world-weary war correspondent, and the flamboyant guest on the *Letterman Show*, there was a midwestern boy who grew up poor and fatherless in the household of an alcoholic and who presented a cheerful face to the community in the halcyon 1950s era of drive-in movies and doo-wop.

Thompson's personality was embodied in the lyrics of his favorite song, "Mr. Tambourine Man." The Minnesota-born songwriter, to whom Thompson dedicated *Fear and Loathing in Las Vegas*, belonged to his inner circle. A photograph of the two embracing was included in *Kingdom of Fear*. The '60s anthem was played at Hunter's wake in Aspen, held on August 20, 2005, which I did not attend because I was climbing Mount Sneffels (14,150 feet) that day as part of an ongoing Fourteener project. At the conclusion of the ceremony, overseen by Thompson's fellow Kentuckian Johnny Depp, his ashes were fired from a cannon. Al Gore, to whom I dedicated *American Nature Writing* (1996) because of his green initiatives, was present, as were George McGovern, who Thompson befriended during the 1972 campaign, and John Kerry, secretary of state in the second Obama administration. All three former presidential candidates were close to Thompson and visited him in Aspen when they were on vacations or attending conferences. Thompson was to these individuals, as he was to peers like Edward Abbey, what the court jester was to King Lear—a trusted ally who was loyal to the cause of truth and justice and who held a mirror up to the mysteries and absurdities of life.

The death of Edward Abbey at a relatively early age was in some ways a more significant loss than that of Thompson, who also died in his sixties. Abbey led an environmental movement. His militancy was in the tradition of John Muir, founder of the Sierra Club, and Aldo Leopold, who fought for the wilderness ideal. Had Abbey lived, he could have, for example, lent his support to my efforts to establish a national park in the southern Rockies to preserve endangered species and help local economies. The author had earlier marshaled supporters, with *Slickrock* (1971), to defeat a planned road system for Canyonlands. If Abbey had not made a stand, there would today be a paved highway to Chesler Park. Because of his efforts, the sanctuary remains a place to commune with the red sandstone, the occasional *Crotalus viridis*, and the radiance of the nearest star. Abbey additionally served as the leader of a nature-writing movement. A constellation of environmental writers, myself included, were influenced by his personality and bound together by his writings. After his death, the ephemeral coalition unraveled. Eventually it devolved into petty feuds, institutionalized mediocrity, and abandoned missions.

Thompson, by contrast, was a commentator in the American tradition of Washington Irving (1783–1859), whose *Sketch Book* (1820) and Oklahoma wilderness narrative (1835) became successful ventures for the independent London publisher John Murray. The progressive Scotsman helped advance the modern age by publishing the works of Byron (who liberated poetry), Jane Austen (who created the novel of manners), Melville (who wrote the nonfiction novel *Typee*), and Darwin (who revolutionized science). The author of *The Gonzo Papers* (1988) was, in my estimation, the finest comic writer of his era, and the preeminent satirist since Swift. He embraced a mode of expression that had been given early life by Aristophanes and was later practiced by Shakespeare. Abbey's admiration for Thompson, expressed in *Abbey's Road*, was justified, as was Thompson's respect for Abbey, as seen in the Abbey epigraph. Will Rogers could make people chuckle. Thompson could make people, from the vice president to the sour apple at the local sports bar, roll on the floor and beg for mercy. His one-liners—"that Joan Jett concert sounded like a pig being eaten alive by a bear"—and funny names—"Hi, I'm Buck Mills from Cheesebox City"— and practical jokes—putting an elk heart on Jack Nicholson's doorstep late one night, thus causing a multi-jurisdictional police response and a national "breaking news" event—gave new definition to American humor.

Both Abbey and Thompson served the needs and interests of American society in the 1970s and 1980s, during an era of national influence, but in different ways. Both were anchored in the West—Thompson at the headwaters of the Colorado River and Abbey in the lower Colorado desert. Both gave proof to the principle that a country needs its independent writers, just as a coral reef depends on the moon that causes the tides that nourish and sustain its biotic communities. Even the ultraconservative Vladimir Putin, a former KGB officer during the Soviet era, acknowledged this universal truth when he paid homage to the Russian dissident writer Solzhenitsyn as another "great humanist" during his remarks on Nelson Mandela's passing (December 10, 2013). It is ironic that some of the best depictions of Abbey or Thompson have come in the form of art—the pen and ink drawings produced by Hunter's artist-collaborator Ralph Steadman and R. Crumb's graphic illustrations of Abbey's milieu in *The Monkey Wrench Gang*.

3

The conversation then took another turn, as Wilson mentioned that I would be teaching at a university in Alaska. Edward Abbey made a face, having heard of the department from his bon vivant on the college lecture circuit, the Alaskan laureate John Haines (1924–2011). He warned me about the resident writers, alluding to the group as "typical AWP [Associated

Writing Programs] invertebrates." Abbey referred to them, in Haines code, as "Morticia, Cousin It, Thing, and Fester." Haines, a two-time Guggenheim recipient, had already provided a written advisory, sent via my editor at the *Bloomsbury Review*, Tom Auer, as had Wallace Stegner, who referred to the department as a "cinderblock outpost." Robert Richardson, the DU biographer of Thoreau, had also counseled against the move, jokingly referring to the school as "Tidewater U." All three supported the original plan, which was to teach at a northeastern university and write a dissertation on Thoreau's *Dispersal of Seeds* (the prospect of residing in New England grew less appealing over time).

John Haines once told me, as we harvested blueberries near his Alaska cabin, that he first met Edward Abbey at a university reading in Missoula in 1975, and that he was "dragooned" into reading Abbey's piece because Abby was too intoxicated to stand at the podium. Haines, the son of an admiral, was, as usual, the essence of dignity and forbearance. He said that he and Abbey became close afterward because they had much in common in terms of life experience. Each also produced a classic work of nature writing. Haines published his contribution to the nature canon, *The Stars, the Snow, the Fire: Twenty-Five Years in the Alaska Wilderness*, in 1989. The literary admiration between the two was mutual. When asked to name the best book about Alaska, Edward Abbey replied on July 3, 1983: "*Winter News*, I say, by John Haines—pure poetry; and by 'pure' I mean poetry about ordinary things, about the great weather, about daily living experience" ("Gather at the River"). Haines's life was as eventful as that of Abbey's. The two can be regarded as parallel entities in the nature-writing genre. They are analogous to John Muir and John Burroughs, who were acquainted and participated jointly in the 1899 Harriman expedition to Alaska. As with Thompson, Haines provides a valuable prism into the life and times of Edward Abbey.

While Abbey served in southern Europe, Haines was assigned to a destroyer in the western Pacific. He was the son of the officer who commanded the USS *Nautilus*, a 375-foot long-range submarine, in the 1942 Makin Island raid. His father received a Navy Cross for sinking an enemy warship with the six-inch deck gun as his crew rescued Major Roosevelt (the president's son) and other members of the marine assault force. The operation, nine months after Pearl Harbor, inspired a 1943 Hollywood film (*Gung Ho!*) starring Robert Mitchum and Randolph Scott. The future writer, who grew up on military bases in the Navy aristocracy, nearly lost his life twice, once during a typhoon that resulted in three sunken destroyers and nine hundred fatalities, and then again during a kamikaze attack that left him clinging, Ishmael-like, to a crate in the middle of the Pacific. The essence of his humanity was apparent in his kind treatment of the Japanese sailors who were pulled from the sea and brought aboard another ship to which he was assigned. After attending a reading by Dylan Thomas in Manhattan, while studying on the GI bill, and receiving a friendly letter of encouragement from William Carlos Williams, Haines abandoned thoughts of a traditional career and devoted the remainder of his life to literature and the preservation of nature. Like Edward Abbey, who established a new home in the desert country, the war veteran set out for the most remote place he could find.

Eight decades after the United States purchased Alaska from Russia, Haines showed up at the territorial office in Fairbanks and applied for a 160-acre homestead. In the spirit of Thoreau, to whom he was devoted, as evidenced in the essay he contributed to my 1992 nature-writing symposium in the journal *Manoa* (University of Hawaii), he built a cabin that stands to this day on a hill above the Tanana River. After I left Alaska, I worked with Senator Ted Stevens, unsuccessfully, to designate the homestead as a national historic landmark. I also enlisted Dana Goia, the NEA chairman, in an effort to name Haines to the laureateship. Donald Hall and Ted Kooser, both fine poets, served in that period. In the outback of the sub-Arctic, and as far from salt water as he could get, the admiral's son began his recovery from combat. Half a continent away, in the Southwest, Edward Abbey, who had witnessed the effects of war in Europe, was similarly coming to terms with what remained of the original American wilderness.

Over the years Haines's reputation grew, as he authored influential essay and poetry collections and hosted a stream of literary visitors, including Raymond Carver (who dedicated a poem to him), John Luther Adams (the Pulitzer Prize–winning composer set one of Haines's poems to music), Robert Stone (who Ken Kesey visited in New York City with Further, his psychedelic bus, in 1964), Ed Hoagland, John Hildebrand (author of the nature classic *Reading the River: A Voyage Down the Yukon*), and Yevgeny Yevtushenko. The Soviet-era poet who was featured on the cover of *Time* in 1962, made a pilgrimage during the Cold War to visit Haines's cabin sixty miles east of Fairbanks. Yevtushenko told Haines that he had been called to literature by the work of Pasternak (1890–1960). He read his poem "Babi

John Haines, the Abbey
of the Far North, at his
Alaskan homestead (July
1993)

Yar" to his American counterpart as they sat beside Haines's wood-burning
stove. The poem is a response to one of the most horrific events in history:
the Einsatzgruppen execution of 33,771 Jewish residents of Kiev over a
two-day period in 1941. Yevtushenko told Haines that he had written the
poem because it was this event, Babi Yar, eliciting no response from Western
powers, that convinced the Nazi leadership at the Wansee Lake conference
outside Berlin that winter that it could proceed with the Holocaust. The
Siberian-born writer had read in his youth about the effects of Picasso's
Guernica in the Spanish pavilion at the Paris World's Fair (1937). He set
about with the same goal of expressing the conscience of the human race. In
1962 Shostakovich composed Symphony no. 13 in B-flat Minor (subtitled
"Babi Yar") based on Yevtushenko's poem. Haines told me that the two
instantly bonded as friends and corresponded for years after meeting.

Abbey and Haines were unique in their peer group for their embrace of what Emerson called self-reliance in an 1841 essay, which also influenced their chief mentor, Thoreau. Both writers declined to make the compromises necessary for a conventional lifestyle or vocation, as did peers such as Wendell Berry (University of Kentucky), Ed Hoagland (Bennington), William Pruitt (University of Manitoba), E. O. Wilson (Harvard), William Kittredge (University of Montana), Wallace Stegner (Stanford), John McPhee (Princeton), N. Scott Momaday (University of Arizona), Archie Carr (University of Florida), and Gary Snyder (University of California). The two lived for decades in an austere manner (Abbey worked as a fire lookout and seasonal ranger; Haines led a subsistence existence) that was consistent with their beliefs regarding personal freedom before accepting regular academic work in the 1980s (Haines taught intermittently at Ohio University and the University of Montana). Like Thoreau and Muir, Abbey and Haines were happiest when they were roaming in the back of the beyond, at a distance from humanity.

That initial correspondence I received from Haines in 1988 was the first of sixty-three letters I received through 2011, when the author died at eighty-seven. His last letter to me, dated December 31, 2010, accompanied a copy of his new book, *Descent*, in the form of a holiday gift. I have always regretted not responding immediately to this incredible act of kindness, considering his age and existential situation. For three decades the creative writers at the local university had refused to hire him, even after the regents presented him with an honorary doctoral degree in 1983. (The standard work on the subject is Steven Rogers's 1995 *A Gradual Twilight: An Appreciation of John Haines*.) Haines died, after falling on the ice, on March 2, 2011, and was remembered with a lengthy tribute in the *New York Times*. In the winter of 2012 I published an essay in the *Sewanee Review* ("A Personal Remembrance of John Haines, 1924–2011") that summarized my twenty-three years of friendship with the Edward Abbey of the North.

Returning to the conversation, I told Edward Abbey that I was the eternal optimist with regard to the professorship at the frosty edges of the academic world in the heart of what Abbey referred to as "Haines Country." I confided that my secondary objectives—none of which could be pursued in New England—were to photograph wildlife in Denali (my camping partner for six years, the photographer Michio Hoshino, was pulled from his tent and killed by a brown bear in 1996), fish the Kenai (in 1992 I shared a 55-pound salmon with students), and hunt in the Brooks Range (after a bush-plane crashed on a 1993 caribou hunt, I hiked twenty miles out of the mountains to the Sheenjek River, where I found a Qui'chin family searching for mammoth ivory along the cutbanks who, in exchange for my rifle, transported me one hundred river-miles to Fort Yukon, in an experience recorded in "From the Faraway Nearby," published in *American Nature Writing: 1998* by Sierra Club Books).

Abbey grimly laughed at my naïveté regarding the isolated campus. He said, "From what the Hainester tells me you're gonna find yourself working as a hunting guide up there." Abbey reminded us of what happened to the nature writer William Pruitt. On the same campus during the 1960s, Pruitt opposed Project Chariot (an Atomic Energy Commission plan to use nuclear bombs to create harbors). The other professors retaliated against him, forced him from his job, and, through a campaign of disinformation, destroyed his reputation and career. Unable to find work, he moved to Canada, where he established the Taiga Biological Station in Manitoba and became a venerated figure in the international scientific and literary community (he is now considered the father of boreal ecology). After Pruitt lost his university position and U.S. academic career, three nuclear bombs were detonated in Alaska (1965, 1969, 1971). Many years later the Alaska legislature honored Pruitt with a citation for his "allegiance to truth and personal integrity," and the state university awarded him an honorary doctoral degree. "It's a weird, dark, Nordic place," Abbey warned. "Be careful."

Abbey was as correct in his advice on this matter as he had been about the trail to Druid Arch in 1975. The frontier campus proved to be, as with the examples cited by Abbey, a dystopian antiworld. After publishing twelve scholarly books in six years, including three with Oxford University Press, while teaching forced overloads every semester (a nonunion school at the time), I was shown the door by the creative writers then running the department. Everything that occurred was consistent with what Abbey had predicted that day at the Mercury Café, when he said, "Trust me. It will be just like an Ibsen play" (referring to such works as *Pillars of Society* and *The Wild Duck*). Abbey understood human behavior in extreme climates and isolated locations from his years in the National Park Service.

After I returned to Colorado in 1994, Thompson, who could find humor in anything, said, "They've gone through the looking glass. These are people who would eat meatballs in front of a vegetarian. The irony is that in demonizing you they destroyed themselves. March them naked into an arena, put cow-bells around their necks, and give them a few jolts from a bull-buster cattle prod." He added, more seriously, seeing the unmerited reversal had a certain Zen aspect to it: "This is a great opportunity. Don't squander it."

Noting the time, I changed the subject and inquired about Abbey's experiences during the filming of *Lonely Are the Brave* (1962), a movie I'd taught at DU (1987) and would include in my forty-first book, *Cinema Southwest* (2000). Abbey had appeared as a police officer in the adaptation of his 1956 novel *The Brave Cowboy* (the once-deleted scene has been restored in some versions). He related a comic anecdote that involved Kirk Douglas's palomino, which escaped the studio wranglers in Tijeras Canyon, near Albuquerque, during the shooting of a helicopter scene with Walter Matthau. Abbey waved off the others, who were only making matters worse, and caught the horse with a technique he learned while growing up in Appalachia, an apple.

He brought up the screenwriter Dalton Trumbo, who, he said, had produced a "first-rate" script. Trumbo was a member of the Hollywood Ten, a group of screenwriters and actors who were blacklisted in the 1950s for refusing to testify before Congress about their political beliefs. Abbey reminded us that the "iron-principled" writer, who would not betray his colleagues in order to advance his own interests, had spent ten months in prison. He saluted Kirk Douglas for championing Trumbo's cause and helping him find work after the repressive 1950s ("the decade of pathetic little lap dogs"). Ed Twining, who had, quite generously, said little through the meal so that Abbey and I could become acquainted, asked Abbey if he had heard about Kirk Douglas's autobiography, *The Ragman's Son*, which told of the actor's struggles as the son of poor Russian Jewish immigrants. Abbey said he was looking forward to reading the book, because the Academy Award nominee had recently said the finest film he had ever been associated with was *Lonely Are the Brave*.

The 1980s were a slower-paced and, in some respects, more deeply lived era, a time long before the frenetic, surface-enchanted era of Facebook postings, tweets, and text messages. The multicourse lunch (paid for by the department's "professional development" fund) and leisurely conversation went on undisturbed for the length of the 1980s film *My Dinner with Andre* and then some. It was a quiet afternoon, and neither Marilyn (still the owner, although she's moved the business, with its annual Neal Cassady birthday party, uptown) nor the waitresses (with whom Abbey was flirting, saluting them as "these sterling representatives of my favorite gender") minded.

Marilyn had hung two reproductions from Andy Warhol's 1983 endangered species series (*Bald Eagle* and *Pine Barrens Tree Frog*) on the wall of the café. Abbey, gazing at the posters as the luncheon concluded, mused about the time he spent working in New York. He said he sometimes wondered if he should have remained in the East and devoted his energies to that region. He conceded that he missed the creative intensity of the Big Apple. He recalled the time, visiting the city, that he saw Warhol. The encounter occurred while Abbey was dashing across Central Park after realizing, while in bed with a waitress he just met, that he was late for dinner with an editor ("There is Eastern Standard Time and then there is Edward Abbey time"). As he jogged along he observed Warhol (who did not drive) advancing on a bicycle. The artist was unmistakable in his platinum wig and sunglasses. The two exchanged waves, although they were strangers. Abbey said that the pop-art leader appeared to be "just another nice guy from Pennsylvania like me." Both were born in the Keystone State in the late 1920s. They grew up within forty miles of one another (Abbey on a farm, Warhol in Pittsburgh). It was an era during which western Pennsylvania, with its natural resources and heavy industry, was gaining national prominence (Frank Lloyd Wright constructed Falling Water at Mill Run in 1937, when Abbey was ten and Warhol was nine).

Abbey then turned to Twining and said, referring to the poster, that he had not known there were tree frogs in the Pine Barrens until seeing the work of art. He said, "I'll bet McPhee doesn't know there are tree frogs in the Pine Barrens!" His eastern rival had published *The Pine Barrens* in 1968. Abbey celebrated "another free meal for being Edward Abbey" with a cigar (public smoking was permitted, even encouraged, then). He humorously referred to me as his "amanuensis," as I had taken several pages of notes during the conversation. I told him that ironically, I had learned the art of recording conversations from Warhol, who I met in April 1968 with my friend Ron Moehle, when the artist was in my hometown (Cincinnati) for the screening of a film at Xavier University. I was initially introduced to Warhol's work in 1964, when I saw his mural at the New York State Pavilion of the World's Fair. Warhol, who signed a book I had with me, taped the exchange on a cassette recorder, as he often did in public settings to triangulate conversations with strangers (two months later he was shot and nearly killed by a deranged individual). The inspirational encounter—during which Warhol, a practicing Catholic, exclaimed "Thank God for the Jesuits!"—proved transformative for Ron, who earned a BFA in printmaking and spent his life in Manhattan. Ron, who I first met in 1959, lived long enough to watch, from his subway stop, men and women on fire jump from the Twin Towers on 9/11, an experience (over two hundred people perished in this manner) that contributed to his decline and death.

Abbey asked what book Warhol had signed. I replied that it was the Penguin edition of the Edward Conze translation of the Buddhist scriptures. He said that he had read the book twice. The first time was while recovering from knee surgery at the VA hospital in Albuquerque in 1960. The second was in 1974, while he was working for the Nature Conservancy at the Aravaipa Canyon preserve near Mammoth, Arizona. On both occasions the writings reminded him of Thales and Democritus, with their penchant for epigrams, although the Eastern texts lacked the Western emphasis on rational inquiry. He pointed to Wilson's plate and said they were, by comparison, like a "turkey sandwich with only the lettuce and mayonnaise." He said that he had never grasped why Herman Hesse, whose 1943 *Das Glasperlenspiel* (he used the German title) was "interesting as a novel of ideas," had become so enthralled with the East. Abbey stated that he preferred the novels of New Mexican writer John Nichols, especially *The Milagro Beanfield War*, which he considered "perfect in every way," to Hesse, Mann, or even Goethe. He surprised us by quoting (in German) from the clown's speech in Goethe's *Faust:* "Das Alter macht nicht kindisch, wie man spricht, / Es findet uns nur nocht als wahre Kinder" (Age is no second childhood—age makes plain, / Children we were, true children we remain). Abbey said that was his favorite line when he was pulled over by the police. He said the technique of reciting it always "brightened up the monotony of another arrest" and "had a calming effect on the situation" (Abbey was arrested several times, beginning with his detention at the age of seventeen for vagrancy in New Mexico). Everyone chuckled at the observation.

Abbey glanced outside at a group of attractive pedestrians as they hurried by, in a rare moment of silence. After craning his neck, he said with a laugh, "Capitol Hill should be designated by the United Nations as a world-heritage girl-watching zone." Our guest then shared a picaresque account. It began simply enough. Once, while returning from Montana, he stopped at a motel in Rock Springs, Wyoming. After he paid for the room, the manager, a middle-aged woman from India, asked if he wanted a "portable heater," as the nights were becoming cold. Abbey said, "Sure, why not?" He was unaware the phrase was a euphemism and that, to her, he appeared to be another oil-field worker. Several minutes later there was a knock at the door. It was his portable heater. Exhausted from the drive, he declined her offer, although the visitor stayed half an hour, watching television and consuming his beef jerky, so as to preserve her reputation. He said it was impossible to sleep "from the beds banging against the walls" and "the pistol duels in the parking lot." He left for Tucson at sunrise. Abbey quipped: "Now there's a bit of rural America you won't find in *Blue Highways*" (William Least Heat-Moon's 1982 travel narrative). As our laughter subsided, Twining suggested to Wilson they fish the Jim Bridger Wilderness that summer, which resulted in more mirth.

Abbey turned serious. He said the most difficult aspect of his life was that he was not in possession of wisdom, and yet people sought him for counsel. He confided that he was "just as lost as anybody." He said, "Let's face it. A priori, life is senseless." Dr. Twining observed that the essence of wisdom was just that—an appreciation of limits. Dr. Wilson said, smiling, that he had always thought "el principio de la sabiduria es el temor de Dios" (the beginning of wisdom is the fear of God). He added that, on the bright side, at least Abbey could always obtain a free meal at any university in the West, "except Cal Tech." Abbey laughed. We parted on the city street with handshakes and friendly slaps on the back. At the last moment Abbey handed me an "I Believe In Life *Before* Death" bumper sticker he had obtained from a street vendor. He said, "I was going to give this to your post commander [the late Tom Auer, the publisher of the *Bloomsbury Review*], but I'll give it to you instead. You can put it on your bicycle." I thanked him. That is my last memory of him, as he stood square shouldered in the spring light with a broad smile. If clean shaven, his face would have evoked the doomed Renaissance philosopher Thomas More, as rendered in the painting by Hans Holbein.

As I watched the group amble off, I realized that if Abbey had been born in a country then under authoritarian control or in the midst of civil upheaval, he might have already been, like his heroes Solzhenitsyn and Marquez, summoned to Stockholm, given his outstanding body of work, his reputation for constructive and informed dissent, and his leadership of a progressive social movement. Writers have in the past received the award for less than he achieved (Bjerstjerne M. Bjornson, Carl Spittler). No other nature writer in our time has enjoyed Abbey's popularity, with the exception of Cheryl Strayed, whose stellar book *Wild: From Lost to Found on the Pacific Crest Trail* held the number one position on the *New York Times* best-seller list for seven weeks in 2012 (five weeks longer than Keith Richards's memoir in 2011). I thought I would surely see the philosopher and author again in a few months, perhaps a year, at some conference or event, and was looking forward to that.

Unaware that the historic era of the printed, paper-based book would soon change forever, and that Edward Abbey's time on Earth was limited, I rode back to the DU campus happily, on an ancient Peugot ten-speed through city traffic.

4

Edward Abbey was, to use a metaphor, the ever-steady hub at the center of a turning wheel that was supported by many individual spokes, each representing a reader or member of the guild who was connected to him. His importance can best be understood in terms of those relationships, as I have tried to document here. He bore within himself all the conflicts— political, environmental, philosophical, literary, academic—of his time. He had as many contradictions as any human being. His early novel *The Brave Cowboy* (1956), for example, was a Remington-like paean to a lost romantic age that he later lampooned mercilessly in essays during the 1970s and 1980s. His estrangement from society and his continual return to nature were the sources of his strength. Despite his reputation as a firebrand, he represented the conscience of his generation and wrote in the tradition of Montaigne and Camus. He never descended into sophistry or embraced an easy falsehood over a difficult truth. Like the Renaissance humanists, he was more interested in life than art. When he committed to publication, he chronicled truth and beauty, as in his last major novel. A rationalist in the Greek, Roman, and Enlightenment traditions, Abbey saw the quest for the supernal as tragic resignation (as in "Down the River"). He understood the wisdom of Paul's and Tertullian's "oportet haereses esse"—that heretics are necessary to prevent society from drifting into complacency and inertia. As time progresses, it becomes increasingly apparent that the age of Abbey in the American West revolved around a single dominant figure, as did the age of Johnson, another consummate rationalist, in eighteenth-century London. To express the concept another way, the author was the apotheosis of an epoch that was even then, in 1988, being destroyed by the forces that had nourished it.

Note

1. The actual Camus quote is "There is no fate that cannot be surmounted by scorn." Abbey apparently (or perhaps intentionally, knowing Ed) mistranslated the French word for fate and replaced it with pain.

PART 4
A NEW GENERATION

Reason is the newest and rarest thing in human life, the most delicate child of human history.
—EDWARD ABBEY, *A VOICE CRYING IN THE WILDERNESS* (1989)

Pariah Canyon, Utah (September 1999)

CHAPTER 13

Faraway

GENOA ALEXANDER

I went for walks. I went for walks. I went for walks and on one of these,
the last I took in Havasu, regained everything that seemed to be ebbing
away.

—EDWARD ABBEY, "HAVASU," *DESERT SOLITAIRE*

THE LEEWARD ISLANDS of the Caribbean tiptoe between Puerto Rico
and Dominica along the forefront of the great Atlantic Ocean in the West
Indies. Generated by volcanoes and surrounded by surf and coral, they
are vacation spots for tourists seeking lush, green rainforest environments
and sunny beaches. About five hundred miles east of Cuba, and about as
far from Edward Abbey's red rock desert as you can get, there is a leeward
island I once called home: Saint Kitts.

Small islands are crowded, busy, noisy places. People flock to the markets, the elfin woodlands, the old fortresses, the mansion gardens, and,
of course, the snorkeling coves. I, however, prefer solitude, as well as
peace and quiet, and so I would often venture over the steep mountain-
ous road overlooking the cliffs of the Atlantic, to the southern peninsula
with my daughter. Surprisingly, the thick rainforests of the island do not
span the entire landmass. At the southern extreme of Saint Kitts I discovered a desert covering thousands of acres. It turned out to be a complete
arid landscape that had everything the southwestern deserts back home
have—sand, rocks, agaves, acacia, and cactus. In fact, it was a lot like
home, where prickly pear cactus and Spanish barbed yuccas grew in our
backyard, and the Chihuahuas regularly chased prairie dogs under the
fence. I suspect that Edward Abbey, who preferred solitude to society and
loved the dry country above all other natural landscapes, would have similarly sought out that place had he been on the island.

As I explored the desert—what ecologists call a microhabitat—the scientist in me began to make field lists. I prepared an inventory of flora and fauna. It didn't take long. As Edward Abbey discovered during his stay on another island—Isla de la Sombre in the Gulf of California ("A Desert Isle" [1979])—the species on an island are not as numerous as elsewhere. After finishing with the lists, I focused my attention on the individual plants and animals, their strategies for existence, their inter-relationships, and the larger macrodynamics of a xerophytic community. I began to perceive a series of lessons. The prickly pear cactus (*Opuntia rubescens*) wore a bristle of spines, just as it did back home. The lesson was to protect yourself in a hostile environment as best you can, which can apply to human society as well. The century plant, or agave (*Agave americana*), taught patience. It grows for twenty years—enduring drought and hurricanes and winds—before it produces its towering main stem, with flowers and fruit. Similarly, the barrel cactus (*Euphorbia pulcher-rima*), which sends down a deep taproot ten or more feet long, showed the importance of having a firm anchor in this world. The wind-flagged acacia trees (*Acacia sp.*) along the more exposed ridges illustrated the importance of being flexible and of bending with the changes while remaining fixed to the earth that gives us life. The guinea grasses (*Panicum maximum*) gave quiet proof to a familiar and ancient lesson from Sunday school—that the humble and least noticed shall inherit the earth (Matthew 5:5). The fauna—scorpions, tarantulas, iguanas, green monkeys, goats, doves, par-rots, warblers, hummingbirds—offered similar variations on the precepts from nature's four-billion-year-old book of proven truths.

The point was not just to survive, though, but also to propagate and flourish.

Edward Abbey was familiar with all these axioms, and more, as I learned upon picking up a collection of his essays—*The Best of Edward Abbey* (1984)—at a garage sale in the overgrown village that passed for a town. It was the first book of Abbey's that I had read. I had visited Abbey's Moab country once before, when my mother took the family to Las Vegas. We traveled across the desert at night in our old family station wagon. I remember looking up with wonder at all the stars in the sky. Arches National Park made a lasting impression, in the light of a brilliant, multicolored dawn. We walked to the Double Arch where River Phoe-nix stood among the reflectors and dangling microphones in the Indiana Jones movie, and the ravens squawked down at us like professors in their black academic robes from the junipers and piñons. The high point of the trip was finding my mother's glasses on the street pavement after they had

Self-portrait of Genoa
Alexander on St. Kitt's

flown off her head on a roller coaster ride atop a Las Vegas skyscraper. Although Edward Abbey was known for his rigorous skepticism, and I am very much a rational skeptic too, I believe he would have accepted that unlikely event as empirical proof that miracles can and do happen in the quintessential desert town of Las Vegas.

Small children can be distracting at times, as every mother knows, and so on my reading days in the Saint Kitts desert I flipped randomly through the Abbey book, beginning with the last essays first, and then the fiction excerpts, and finally the middle essays. It was there that I discovered his essay about the desert island in the Gulf of California, as well as a little gem entitled "Havasu." The latter was destined to play a major role in my life journey. In Havasu Canyon Abbey found himself in much the same predicament I was in on Saint Kitts. He was residing in a place that, based on appearance, seemed to be paradise. The canyon had everything—a waterfall, a secluded woods, a pristine campsite, hiking trails—and yet it had nothing. It was—and this became increasingly apparent to him—in many ways the opposite of paradise. He remained there for weeks. He roamed and rested and meditated. He felt like Adam in the Garden of Eden. Or like a prisoner trapped in a cell. Eventually he went a little crazy. He realized that paradise was somewhere else. It was—and this took him a while to perceive—not located in the most beautiful place he could find. It was elsewhere—somewhere, *out there.*

On my daily trips to read in the shade of my favorite acacia in the St. Kitts desert, I delved deep into the wit and wisdom of Edward Abbey. After a week of wandering through his writings, I began to realize some hard facts about myself and my situation. Basically, I needed to do what Abbey had done. I needed to pack up, walk through the gates of a utopia that turned out to be the un-Eden, and move on toward another realm. My place was not there, sitting stagnant on island time, but somewhere else, with a life and a career of my own, as a science educator. I'm not sure I could have done that without the insights provided by Abbey's essay. Perhaps I would have, but it probably would have come later, and my future would have been postponed that much more. That was the lesson—go home and get to work and do what you were put here to do with what little time you've got in this vast and eternal universe.

The writings of Abbey helped me at a difficult period in my life, when I faced a strategic decision about whether to stay in one landscape, both literally and figuratively, or return to another. His words provided guidance and for that I am grateful. I suspect I am not the only reader who Abbey and his writings have changed, nor am I the last. That is what a good teacher always does: help guide and clarify. Confucius said that the student is like a raw piece of jade that the teacher shapes into a work of art—the educated person. That is what the words, and teachings, of Edward Abbey did for me.

I remember my last day in my desert by the sea. The cactuses were covered with bright yellow flowers. I never knew what month it was in the tropics. That must have been the right time for them. The honeybees—dressed in orange and black like tiny clowns, my daughter said—were everywhere, and so were the songbirds. There was great excitement in the air. I knew I would never see the place again, but it had served me well. The sea formed a vast blue arc in all directions but one, and in my daughter's eyes there was a blue more like the skies of home than the maritime skies over the Caribbean. I took her hand. Together we walked from the peninsula toward the car and the airport and the flight back to the familiar past that turned out, in the end, to be a journey into an exciting future.

CHAPTER 14

Valle de la Luna

ESTHER ROSE HONIG

*Out there is a different world, older and greater and deeper by far than
ours, a world which surrounds and sustains the little world of men.*

—EDWARD ABBEY, "CLIFFROSE AND BAYONETS," *DESERT SOLITAIRE*

THE HYDRAULICS HISS. The bus door swings open. A burst of hot desert air welcomes me and the other passengers to San Pedro. I can feel my
lips chap almost immediately. This is exactly what I've been waiting for. I
step out into a scene that evokes a passage from Edward Abbey's journals,
had he been born in South America instead of North America. San Pedro
is the last forlorn (or cheerful, depending on your point of view) outpost
of civilization in this high Andean plateau. This is the way the world will
look at the end and how it has appeared on every frontier of civilization
that ever was.

A single bus terminal anchors the corner of the sandy lot. In between
are a couple of dogs, several parked taxis, and an elderly man in a fedora
who is either the mayor welcoming us or the only survivor of the last
windstorm. The town has been here for hundreds of years. It will still be
standing hundreds of years from now. All around this settlement—narrow
streets and adobe bricks baking in the sun—is the Atacama desert (named
for the indigenous Atacameno people). Everyone here, even the kinder-
gartners and especially the teenagers leaving (for good) for the big cities
on the Pacific coast, will tell you the Atacama is the oldest and driest hot
desert on the planet.

The desert appears at first glance to be like any desert in Arizona, or
Algeria, or Outer Mongolia. On the eastern horizon is a snow-capped
volcano, called Licancabur (19,423 feet). It serves as a reminder to everyone of the ultimate authority of nature in these parts. There is nothing
like this landform in the American Southwest. It is nearly the height of

Esther Rose Honig in the Atacama Desert of Chile

Denali, the tallest mountain in North America. It commands your attention. Your eyes keep returning to it. It doesn't move. It is twenty miles
away—a single day's walk. It has dominated the view in that direction for
eons, an Olympian salience forever beckoning to climbers and prophets.
The native people gave it the name Licancabur, which translates as "the
mountain of the people." With all due respect to the deserts of Edward
Abbey's Southwest, the prodigious massif puts Blanca Peak and Navajo
Mountain into perspective. I will leave the ascent of the peak for another
trip, if there is one. I have come on this excursion to see the surrounding
countryside for myself and report back to everyone on the experience.

Half an hour later I check into the local hostel. Another American has
arrived, only this one speaks Spanish as well as she does English. After
planting the flag, I wander around the place. As I suspected, there is not
much. The center of activity today is the artist's market, which is as colorful as any of those in Santa Fe or Monument Valley. I carefully navigate
through the long narrow aisles lined with stalls selling jade and silver
jewelry, alpaca sweaters, pan flutes, and large pendant earrings (no doubt

made in China). The vendors here are mostly women. They wear long, wool skirts and keep their long black hair in a braid, caped by a black fedora—customary *altiplano* dress. I pass by dozens of these stalls, all selling mostly the same trinkets, and exit through the other side of the market, which brings me to the middle of the town's center. The main street is narrow, unpaved and lined by tan and white, single-story adobe buildings. It's easy to imagine that not too long ago these were houses, lived in by families. Now they're filled with gift shops and tour operators. Glossy canvas banners hang over doorways, advertising guided tours to snow-white salt flats, fields of geysers, and red volcanic lakes. According to the most recent census, San Pedro's population is less than five thousand. Each year thirty-five thousand travelers come to the village. The price of change is visible.

The town is reminiscent of the old Spanish settlements—Conejos, Antonito, La Jara—in the San Luis Valley of Colorado, my home state. In fact, the altitude—about eight thousand feet across the sage and cactus flats—is approximately the same in both places, as is the great wash of alpine desert light. I think also of the dusty Italian villages in the Sergio Leone westerns from the 1960s that my father's generation loved to watch. If Clint Eastwood rode his mule down the main street of this town, in his dusty hat and Mexican serape, he would not seem out of place. Thankfully, Hollywood has yet to discover this remote location, although it probably will someday.

I keep glancing at the volcano. It is truly bizarre to see snow, with all that snow connotes, in the midst of so much heat and aridity. One thing is certain. There is nothing like this geographic province—roughly at the point where Bolivia, Argentina, and Chile converge—in the Painted Desert of Edward Abbey. Not in Kayenta or Keet Seel or Canyon de Chelley or any of those other places he wrote about.

Yes, Edward Abbey.

In my pack is a copy of Edward Abbey's *Desert Solitaire*. I brought the book along for the trip, just as Abbey carried copies of works by Major Powell and Thoreau on two of his desert adventures. Having Abbey along on the journey is like having a trusted friend nearby. There is some comfort in hearing a familiar voice from that other continent to the north and from my native province, the American West. I recall Abbey's fierce polemic about what tourism does to the rare places of this Earth. "No more cars in the national parks," he wrote. To which I say, "Good luck with that." Tourism has been around forever. Tourism began with our first steps out of Olduvai Gorge, as we started the long walk to Tel Aviv and Toronto and Tokyo. Ulysses was a tourist, roaming the eastern Mediterranean. Columbus was a tourist, off to discover a new route to China. The Apollo astronauts were tourists, picking up rocks to take back home and show everybody. Abbey was a tourist, exploring Europe, Mexico, and Australia. It's part of our nature. It's why we are successful as an animal species—our innate fascination with the unknown. It's part of the reason the wheeled rover currently exploring the red deserts of the fourth planet, and about to climb a mysterious mountain at the center of a large impact crater, is called Curiosity.

Curious people—tourists really—have been coming to South America for ten, or fifteen, or even twenty thousand years, depending on which scientific source you consult. Darwin, who at one point ventured inland as far as the Atacama region, poked around the beetled coasts, inspired by the expedition of Von Humboldt, who, in turn, was intrigued by the breathless chronicles of those early explorers—like the intrepid Sir Walter Raleigh—who came before him. A hundred years ago, the ever-restless Theodore Roosevelt ventured deeper inland, along an Amazon tributary, searching for the jungle trail that would lead him back to childhood. More recently, Bruce Chatwin, with notebook and pencil in hand, roamed the Patagonian deserts.

But none of them have come here, to this place where I am now.

Everyone who makes the journey to San Pedro comes, in part, to see the Valle de la Luna. The analogy, in Edward Abbey's southern Utah canyon country, would be the mile and a half trail through the sagebrush and sandstone outcrops to Delicate Arch. The geological point of interest in the Atacama desert, appropriately called the Valley of the Moon, is a transcendent feature of the Andean landscape. Everyone I've talked to in the city eight hundred miles to the south (Santiago) insists the unusual valley must be *seen*. People in Salt Lake City similarly make at least one pilgrimage over the course of their lives to see the legendary arch near Moab that is featured on every license plate in the state.

The first day ends anticlimactically, with a hurried meal and an early bedtime. If I have any dreams I don't remember them the next morning, which begins at 5:30 a.m. I grab as many layers as I can fit into my daypack. The desert can be brutally hot and surprisingly cold depending on your elevation. I meet the bus at the front gate of my hostel. Once aboard

I find there are only three other couples on my tour, a huge waste of space for a full-sized bus. After a quick stop for a complimentary breakfast of toast and hot coffee we leave for the open desert. We speed along through plains of yellow sands interspersed with red peaks. White salt crystals frost the desert floors, jagged cliffs, rolling hills, narrow valleys, and fat gypsum boulders. I imagine what it must have been like for Pedro de Valdivia, the Spanish conquistador who traversed this unforgiving landscape five hundred years ago to found the Chilean capital. For months he marched from Peru through the Atacama Desert with more than one thousand indigenous servants. They were unprepared for the extreme conditions, and many died. Valdivia only survived by robbing natives of their food and livestock. Today we breeze over the paved highways and relax in the air-conditioned bus.

As we start on the first leg of our trip, a tall skinny boy, who looks no older than seventeen, stands up at the front of the bus and shyly introduces himself as Jorge, our tour guide. He wears jeans and a grey hoodie and has a head of long black hair—he looks like he's been plucked from the high school skate park. We shall be at his mercy, for better or for worse. Almost immediately, Jorge launches into what is obviously a very practiced speech, a sort of monotone rap, in which he explains the history and geography of the surrounding area. The whole thing takes less than ten minutes. Then he sits back down. He gives several of these "informative statements" throughout the tour, each time ignoring any raised hands and disregarding the German couple who don't understand any Spanish.

On our first stop, we go bird watching at the national flamingo reserve. A pair of giant, shallow lakes hold a perfect reflection of the surrounding mountain range. Here dozens of flamingos gather and feed in small clusters. These feathered ballerinas are Andean flamingos, the rarest flamingos in the world. Chile's Nobel Prize–winning poet Pablo Neruda (1904–1973), once wrote a poem, which appears in his book *Arte de pajaros* (*Art of Birds*), about the Chilean flamingo (*Phoenicopterus chilensis*). He refers to the flamingo as "a flying rose / swinging toward sweetness." People sometimes forget—especially those who are quick to criticize Abbey's conservative views on immigration—that the literary revolutionary Pablo Neruda was a writer of great importance to Edward Abbey. With a universe of choices, Abbey selected an epigraph from the Spanish-speaking Neruda for *Desert Solitaire*: "Give me silence, give me water, hope. Give me the struggle, the iron, the volcanoes." In Spanish it sounds this way:

"Dadme el silencio, el agua, la esperanza. Dadme la lucha, el hierro, los volcanes."

Either way it is beautiful.

I ask Jorge why the earth here looks so jagged. Around the edge of the lake the mud has dried into small stiff peaks. Jorge explains that it's because the sun here is so strong that it pulls the mud up toward the sky, as it is drying. His answer seems questionable, almost mystical, and I wonder if he's just making it up. But the environment here is so foreign to me anyway that I couldn't rebut him if I tried.

We drive for hours and stop periodically to deboard at desert springs and salt fields. We leave the comfort of our seats to meander outside for a brief twenty minutes or so at each destination. Then the driver shouts for us to climb back inside. We visit a handful of tiny towns to see their ancient adobe churches: the footprints of evangelism. Inside, Jorge rattles off the dates of their founding, destruction, and reconstruction. Outside in the sun-bleached plaza, young women selling handwoven tapestries and scarves peek around the corner at the group of approaching tourists. In their black fedoras, a baby strapped to their backs, they stand in bashful silence as we browse their shops and handle their goods. After visiting what feels like the seventh town, I can't help but think about the precariousness of life in such a place and how fragile these lives are, in this giant, ancient desert, where life should not exist at all.

The conclusion to our first day's trip is an excursion to the Laguna Miscanti. The briny lake sits at the edge of a volcano and supports little life besides desert rats and vicunas (small llamas the size of dogs). One by one we leave the bus to face a chilling wind. Everyone snaps a few photos of the amazing scenery and walks down a short path to the other side of the valley. There, just before we get too cold, the bus comes to pick us up and we're shuttled back to San Pedro in heated comfort.

The experience is slightly surreal, and is not my preferred way of traveling, but sometimes in life one must surrender to absurdity, and of course a little humor always helps.

That night I dip back into Abbey's book, and read some more about that *other* desert. Abbey never made it here. He did go to Australia once, on assignment for *National Geographic*, and he wrote some nice essays about the experience. Had he lived longer, he might have come here. The way he would have written about this place would have been different from me. He would have said something like this, which he writes in

Desert Solitaire ("Episodes and Visions"): "The desert says nothing. Completely passive, acted upon but never acting, the desert lies there like the bare skeleton of Being, spare, sparse, austere, utterly worthless, inviting not love but contemplation."

Each person sees things differently. I look at the people of this desert and I see the poverty and the despair before I see anything else. Each person, their life, their story, is unique. People are like the stones in a dry riverbed. At a distance the cobblestones appear the same, but when you sit down and examine them, each one is different and bears the marks of its own origin and history. Georgia O'Keeffe, who lived for many decades in an outlier of the Painted Desert, along the Upper Chama River, was fond of painting river stones. An entire thirty-by-forty canvas would be devoted to a single stone, with perhaps a random feather or flower or leaf in the corner to catch the wandering eye. After years of living in the desert, the artist had learned that one of the most valuable secrets of nature—either wild nature or human nature—is that the smallest fragment contains the key to the whole.

The next morning, weary with the organized tour approach to the desert, I rent a rattled mountain bike from the Internet café in San Pedro and take off for Valle de la Luna, the local national park that just thirty years ago was the site of a large salt mine. With me I've brought a large bottle of water, a roll of bread with cheese, sliced turkey and olives, enough I think for my day biking. The valley is about eight miles away, and the trip takes about an hour and most of my water. I think of Abbey descending by rope with his friend Waterman into the Maze, a similarly exotic geological landscape in the Utah Canyon country, which he describes in the last chapter of *Desert Solitaire*. Everyone yearns to have that close, intimate experience with a particularly vivid example of wild nature. In such places we observe firsthand the capacity of nature to create a landscape that the human mind apprehends—through the symmetry or through the fractal patterns—as beautiful.

The Valle de la Luna does not disappoint.

There is only one road through the park, and I follow it. The thoroughfare is sandy in places and deeply rutted in other places. I wish constantly that I had rented a helmet. The surrounding countryside is, indeed, a lunar-like— even Martian-like—countryside. Death Valley is such a place. So is the Dead Sea in Israel. These are the raw materials of the earth. This is the ancient quarry from which cities and civilizations are built. Here there are no fish-filled streams with bridges or enchanted woodlands. Here is the original surface of the third planet from the sun, as it was in the beginning and as it will be in the end. Here is the place to confront the elements and ask them, as Gauguin did in his paintings, "Where do we come from? What are we? Where are we going?"

"But what exactly does it look like?" asks the reader. Open the latest issue of *National Geographic* and examine the pictures sent from the Mars rover. That is exactly what it looks like. There is no need to travel nine months through outer space to see the deserts of the fourth planet. Just take a bicycle ride through the Valle de la Luna in the Atacama desert of Chile. You will have the added advantages of an oxygen atmosphere and normal Earth gravity, as well as an Internet café at the end of the day. It will help if you have some knowledge of conversational Spanish.

At intervals I hop off the bike and hike the designated trails. One leads to a sandy hilltop viewpoint, where I take a long break to eat part of my lunch, pour the sand from my shoes, and appreciate the view. The landscape in every direction is austere, disciplined, and wholly devoid of vegetation. This desert has been around for more than 150 million years. These mountains and valleys that I see now have watched the dinosaurs die out and humans arrive and disperse.

It gives you pause. You think of home, family, friends, and always there is that relentless wind—a cosmic wind really—blowing hard from some place far away.

My final destination for the day is Las Tres Marias (the Three Marias), a cluster of tall delicate rock formations, skinny, gnarled and twisted, that were formed by wind and weather over the course of time. There are so named for their exaggerated resemblance to the Virgin Mary. With some imagination and a bit of Catholic faith, you can see three crude figures posturing in prayer and vigilance. In Latin America there is a very old and steadfast culture of the *aperations*, when the image of the Virgin appears miraculously on a piece of toast or on the side of a burning building. For Catholics, an *aperation* is a divine message, as if Mary herself has reached out to lend her love and guidance.

We all know how Edward Abbey regarded such matters. In *Desert Solitaire* he devoted an entire section to his beliefs regarding the supernatural: "If a man's imagination were not so weak, so easily tired, if his capacity for wonder not so limited, he would abandon forever such fantasies of the supernal. He would learn to perceive in water, leaves and silence more than sufficient of the absolute and marvelous, more than enough to console him for the loss of the ancient dreams."

In the valley of the moon, the miners who once lived here canonized these rocks. Also called "los vigilantes" (the vigilantes), the miners, whose camp was just a mile or so from the site, toiled in agony hauling salt from deep within the hills. They risked their lives in dark and narrow tunnels and endured a lifetime of brutal labor in exchange for little of substance, no rest, and poor health. It was these unbearable conditions, faced by miners all over the Atacama, that spurred Chile's socialist movement in the 1960s. And for many years, it was the Three Marias that these miners passed each morning on their way from their camp to work in the mine—three faceless figures that lent them a quiet moment of solace each day.

In their footsteps, I walk from the Three Marias and climb a path that leads up a hill to the mine. Left to its own devices, the desert preserves everything (the Egyptians knew something about this) with immaculate care. I spot the remains of an adobe hut. The boulder it was built against is charred black. Perhaps it was a kitchen, a place where the miners were served lunch. A black piece of cloth is matted into the desert floor. Maybe it was a handkerchief or some parcel of clothing. It's another twenty-minute walk up the hill before the narrow path sinks into a gaping black hole in the rocks. The old mine is barricaded with warning signs, and it seems as though one could slip and fall to the center of the earth.

Pablo Neruda wrote about these mines in his poem about the Atacama. It begins: "Insufferable voice, disseminated salt, substituted ash, black bouquet on whose extreme dewdrop the blind moon rises, through grieving galleries of copper" (*Canto General* [1950]). For Neruda, the Atacama is a mysterious woman, her body a striking landscape, bearing little life and plenty of precious minerals. She is powerful in her own right but has long been a place of agony and greed.

When I return to the site of the Three Marias, the sun is setting. The shadows are lengthening from every ridgetop and rock, and the desert is falling back into repose. The whole countryside is gradually falling asleep. I rest against a boulder and face the three maidens while I finish the rest of my water and food. I'm completely exhausted and likely very dehydrated, but I disregard my body and instead focus on the sky above, glowing bright orange and pink. The mood is peaceful, the view sublime. Suddenly the harmonic moment is interrupted. Several tourist buses appear on the horizon. The noise of the diesel engines grows louder, almost unbearable.

They hiss and grind to a stop in front of me and completely block my view. The passengers inside unload, listen to a ten-minute speech on the significance of these three rocks, and then pile back into their buses for dinnertime back in San Pedro.

I'm left alone then with the desert and the great silence that was here before they came. In another desert, on another evening twenty years before I was born, Edward Abbey wrote, at the end of his essay on his ascent of Mount Tukuhnikivats in *Desert Solitaire*: "Mesa, canyon and plateau, the pacific desert lies in whiskey-colored light and lilac dusk, a sea of silence. Clouds edged with fire sail on the clear horizon."

After awhile, watched by the Three Marias, I get on my bicycle beneath the violet sky and return along the grey road to this world.

Afterword

Assailed at times by a sense of desperation—in seven weeks I'll be forty years old and still don't know with any precision who or what I am. . . . Am resolved to continue on my present course: to compose somehow the one good novel; to run Cataract Canyon in a kayak; to raze more billboards; to build that solid house of rock and wood far out somewhere where my sons and grandsons can find at least a temporary refuge from the nightmare world of 2000 A.D.

—EDWARD ABBEY, LETTER TO AL SARVIS, DECEMBER 13, 1966

1

Fifteen days after Edward Abbey's passing, on March 29, 1989, Clarke Abbey, his widow and the mother of two of his children, wrote me a note at the University of Alaska from their home in Tucson. She thanked me for a review of *The Fool's Progress*, which had appeared that month in *Bloomsbury Review*. She reported that the last thing Abbey read before he died "during one of his last lucid periods" was that piece of writing. Many other reviewers, from the *New York Times*, the *Los Angeles Times*, the *Washington Post*, to (most disappointing of all) Ed Marston of the *High Country News*, writing in the *National Review*, had criticized the work, which Abbey had described to us as his "fat masterpiece." These reviewers, and particularly Marston, dismissed Abbey in the same manner that establishment stalwarts like James Lowell, editor of the *Atlantic Monthly*, sought to marginalize the nonconformist Thoreau, or as Sartre regularly parried at a distance with the free-thinking author of *The Rebel*.

Unlike the others, I had found reason to praise Abbey's novel, which represented a large-scale, multiyear effort that was conceived in the context of those European works produced by Camus and others that Abbey admired. The book employs a parallel narrative with a converging timeline, which is a challenging contrapuntal structure in which to compose a lengthy work. Its conceptual inventiveness builds upon the twentieth-century experiments of William Burroughs, with his nonlinear cut-up novels, and Peter Matthiessen, with his spare Caribbean narrative *Far Tortuga* (1975). Abbey's novel anticipated later eclectic works, such as David Mitchell's *number9dream* (2001), which took its title from the sound collage on the Beatles' *White Album* (1968), and was followed by the even more daring *Cloud Atlas* (2004). Both were conceived in the free-spirited British tradition of Laurence Stern (*Tristam Shandy* [1750]) and James Joyce (*Finnegans Wake* [1939]). Abbey had, with considerable skill, achieved a Bach-like resonance between two opposites: life and death. Although uneven in terms of literary quality, because of Abbey's declining health, the text provides the reader with useful insights into the author and his time. It is clear that Abbey was striving for the universal standard of enduring works—to bear witness to the truth, to comfort the afflicted, and to provide intellectual and spiritual sustenance to humanity.

The book is at one level an autobiographical narrative, but the author avoids direct personal reference, as Hemingway did when writing of postwar Paris in *The Sun Also Rises* (1925). Indeed, much of what we know of Abbey's personal life only came to light in the posthumous journals (1994) and letters (2006) edited by David Petersen. This delayed revelatory process was also the case with Mark Twain, whose autobiography was not published, in accordance with the author's instructions, until a century after his death (2010), and Eugene O'Neill, whose *Long Day's Journey into Night*, written in 1941, was not published, as the author directed in his will, until after his passing (the play received a Pulitzer in 1957).

Most of the other reviewers had reacted to the standard Abbey provocations. I ignored the subversive rhetoric and focused on the compelling aspects of what I considered an original contribution to American literature. It is not *The Grapes of Wrath* or *Legends of the Fall*, in terms of sustained excellence, but it is not the opposite of those works either. If I had been his editor, I would have encouraged him to produce another work of nonfiction, which was his area of strength. I would have suggested that he take a year to explore an unfamiliar part of the greater Southwest. He could have, for example, written a book about Sonora that focused on the exotic biota, as well as a complex human realm dating to the Aztec era. Such a work might have prompted Abbey to reexamine his thinking on Mexico, which tended toward superficial reductions and modes of discourse that were not consistent with his normal standards of rigor and objectivity. It could have also served to advance literature in the border province beyond the quaint nonfiction of J. Frank Dobie and Charles Sheldon and the genre fiction of Carlos Castenada and Cormac McCarthy (Abbey had included a brilliant, Coover-esque short story titled "Rocks" in *Desert Solitaire*).

The two books together—*Desert Solitaire* and a northern Mexican book laced with Abbey irreverence, humor, and irony—might have been his *Iliad* and *Odyssey*, or, to use a nonfiction analogy, his *Seven Pillars of Wisdom* and *Revolt in the Desert* (T. E. Lawrence, 1926 and 1927). As can be seen in his four Australian essays ("The Reef," "Anna Creek," "The Outback," and "Back of Beyond") from the late 1970s, the author could write with power and vigor when inspired by new people, fresh adventures, and unknown landscapes. Abbey, however, had come to age in a generation that considered the novel to be the supreme prose work. It was toward that elusive goal, in a form that, after two centuries of use by Bronte, Hugo, Tolstoy, Balzac, Flaubert, and Dickens, was approaching a state of depletion, that he devoted his remaining years. Unfortunately, Abbey at that point had been significantly undone by the course of his illness, which adversely affected his cognition, as well as by his celebrity, which also subverted his perception of himself and his efforts to sustain a high literary standard.

Abbey's widow wrote of the review: "I believe it's the most perceptive and the best review that Ed's had of any of his books. I know how much it meant to him to have his book receive its due recognition. You said it all so beautifully." In a subsequent conversation I learned that she had read it to him aloud, as he was not able to read in his final hours. My editor Tom Auer had overnighted the issue of *Bloomsbury Review* to Abbey to make certain the author, who had recently published an entertaining John Updike critique in our pages, was provided with the opportunity to familiarize himself with the review before he passed. That note reporting that the last written words that Abbey processed before leaving this world was my response to his final work, together with my correspondence with him, have always made me grateful for my brief acquaintance with the author.

Because I lived thirty-five hundred miles away and had a full teaching, committee, and publishing load, as well as a wife who was close to giving birth (my now twenty-six-year-old son, Steven, an Atlanta businessman), I was unable to attend the wake in Moab. The gathering of remembrance was attended by such Abbey intimates as Wendell Berry, Peter Matthiessen, and John Haines. My father and older brother, both EPA officials in

Denver, were able to make the pilgrimage and provided a report (my father made a photographic record). It was clear to me, from their observations, that Abbey was cherished, as a person as well as an author, by a large number of people in the West and elsewhere in the country.

Had Abbey lived, I believe we would have seen him at Burning Man, South by Southwest, and Coachella, cheerfully urging the young crowds on to a greater purpose than hedonism and self-indulgence. Abbey liked to have fun as much as anyone, but he saw recreation as only one part of the larger round of existence. His final writings—as in "A Writer's Credo" (1988), which he read at Trinity United Methodist Church in Denver in 1989—emphasize the duties to nature and society that attend our journey. He may have, in that spirit, joined ranks with those in Congress, from Jared Polis on the left to Jim Sensenbrenner on the right, who have denounced the triumph of irrationality known as metadata mining, with its misapplication of the Patriot Act and its undermining (to use an Abbey-esque pun) of the Fourth Amendment (his fellow insurgent Hunter S. Thompson was co-creator of the Fourth Amendment Foundation).

Or perhaps not.

Perhaps, given twenty, or twenty-five, or thirty more years of longevity, in the end he would have turned his back on the never-ending travails of the human race, and retreated, as Hunter S. Thompson did to his sanctuary on Woody Creek, to find the time, as the light angled low from the west, to contemplate the mysteries of the broader nature he loved to ponder. Like Camus, whose mother was a deaf-mute and who grew up in a household of silence, Abbey believed that solitude, meditation, and estrangement were necessary to the social task of writing. The author was an attentive listener, as evidenced by Robert Redford's observation cited in the introduction. He embraced the principle of disciplined utterance and informed statement. A remote Southwestern perch from which to survey the world-at-large might have suited Abbey's nature as much as another lecture tour promoting his beliefs regarding the human experience.

2

Abbey was, to be sure, not just another member of the literary community. His writings captured the zeitgeist of the American West during the 1970s and 1980s. Radiant works such as *Desert Solitaire* and *Abbey's*

Road helped to shape and define a literary era. Only a handful of authors west of the Mississippi—among them Hunter S. Thompson, John Haines, and Wallace Stegner—were his peers in nonfiction. Others, such as David Rains Wallace (who I interviewed for the *Bloomsbury Review* in 1990) and Ken Brower (who I published on several occasions), at times came close to, or matched, his standard of excellence. With his Thoreau-like emphasis on the natural world, Abbey softened the asperities of Thompson's hard-driven Epicurean doctrine. Both authors were committed literary, social, and political activists. Both shared a gift for aphorism and granular narratives of personal synthesis. Although they were quite different as people—Thompson watched television constantly, loved popular music, embraced the cold weather months, regularly socialized with political leaders and popular culture icons, and reveled in pursuits that Abbey studiously avoided—they were kindred in their literary endeavors. Both rebelled against stale and obsolete formulas of expression, whether it was Abbey exploring the practical ramifications of ethical imperatives, or Thompson probing the permeable boundaries between literary genres. Thompson was an intensely social being, while Abbey preferred solitude and socialized only when absolutely necessary. As Abbey states in "Coda: Cape Solitude" (1979): "All my life, a loner, an outsider, a barbarian from the steppes, the wolf on the snow-covered hill looking down at the lights of the village. I think I've never been accepted by my fellow men, fellow women, never been a bona fide member of the club. And looking back at the human race, feeling I never belonged, my first thought, right now, is—thank God."[1]

Thompson's most noticeable effect upon Abbey was to convince him, by the commercial and critical success of the winning Hunter S. Thompson formula, that comic and satiric writing was a form of serious literature. As a result, Abbey's writing, and modes of presenting himself, changed significantly over the course of the 1970s. The contrast is striking between the tightly controlled, formal writing in *Desert Solitaire*, published in 1968, when Abbey was still under the influence of Joseph Wood Krutch (*The Desert Year*), and the more lighthearted and liberated prose in *Abbey's Road*, written a decade later, by which time he was firmly in Thompson's revolutionary camp. While it is true that both authors were part of the same milieu, and were responding to the same societal changes and contemporary sources of inspiration, Thompson was the more radical and innovative of the two. One can, to make a distinction between Abbey and Thompson, imagine Thompson evolving independently of

Grandview
Overlook, Utah
(March 1997)

Abbey, had Abbey never existed, but one cannot easily imagine Abbey becoming quite so liberated in the mid to late 1970s without the colorful influence of Thompson. Abbey was familiar with the universal dynamic of cross-fertilization and wrote about it in his essay on Ralph Waldo Emerson: "Without Emerson there would have been only a lesser Thoreau and maybe no Walt Whitman at all."[2]

On one level, Abbey and Thompson embodied the creative archetypes expressed in the ancient Greek formulations of Apollo, who represented the ordered and rational (Abbey), and Dionysius, who evoked the spontaneous, disordered, and emotional (Thompson). Thompson published his first work of revolutionary journalism, *Hell's Angels: A Strange and Terrible Saga*, in 1966. Abbey followed two years later with his groundbreaking work of nature nonfiction, *Desert Solitaire*. Thompson developed the *Fear and Loathing* series in the 1970s, as Abbey refined and adapted his literary approach during the same decade. Their relationship evolved over time, as they competed in a friendly manner at a distance, both with each other and with other writers of the era. Abbey was, by most objective standards, the more ordered and rational of the two, although at times he was capable of personal behavior and literary improvisations every bit as wild as Thompson. The author of *The Gonzo Papers* was the embodiment of the Dionysian ideal but could also shift to the discipline and restraint of the Apollonian school. He quotes the venerable Dr. Johnson, for example, in "Ashes to Ashes and Dust to Dust: The Funeral of Mother Miles" (1966): "He who makes a beast of himself gets rid of the pain of being a man."[3] For his part, Abbey could make humorous, Thompson-like topical references to the mundane artifacts of consumer culture—"Elmer's Glue" and "Lady Clairol Spray-Net."[4] Both stood opposed to the vapid, mannered, and artificial in literature, as seen in eastern writers like John Updike and John McPhee, who Abbey detested, and the staid establishment journalists who supported follies like the Vietnam War and the administration of Richard Nixon and who Thompson delighted in mocking. They were united in their comical and humane vision of the world and of themselves.

The two kindred spirits never met socially, but quoted each other in print and referred to each other admiringly in their books, as Abbey does in the Preface to *Abbey's Road* and elsewhere. Thompson, in tribute to Abbey, included an epigraph from Abbey in his final book. These references underscore their close literary relationship and mutual cross-fertilization during the 1970s, when they shared a progressive approach to writing and social commentary. To an extent this process continued through the mid-1980s, although by then Abbey's health had begun to deteriorate. Thompson would remain intact, in terms of literary skills, through the 1990s. The author would complete one last major novel, *The Rum Diaries*, which he had begun in 1959 (the Hemingway influence of the early period is noticeable) and finally published in 1998. The dynamic between the two is analogous to that between Hemingway and Steinbeck, as the former strongly influenced the latter, even though they were not formally acquainted and traveled in different social circles. A second example can be seen in the relationship between the modern Latin American writers Jorge Luis Borges and Gabriel García Márquez, who were deeply rooted in the imaginative world of Cervantes, and several members of the postwar literary generation in America, including Robert Coover and the very early Barry Lopez.

John Haines, who lived the Thoreau ideal at his remote Alaskan retreat, was, by contrast with both Abbey and Thompson, a focused topical writer with a disciplined Scandinavian style and a short-format preference. His forte was the self-contained essay. A respected poet, Haines acquired the lapidary skills necessary for that genre. He was deeply influenced by such poets as Dylan Thomas, Edwin Muir, and the Nobel laureate Czeslaw Milosz (with whom I corresponded from 1980 until his death). The many years Haines spent writing poetry had a salutary effect on his prose, which tended to be more polished than that of either Abbey or Thompson, who often wrote on deadline. At times, Haines's nature prose evoked the measured cadences of Thomas Merton (1915–1968), a Trappist monk who also wrote in social isolation with few daily distractions. Merton's northern Kentucky hermitage, which I visited on a religious retreat at St. Xavier in 1969, was opulent compared to Haines's rustic cabin along the Tanana River. The same might be said of Thompson's multimillion-dollar mountain residence along Woody Creek near Snowmass Village and Abbey's comfortable 4.5-acre estate in the west Tucson suburbs (contrary to what he wrote, Abbey never lived in nearby Oracle or in Wolf Hole). Like Abbey and Thompson, as well as their precursor Thoreau, Haines was a nonconformist who approached life and literature with the opposite of methodological rigor. That independent spirit can be seen throughout his body of writing.

Haines alone, among his larger circle of peers, resided in an authentic wilderness setting. North of his cabin there were no paved roads for five hundred miles to the Arctic Ocean. His secluded mode of living was consistent with his belief system regarding nature, literature, and civilization. As a result of his simple, self-sufficient approach to the journey, growing his own vegetables, harvesting the berries and mushrooms of the forest, and killing one moose a year, Haines remained productive as a writer nearly to the age of ninety. Many of his finest books were published in his seventies and eighties, as he had a burst of creative activity in his last years. At seventy-six he and his wife made a pilgrimage to Florence, Italy, and the Wordsworth cottage. At the same age, the hard-living Abbey and the swash-buckling Thompson had been dead for ten or more years. In retrospect, it may have been a blessing that Haines never taught at the local university, as a result of the insecurities of the writing faculty who refused to hire him, and remained sixty miles away at his homestead. His isolation from that often cynical world and its various hierarchies, coupled with the physical benefits of a hardy outdoor existence, spared him from other fates, and the well-documented effects of toxic work environments upon health.

Although not as well-known during his lifetime as Edward Abbey and Hunter S. Thompson, Haines, like the once-obscure William Blake among the romantic nature poets, may see his reputation grow in the next century. The former NEA chairman Dana Gioia, who delivered the commencement address at his alma mater Stanford in 2007 and currently (2015) holds an endowed professorship at the University of Southern California, wrote insightfully of Haines in a foreword to *A Gradual Twilight* (2003) that "in a literary age characterized by middle-class professionalism and institutional security, especially among academic writers, Haines reminds one of the deep historical connections between the artistic vocation and voluntary poverty. . . . By spiritual necessity, the prophetic writer must stand apart from his or her milieu and renounce the compromises that solicit its rewards. Renunciation, sacrifice and dedication . . . [permit] the sort of freedom, candor and purity that characterize Haines' work. . . . In a literary era dominated by institutional life, he stands out as both a singular and exemplary figure."[5] Gioia was nominated by President Bush to the NEA chair and fully vetted by Congress. He served in that position for six years. He may be considered one of the more credible contemporary sources on Haines, who has often been mythologized and vilified by his academic antagonists and guild competitors in Alaska, in a manner that recalls the campus experiences of William O. Pruitt, as well as my own. Edward Abbey's great respect for John Haines, expressed in his Alaska essay (1983), was well founded and shared by other knowledgeable observers of the era.

Only Wallace Stegner, who was of an older generation (born 1909), came close to equaling Edward Abbey's comprehensive knowledge of literature, history, and philosophy. Neither Thompson nor Haines could approach Abbey in this regard. Stegner, a career academic at Stanford who had earned a doctoral degree, was an influential force in the national guild during his maturity, but he lacked Abbey's ability to energize and mobilize a vast constituency of young people for environmental purposes. Although he wrote many fine essays, he failed to produce a unified work on the order of *Desert Solitaire*. The professor's books sold sparsely compared to Abbey's (*The Monkey Wrench Gang* sold half a million copies, *Desert Solitaire* a million). His fiction, reflecting limitations of ability, life experience, and perspective, attracted no interest from the film community, in contrast to the lively, earthy works of Hunter S. Thompson (who freely mixed genres), Jim Harrison (based in northern Michigan at the time), John Nichols, and his former students Edward Abbey, Ken Kesey, Tom McGuane, and Larry McMurtry. Stegner's Pulitzer Prize–winning novel *Angle of Repose* (1972) has long been questioned for incorporating the letters and memoir of Mary Foote with insufficient attribution.[6] The author's harshest critics, among them feminists, have accused him of plagiarism.

Stegner's functional role during his era was to manage a well-regarded writing program at the finest institution of higher learning in the American West. Edward Abbey left the vaunted program in midterm (1957), disillusioned with the workshop method and uninspired by its primary architect. Stegner, who had a history of conflicts with those who questioned his authority (as with Ken Kesey), then purged Abbey from the list of fellows, as is confirmed in the online record. In retrospect, the professor appears a well-intentioned but dogmatic pedagogue who linked his career and reputation to the corporate Association of Writers and Writing Programs (AWP) approach, which the former U.S. poet laureate Donald Hall pilloried with the phrase "McPoem" in *Poetry and Ambition* and that, more recently, Mark McGurl, a literary scholar at Stanford, has thoroughly dissected in *The Program Era*.[7]

McGurl concludes that the era of writing programs systematized writers in a way that "lays bare the recruitment of creativity to the inhuman ends of the economic order we serve," produced a "literature of solipsism," and fostered an anti-intellectual environment.[8] Abbey stands out, in this context, for his independence and clearheadedness. He saw, in the powerful established literary order that Stegner embodied (in the 1980s there were over two hundred AWP programs), a series of contradictions. The programs existed, and still do, to the significant financial benefit of universities and those who taught in them. In other countries they do not exist, nor have they ever existed at any other time in the history of the written word. They represent the archetypal American approach, as orthodoxy and conformity are imposed in a factory model and a low-wage labor base—graduate teaching assistants and part-time faculty—is exploited.

Like many, Edward Abbey taught in a writing program out of economic necessity. His aversion to academia began while he was a university student in the 1950s: "Gawd but I hate school. . . . [T]edious and painful and full of gray smog and hateful to life."⁹ According to his journal entries in the 1980s, he dreaded each spring semester at the University of Arizona. Two decades earlier, he taught for one semester at Western Carolina University in the southern Appalachians. His comments are illustrative of his point of view: "Like a bloody idiot I accepted a teaching job here at Redneck U. . . . But oh! The horror the tedium the *drudgery* of academic life. How I despise it. How I loathe it. . . . [F]ive fucking days per week. . . . The ceaseless pressure of the fucking job—no time to relax—always there's tomorrow's shit to prepare. . . . Of course, I could always shoot myself. But I haven't even got a gun."¹⁰ To those familiar with the history of education, such observations are nothing new. It was the Roman satirist Juvenal, a literary ancestor of both Thompson and Abbey, who wrote: "Do you teach? Bowels of iron are what a teacher needs. . . . The same daily fare again and again—it's death to the wretched master."¹¹

A student of Abbey's, Nancy Mairs, wrote an essay that was included in James Hepworth's *Resist Much, Obey Little* about Abbey's advanced writing class at the University of Arizona. She states that the rigorous course generated graduate student complaints. Abbey's reading requirements and standards of excellence, colliding with the universal tendencies toward mediocrity and indolence, were not appreciated by the class. Mairs blames the "graduate students, who bear a heavy responsibility, it seems to me, when a class goes badly."¹² Abbey told us during our March 1988 conversation that he was concerned about the pernicious effects on his writing of working in academia. He joked that a book about his experiences in academia would be entitled *Hobbit Life: My Experiences with Gigantic Dwarfs*. Elsewhere in his published writings he was equally frank: "Writers should avoid the academy. When a writer begins to accept pay for talking about words, we know what he will produce soon— nothing but words."¹³

No writing professor I have known—and I have studied under, worked in departments with, and published dozens of them over the last five decades (my first creative writing class was in 1970 at Mt. Hermon with Harvard poet Paul Smyth)—would support the current system without some reservations. Most would prefer an arrangement along the lines of the European tutorial model, while conceding the approach would not be viewed as cost effective by administrators. Any twenty-first-century reform movement, based on an acceptance of Edward Abbey's perspective and that of prominent academic dissidents like Hall, Gioia, and McGurl, would have to begin with an examination of assumptions and proceed to a consideration of alternative approaches. At their best, as in the case of the stellar University of Denver program from which I graduated, led by the distinguished poet Bin Ramke, they are constructive and beneficial to young writers. At their worst, as in the Alaskan program I describe in "The Age of Abbey" in this volume, they degenerate into a counterproductive tyranny of the weak. Most fall somewhere in between those two extremes. Abbey's position for much of his life vis-à-vis the programs that dominated his literary era (as well as that of the martyr John Haines in Alaska) recalls the insight of Camus: "In an era of bad faith, the man who does not want to renounce separating true from false is condemned to a certain kind of exile."[14]

I might say, in summary, that I learned much from my acquaintance with Abbey, Thompson, Haines, Ginsberg, Burroughs, and other twentieth- and twenty-first-century authors who I either knew informally or interviewed in my capacity as an editor for a literary journal. My background— born the middle son of a middle-class family in the middle of the country during the middle of the last century—may have helped in this role. By upbringing as well as by nature, I am most comfortable in the center of a discussion and tend, perhaps in part because of my midwestern origins, to be easygoing and to withhold judgment of people. These characteristics can be useful with respect to the task of engaging another personality and intellect in meaningful dialogue, and then recording that exchange of ideas for the sake of posterity.

3

My favorite Abbey passage, and one I have cited when teaching his works, has always been the critique he made of Shakespeare in his journal. Abbey was not intimidated or impressed by any person or institution, and that includes the most esteemed member of the canon. His startling, irreverent observations have led me to regard Shakespeare and other Olympian figures in new and liberating ways. Any revolution begins with a simple and plainspoken critique:

Certainly [he is] a master poet—but his plays are archaic bores: the

childish humor of his comedies; the farcical nonsense of his trage-
dies; the tedious sycophancy of his histories. One of the many things
I dislike is the total absence of any real, free, independent men in his
world. All we have are masters and slaves, bosses and the bossed, and
the prevailing slime of servility by which the hierarchical machinery
is lubricated; in short, no men. Therefore, no heroes. No tragedy.
Shakespeare, the immortal bard—vastly overrated. Really belongs
in the company of other distinguished hacks, such as S. N. Behrman,
J. T. Racine, Ben Jonson, J. M. Barrie, Gilbert & Sullivan, etc. The
characters I admire most in Shakespeare are his villains: Jack Cade,
Caliban, Edmund the Bastard, Macbeth, Iago, that chap who married
Hamlet's mother—what's his name, etc. In all of Shakespeare there
is no Spartacus—not a single one. Ah, Ah, you say, but such a figure
could not have been regarded as heroic in Shakespeare's time, and
Shakespeare was very much a product of his time. To which I reply,
"Precisely." I think it's unbecoming of a writer to submit, supinely, to
evil institutions, merely because they constitute the prevailing order of
things. Raleigh serves as an example of a man who was capable, unlike Shakespeare, to rise above and see beyond the narrow limitations
of his own time. Marlowe another.[15]

Time may reveal that passages such as this will inspire some gifted
young talent, in the years to come, to lead a revival of a literary genre,
perhaps verse drama, in English. This was certainly the case, a century
ago, with the bold, plangent writings of James Joyce, which prepared
the literary ground for the emancipated modernists who followed. These
authors included Ernest Hemingway, who made the journey to Paris in
1921 specifically to meet Joyce; Edward Abbey, who ranked Hemingway
among his chief influences and chose an epigraph from Joyce's *Finnegans Wake* for *Abbey's Road*; and Hunter S. Thompson, who, early in his
career, typed out an entire Hemingway novel in order to learn how the
master created prose. In this same period the Air Force veteran became so
absorbed with the Nobel laureate's example that he traveled to Ketchum
to view the author's fresh grave (1964) and visit the Sawtooth Club on
Main Street where his idol had spent many a night. The locals, according to Thompson, all appeared to have "escaped" from Hemingway's
stories. They assured him that, once the author was relaxed among intimates, his informal recollections of his life—riding a landing craft toward

Normandy Beach on D-Day, hunting big game in Africa, filming *The Old Man and the Sea* with Spencer Tracy—were better than anything in his books. The same was true, for those who had the opportunity to meet him, of Edward Abbey.

4

Abbey stated several times before his death that he wanted the words "No Comment" inscribed on his tombstone, which they were. The phrase "question authority," uttered by the quintessential rebel Walt Whitman, in the contrarian spirit of Abbey's idol Socrates, offers a more apt summary of Abbey's philosophy and of the age of Abbey. The phrase provides a journey-ending conclusion that can also serve as a useful point of departure. The only other formulation that might resonate with similar clarity would be the Roman epitaph from Camus's Algeria: "Non fui, fui non sum; non desidero" (I was not, I was, I am no more; I have no regret). As a philosopher, Abbey knew there are no answers, only questions that are continually refined. As a naturalist, he was keenly aware that life is short and death is long and that absent the illusory consolations of the supernatural, the only justice, truth, and love that exist is that which is made here on Earth. As a novelist, he understood that most human beings exist in shades of gray, that every sinner has done a few good things, and that every saint has a closet somewhere. As a student of history, the author was cognizant of the fact that he lived in a barbaric era long before the birth of civilization. Despite his lighthearted approach to life ("Be loyal to what you love, be true to the earth, fight your enemies with passion and laughter"), Abbey was familiar with Primo Levi's "Hier ist kein warum" (Here there is no why), what an SS officer at Auschwitz told Levi.[16] In "A Writer's Credo" Abbey quotes the novelist Kurt Vonnegut on the subject: "You want to know something? We are still in the Dark Ages. The Dark Ages—they haven't ended yet."[17] Abbey's eyes were always fixed on that bright horizon of freedom and justice, where his benevolent monarch—reason—would finally prevail.

Several years after his passing, the author's widow Clarke related to me in a telephone conversation the manner in which her husband had been laid to rest in the furthest outlier of the Arizona desert. As is widely known in the literary community, Edward Abbey asked to be interred in the heart of his favorite cactus country. She described how she and the children made pilgrimages to the remote location, which can only be reached on foot. At the fugitive site they left beautiful rocks, wind bells, and other artifacts to amuse the mule deer and coyotes and ravens.

Those who knew and loved Edward Abbey, the mortal man, and who travel in remembrance to that final set of coordinates continue to miss him, but the life systems of the desert do not. His remains have been carried off in the pincers of ants and beetles and scorpions and centipedes into the underworld upon which this world of light and life and reason is based. The author's physical nature has deliquesced into bacteria and molecules and atoms. It has been returned to the cauldron in which all organic forms are made into new things. Just where the eternal part of him is now only the four winds can tell us, and they are not saying.

Notes

1. Edward Abbey, "Coda: Cape Solitude," in *Abbey's Road* (New York: Plume, 1991), 192.

2. Edward Abbey, "Emerson," in *One Life at a Time, Please* (New York: Holt, 1988), 216.

3. Hunter S. Thompson, "Ashes to Ashes and Dust to Dust: The Funeral of Mother Miles," in *The Great Shark Hunt: Strange Tales from a Strange Time* (New York: Simon and Schuster, 1979), 614.

4. Edward Abbey, "Cliffrose and Bayonets," in *Desert Solitaire: A Season in the Wilderness* (New York: Touchstone, 1990), 36.

5. Dana Goia, foreword to *A Gradual Twilight: An Appreciation of John Haines*, ed. Steven Rogers (Fort Lee, NJ: CavanKerry Press, 2003), xv.

6. See, for example, Philip Fradkin, "A Classic, or a Fraud?," *Los Angeles Times*, February 3, 2008, M-8.

7. Donald Hall, "Poetry and Ambition," in *Poetry and Ambition: Essays, 1982–88* (Ann Arbor: University of Michigan Press, 1988), 8.

8. Mark McGurl, *The Program Era: Postwar Fiction and the Rise of Creative Writing* (Cambridge, MA: Harvard University Press, 2009), 320.

9. Edward Abbey, *Confessions of a Barbarian: Selections from the Journals of Edward Abbey, 1951–1989*, ed. David Petersen (New York: Little, Brown and co., 1994), 221.

10. Ibid., 235–36.

11. Juvenal, qtd. in Edith Hamilton, *The Roman Way* (New York: Avon, 1973), 194.

12. Nancy Mairs, "597ax," in *Resist Much, Obey Little: Some Notes on Edward Abbey*, ed. James Hepworth and Gregory McNamee (Tucson, AZ: Harbinger House, 1985), 46.

13. Edward Abbey, "On Writing and Writers, Books and Art," in *A Voice Crying in the Wilderness (Vox Clamantis in Deserto): Notes from a Secret Journal*, ed. David Petersen (New York: St. Martin's, 1989), 56.

14. Albert Camus to Jean Gillbert, 1956, qtd. in Herbert R. Lottman, *Albert Camus: A Biography* (New York: Doubleday, 1979), 577.

15. Abbey, *Confessions of a Barbarian*, 258–59.

16. Ibid., 133.

17. Kurt Vonnegut, *Deadeye Dick* (New York: Dial Press, 2010), 271.

The Fool's Progress: An Honest Novel

A Review by John A. Murray

(March 1989, *Bloomsbury Review*)

In a note to me dated March 29, 1989, Edward Abbey's widow Clarke wrote that this review was the last piece of writing that Edward Abbey read "during one of his last lucid periods" before he died. She later stated in a telephone conversation (1996) that it had brightened his final moments on Earth, given the overall critical response to the novel.

Since Ulysses returned to Ithaca after ten years of wandering across the Mediterranean, the story of the homecoming—of the lost, fallen, or failed hero struggling to regain his birthplace through epic trials—has proven to have enormous and enduring appeal. *The Fool's Progress* is a modern version of the story of Ulysses. It is the tale of a man who, after thirty years of wandering through the Southwest in search of the honest life, learns that he is dying and returns in his 1962 Dodge Carryall truck to his hometown in Stump Creek, West Virginia. Edward Abbey, well known through his six earlier works of fiction and twelve works of nonfiction, has attained in *The Fool's Progress* the full promise of a fertile career that began in 1956 with his first novel, *The Brave Cowboy*, which was subsequently made into the film *Lonely Are the Brave*. Readers (and reviewers) have waited many years for this important novel to be released. It is, as the author often said it would be, a "fat masterpiece" (some 485 pages) and tells the oldest story with the newest narrative tools in such a way as to produce what may be considered by posterity as one of the classic American novels of the 1980s.

There are two narratives in *The Fool's Progress*. First, we have Henry H. Lightcap (a thinly veiled self-portrait of the author) traveling from Tucson, Arizona, to Stump Creek, West Virginia, circa 1977. This is told usually in the first person and present tense, but sometimes changes to the third person and past tense. Second, we have the *compleat* story of Lightcap's residence on Earth (1917–1977) told in a series of flashbacks beginning with birth and progressing chronologically through childhood, boyhood, youth, early travels, military services, university years, and adulthood (1940–1970), also known as "The Lost Years," a period that includes various part-time jobs, lengthy periods of unemployment, and several wives and children. The second story line is often told in the third person and past tense but can change at any time to the first person and present tense. A powerful and suspenseful effect results from all this, much as Tolstoy attained in *War and Peace* by shifting between the story chapters and the history essays, or as Melville achieved in *Moby Dick* by alternating between the story chapters and the whale essays. Think of a sonata. In a sonata we have two opposing keys, interwoven in such a way as to heighten the contrast between the conflicting ideas they evoke. The contending keys in *The Fool's Progress* are life and death (the living voice of present time, the dead voice of past time). The melodic line—Lightfoot's story—functions identically in both keys. It is, in effect, transposed seamlessly from one to the other. And of course the novel—as with a sonata—ends in harmony: Lightcap's reconciliation of life and death through the transcendence of love. That Edward Abbey is able to do so much so effortlessly—and with the twin challenges of the Anti-Hero (Lightcap as a flawed and unfulfilled man) and the Anti-Western (the trip from west to east instead of from east to west)—is a tribute to his mastery of the novel as both a storytelling and an art form, an ease many strive for but few attain.

Despite what it says on the cover, *The Fool's Progress* is not a picaresque, at least in the conventional academic sense of an episodic adventure narrative, as in *Lazarillo De Tormes*; far more is at work here. The novel is about the eternal verities—evil, injustice, suffering—and about how a common, earthy, ordinary man—Henry Lightcap—endures with dignity, despite what Hamlet called "the thousand natural shocks that flesh is heir to." Durability is achieved through intelligence and humor. A word about humor: much of Lightcap's universality is achieved through Abbey's warm and comic portrait of him. Humor—as dramatists from Aristophanes to Woody Allen have known—instantly universalizes and democratizes the protagonist. The novel is funny—no, make that hilarious—in places and will inevitably be compared to the best of Twain, Swift, Rabelais, Erasmus, and that grand old master, Chaucer. A sampling: As Lightcap ruminates about sex—"I've never met a nymphomaniac I didn't like." After Lightcap shoots his home refrigerator—symbol of all that is artificial—with a magnum revolver—"I've settled that bastard's hash." On his third wife's attempt at *oeuf poche en aspic*—"boiled sewage efflu- ent." On another of his third wife's dinner—"resembled something out of a nightmare by Poe." And a favored quote from Brahms—"If there's any- one here I've failed to insult, I apologize." This is vintage Edward Abbey, and there is enough comedy vérité—particularly in the early, earthy, and angry chapters when Henry is wrestling with the suppressed knowledge of his fatal disease—to keep David Letterman supplied with a season's worth of one liners.

The novel is also serious, of course, and becomes more so as the story line advances. There is some extraordinarily fine writing in this book, as when Abbey writes of Lightcap's birth from "the dark radiant chamber of conception," a wonderfully Miltonic inversion, and then describes how Henry's father "swabbed away the silvery caul, that shining suit of lights, like the garb of a traveler from outer space." Later, Henry sees the moon "rising round as a banjo through the mists above the eastern hills" of his native West Virginia. And then there is this fine passage, again written of his beloved eastern mountains:

> He [Henry] loved the lament of the mourning doves, echoing his own heartache, when they returned each spring from wherever they went in the winter. He loved the soft green of the linwood trees, the bright green of the Osage orange against the morning sun. . . . He loved the red-dog dirt road that meanders through the smoky hills beside the sulfur-colored creek, . . . the gray good gothic two-story clapboard farm-house that remained, after a century, still the Lightcap family home. . . . He loved the beagle hounds that ran to meet him each evening. He loved . . . the sight of the family wash hanging from the line, the sound of his father's axe in the woodyard as the old man split kindling for the kitchen stove. . . . But most of all and above all and always in April Henry loved the sound of a hardball smacking into leather.

There are as many definitions of a classic as there are literary critics. Samuel Johnson wrote of works that are "just representations of general nature." Coleridge posited a characteristic of organic unity. T. S. Eliot used the word *maturity* to define the word classic; a work that displayed the comprehensiveness expected of age, learning, and wisdom. All of these are fine, but have their limitations. Five characteristics can be used to judge a classic with greater precision: universality of character and action, excellence of craft, moral and not equivocal truth of theme, integrity of style, and depth of feeling. Not only does *A Fool's Progress* measure up well when judged by these standards, it also stands up well when put beside the preexisting classics of the genre of the western American novel: *The Big Sky*, *The Grapes of Wrath*, *On the Road*, and others. It just may be, as was suggested earlier, that *A Fool's Progress* will, like its stubborn and tenacious protagonist, endure. There is really no higher praise a reviewer can bestow upon a work.

There has been and will continue to be criticism of *A Fool's Progress*—particularly from those who come to the work with a set of assumptions ready to be verified—but for those who read the novel without prejudice or preconception, the reading will be a pleasurable and memorable experience. Abbey tells a good story simply and well—a little too earthy for some, no doubt—but communicating truths is what writing is all about. It is, in the end, ironic, but something fitting, that an author widely miscast as a misanthrope should present so humane a vision in his finest novel.

Further Reading

The following represents a partial list of primary works by and secondary works on Edward Abbey (excluding fiction), as well as related works of interest, in terms of his milieu and larger cultural context. The academic field of Abbey studies is vast and growing. In making these selections, literary value and historical importance were factored in, as well as relevance to particular essays in this book.

Primary Sources

Abbey, Edward. *Desert Solitaire: A Season in the Wilderness*. New York: McGraw-Hill, 1968.

———. *Appalachian Wilderness: The Great Smoky Mountains*. With Photographs by Eliot Porter. New York: Dutton, 1970.

———. *Slickrock*. With Photographs by Philip Hyde. San Francisco, CA: Sierra Club, 1971.

———. *Cactus Country*. New York: Time-Life, 1973.

———. *The Journey Home: Some Words in Defense of the American West*. New York: Dutton, 1977.

———. *Abbey's Road*. New York: Dutton, 1979.

———. *Down the River*. New York: Dutton, 1982.

———. *Beyond the Wall: Essays from the Outside*. New York: Dutton, 1983.

———. *The Best of Edward Abbey*. San Francisco, CA: Sierra Club, 1984.

———. *Edward Abbey Reads from His Own Works*. Laguna Beach, CA: Audio Press, 1987.

————. *One Life at a Time, Please.* New York: Holt, 1988.

————. *A Voice Crying in the Wilderness (Vox Clamantis in Deserto): Notes from a Secret Journal.* Ed. David Petersen. New York: St. Martin's, 1989.

————. *Confessions of a Barbarian: Selections from the Journals of Edward Abbey, 1951–1989.* Ed. David Petersen. New York: Holt, 1994.

————. *Earth Apples: The Poetry of Edward Abbey.* Ed. David Petersen. New York: St. Martin's Press, 1994.

————. "Cactus Chronicles, The Unpublished Letters." *Orion* 25.4 (2006): 44–53.

————. *Postcards from Ed: Dispatches and Salvos from an American Iconoclast.* Ed. David Petersen. Minneapolis, MN: Milkweed, 2006.

Secondary Sources

Austin, Mary. *The Land of Little Rain.* Introduction by Edward Abbey. New York: Penguin, 1988.

Berry, Wendell. *The Gift of Good Land: Further Essays Cultural and Agricultural.* Berkeley, CA: Counterpoint Press, 1981.

Bezner, Kevin, and Kevin Walzer. *The Wilderness of Vision: On the Poetry of John Haines.* Brownsville, OR: Story Line Press, 1996.

Bowden, Charles. *Blue Desert.* Tucson: University of Arizona Press, 1986.

Calahan, James M. *Edward Abbey: A Life.* Tucson: University of Arizona Press, 2003.

Crawford, John, William Balassi, and Anne O. Eysturoy. *This Is About Vision: Interviews with Southwestern Authors.* Albuquerque: University of New Mexico Press, 1990.

Dillard, Annie. *Pilgrim at Tinker Creek.* New York: Harper and Row, 1975.

Douglas, William O. *My Wilderness: East to Katahdin.* New York: Doubleday, 1961.

Dutton, Clarence E. *Tertiary History of the Grand Canon District.* Washington, D.C.: Government Printing Office, 1882.

Ehrlich, Gretel. *The Solace of Open Spaces.* New York: Viking, 1985.

Fletcher, Colin. *The Man Who Walked Through Time.* New York: Knopf, 1968.

Ginsberg, Allen. *Howl*. San Francisco, CA: City Lights, 1956.

Glacken, Clarence J. *Traces on the Rhodian Shore: Nature and Culture in Western Thought from Ancient Times to the End of the Eighteenth Century*. Berkeley: University of California Press, 1967.

Haines, John. *Descent: Selected Essays, Reviews, and Letters*. Fort Lee, NJ: CavanKerry Press, 2010.

———. *Fables and Distances: New and Selected Essays*. Minneapolis, MN: Greywolf, 1996.

———. *Living Off the Country: Essays on Poetry and Place*. Ann Arbor: University of Michigan Press, 1981.

———. *News from the Glacier: Selected Poems, 1960–1980*. Middleton, CT: Wesleyan University Press, 1982.

———. *The Stars, the Snow, the Fire: Twenty-Five Years in the Alaska Wilderness*. Minneapolis, MN: Greywolf, 1989.

Harrison, Jim. *Just Before Dark: Collected Nonfiction*. Boston, MA: Houghton Mifflin, 1991.

Hepworth, James, and Gregory McNamee, eds. *Resist Much, Obey Little: Some Notes on Edward Abbey*. Tucson, AZ: Harbinger House, 1985.

Hildebrand, John. *Reading the River: A Voyage Down the Yukon*. Boston, MA: Houghton Mifflin, 1987.

Hoagland, Edward. *Notes from the Century Before: A Journal of British Columbia*. New York: Random House, 1969.

Inskip, Eleanor. *The Colorado River through Glen Canyon before Lake Powell: Historic Photo Journal, 1872 to 1964*. Moab, UT: Inskip Ink, 1995.

Jackson, William Henry. *Time Exposure: The Autobiography of William Henry Jackson*. New York: G. P. Putnam's Sons, 1940.

Journal of Energy, Natural Resources, and Environmental Law 11.1 (1990).

Krutch, Joseph Wood. *The Desert Year*. New York: William Sloane, 1952.

Larson, Debbie. *The Deserts of the Southwest*. Foreword by Edward Abbey. San Francisco, CA: Sierra Club, 1977.

Lawrence, D. H. *Selected Letters*. London: Heinemann, 1935.

Leopold, Aldo. *A Sand County Almanac and Other Writings on Ecology and Conservation*. Ed. Curt Meine. New York: Library of America, 2013.

Lincoln, ML. *Wrenched*. Film documentary, 2013.

Loeffler, Jack. *Adventures with Ed: A Portrait of Abbey*. Albuquerque: University of New Mexico Press, 2002.

Lopez, Barry. *Desert Notes: Reflections in the Eye of the Raven*. New York: Scribner's, 1976.

Lyon, Thomas J. *This Incomparable Land: A Guide to American Nature Writing*. Minneapolis, MN: Milkweed, 2001.

McCann, Garth. *Edward Abbey*. Western Writers Series. Boise, ID: Boise State University, 1977.

McPhee, John. *Encounters with the Arch-Druid*. New York: Farrar, Straus and Giroux, 1971.

Milosz, Czeslaw. *The Captive Mind*. New York: Random House, 1981.

Murray, John A. Review of *The Fool's Progress: An Honest Novel*, by Edward Abbey. *Bloomsbury Review*, March/April 1989, 3–4.

Nabhan, Gary Paul. *Counting Sheep: Twenty Ways of Seeing Desert Bighorn*. Tucson: University of Arizona Press, 1993.

———. *The Desert Smells Like Rain: A Naturalist in Papago Indian Country*. San Francisco, CA: North Point, 1982.

Nichols, Tad. *Glen Canyon: Images of a Lost World*. Santa Fe: Museum of New Mexico Press, 1999.

Peacock, Doug. *Grizzly Years: In Search of the American Wilderness*. New York: Holt, 1991.

Powell, John Wesley. "Exploration of the Colorado River of the West." *Scribner's Monthly*, January, February, and March 1875.

Redford, Robert. *The Outlaw Trail: A Journey through Time*. New York: Grosset and Dunlap, 1978.

Rogers, Steven B. *A Gradual Twilight: An Appreciation of John Haines*. Foreword by Dana Goia. Fort Lee, NJ: CavanKerry Press, 2003.

Ronald, Ann. *The New West of Edward Abbey*. Reno: University of Nevada Press, 1982.

Rusho, W. L. *Everett Ruess: A Vagabond for Beauty*. Layton, UT: Gibbs Smith, 1983.

Stegner, Wallace. *The Sound of Mountain Water: The Changing American West*. Garden City, NY: Doubleday, 1969.

Steinbeck, John. *The Log from the Sea of Cortez*. New York: Viking, 1951.

Stewart, Frank. *A Natural History of Nature Writing*. Washington, D.C.: Island Press, 1995.

Temple, Eric. *Edward Abbey: A Voice in the Wilderness*. VHS, Eric Temple Productions, 1993.

Thompson, Hunter S. *Fear and Loathing in Las Vegas: A Savage Journey to the Heart of the American Dream*. New York: Simon and Schuster, 1972.

———. *The Great Shark Hunt: Strange Tales from a Strange Time*. New York: Simon and Schuster, 1979.

Van Dyke, John C. *The Grand Canyon of the Colorado*. New York: Scribner's, 1920.

Wild, Peter. *John Haines*. Western Writers Series. Boise, ID: Boise State University, 1985.

———, ed. *The Desert Reader*. Salt Lake City: University of Utah Press, 1991.

Williams, Terry Tempest. *Refuge: An Unnatural History of Family and Place*. New York: Pantheon, 1991.

Wilson, E. O. *Biodiversity*. New York: Norton, 1998.

———. *Naturalist*. Washington, D.C.: Island Press, 2001.

———. *Sociobiology: The New Synthesis*. Cambridge, MA: Harvard University Press, 1975.

Zwinger, Ann. *A Desert Country Near the Sea: A Natural History of the Cape Region of Baja California*. Tucson: University of Arizona Press, 1987.

Contributors

JOHN ALCOCK is the Regents Professor Emeritus of Biology at Arizona State University. He received his doctoral degree from Harvard University under the direction of Ernest Mayr. Alcock's research interests include the evolution of diversity in insect populations and the social behavior of insect populations. His research projects have taken him to Australia and across the American Southwest. The many natural history books of Alcock include *The Evolution of Insect Mating Systems* (1983, with Randy Thornhill), *The Kookaburras' Song* (1988), *Sonoran Desert Summer* (1990), *Sonoran Desert Spring* (1994), *In a Desert Garden: Love and Death Among Insects* (1999, received the Burroughs Award for Natural History Writing), *The Triumph of Sociobiology* (2003), *Animal Behavior: An Evolutionary Approach* (ninth edition, 2009), and *When the Rain Comes: A Naturalist's Year in the Sonoran Desert* (2009).

GENOA ALEXANDER is a twenty-five-year-old public-school educator in Denver, Colorado. She holds two degrees in science from colleges in Colorado. Her primary area of professional interest and research is the education of gifted and talented children. She has explored and studied the deserts of the American Southwest, southern Europe, and northern Mexico, as well as the desert microhabitats of the Caribbean.

CHARLES BOWDEN was for many years an investigative journalist with the *Tucson Citizen*. In 1996 he received the Lannan Literary Award for Nonfiction. He was the author of a host of works on the Southwest, including *Killing the Hidden Waters* (1977), *Blue Desert* (1986), *Frog Mountain Blues* (1987), *Mezcal* (1988), *Red Line* (1989), *Desierto* (1991), *The*

Sonoran Desert (1992), *Chihuahua* (1996), *Stone Canyons of the Colorado Plateau* (1996), *The Sierra Pinacate* (1998), *Juarez* (1998), *Inferno* (2006, Southwest Book Award winner), and *Dead When I Got Here* (2014). In a letter to Jack Shoemaker of North Point Press, Edward Abbey described Bowden as the natural inheritor of his literary mission in the Southwest: "[Bowden is] a very good writer, with a shrewd eye for human folly and a sympathetic heart for the used and abused, both human and other. He writes in a laconic, highly compressed, indirect style, laced with irony humor and a wholesome dash of Cyanide. I.e., he regards the human race with less than total admiration. He deserves, in my opinion, a better publisher and a much larger audience than he has to date." Charles Bowden died at his home in Las Cruces, New Mexico, on August 30, 2014.

MICHAEL BRANCH is a professor of English at the University of Nevada, Reno. He is cofounder and past president of the Association for the Study of Literature and Environment (ASLE), and he served for sixteen years as the book review editor for *ISLE: Interdisciplinary Studies in Literature and Environment*. Branch is cofounder and series coeditor of the University of Virginia Press book series Under the Sign of Nature: Explorations in Ecocriticism, with twenty-five titles to date. His scholarly works include *John Muir's Last Journey: South to the Amazon and East to Africa* (2001), *The ISLE Reader: Ecocriticism, 1993–2003* (2003), and *Reading the Roots: American Nature Writing before Walden* (2004). He lives with his wife and children in the high desert at Piedmont, a passive solar home of their own design near Reno, Nevada.

EDWARD HOAGLAND graduated from Harvard in 1954, and later taught at a number of colleges and universities, including Columbia, Brown, and Bennington. Now retired from teaching, he spends his summers in the mountains of Vermont and his winters at his family's ancestral three-hundred-year-old colonial home on Martha's Vineyard. His nonfiction works include *Notes from the Century Before: A Journal from British Columbia* (1969), *Red Wolves and Black Bears* (1976), *African Calliope: A Journey to the Sudan* (1979), *Balancing Acts* (1992), *Hoagland on Nature* (2003), *Alaskan Travels* (2012), and *The Devil's Tub* (2014). He was the series editor for the Penguin Nature Series. Hoagland's professional awards include two Guggenheim Fellowships (1965 and 1975), an American Book Award (1982), a Lannan Foundation Award (1993), election to the American Academy of Arts and Sciences (2011), and a John Burroughs Medal in Natural History Writing (2012).

ESTHER ROSE HONIG is a twenty-five-year-old radio journalist and contributing reporter for KCUR, Kansas City's NPR station. In 2012 Honig graduated from Mills College in Oakland, California. While living in Oakland, Honig contributed to the local public radio station KALW. She recently returned from a fellowship program in Santiago, Chile. Honig is best known for her project "Before and After," which used Photoshop to explore global standards of beauty. In 2014 it went viral and was reported in more than thirty countries by news outlets such as *Time*, CNN, and *Good Morning America*.

JACK LOEFFLER was the recipient of the 2008 Governor's Award for Excellence in the Arts in New Mexico for aural history. A professional musician (jazz trumpet) and musical historian, he has devoted a large part of his life to preserving the indigenous music of the Southwest, much as Alan Lomax worked to preserve the folk and blues music of the Appalachians and American South. Loeffler was a close personal friend of Edward Abbey's, and in 2002 he published *Adventures with Ed: A Portrait of Abbey* with the University of New Mexico Press. The book provides readers with a valuable portrait of the author across the span of his most interesting decades.

NANCY LORD lives near Kachemak Bay in Homer, Alaska, and teaches in the low-residency MFA program at the University of Alaska, Anchorage, as well as in the Kachemak branch of the same state university. She was the Alaska writer laureate, 2008–2010, and is the author of numerous works of literary nonfiction, including *Fishcamp: Life on an Alaskan Shore* (1997), *Green Alaska: Dreams from the Far Coast* (1999), *Beluga Days: Tracking the White Whale's Truths* (2007), *Rock, Water, Wild: An Alaskan Life* (2009), *Early Warming: Crisis and Response in the Climate-Changed North* (2011). She has also authored many fine works of fiction, including the outstanding short story collection *Survival* (1991).

CURT MEINE received his undergraduate degree in English and history from DePaul University in Chicago and an interdisciplinary doctoral degree from the University of Wisconsin, Madison. After working for the National Academy of Sciences and the International Crane Foundation, he became a senior fellow with the Leopold Foundation. He is the author of *Aldo Leopold: His Life and Work*, the definitive biography of Aldo Leopold (University of Wisconsin Press, 1988), as well as *Correction Lines: Essays on Land, Leopold, and Conservation* (2004). Meine, who grew up in Chicago, is an accomplished folk and blues guitarist and musician and owns a collection of fine vintage instruments.

BEN A. MINTEER is the Arizona Zoological Society Endowed Chair in the School of Life Sciences at Arizona State University. He received his master's degree in natural resources planning and doctoral degree in natural resources from the University of Vermont. His research interests include environmental policy, ecological ethics, the historical foundations of ecological management, and conservation biology. Minteer's books include *The Landscape of Reform* (2006), *Nature in Common? Environmental Ethics and the Contested Foundations of Environmental Policy* (2009), and *Refounding Environmental Ethics* (2012).

KATHLEEN DEAN MOORE is Distinguished Professor of Philosophy at Oregon State University and cofounder and senior fellow of the Spring Creek Project for Ideas, Nature, and the Written Word. Moore's published books include *Riverwalking: Reflections on Moving Water* (1996), *Pardons: Justice, Mercy, and the Public Interest* (1997), *The Pine Island Paradox: Making Connections in a Disconnected World* (2005), *Holdfast: At Home in the Natural World* (1999), *How It Is: The Native American Philosophy of V. F. Cordova* (2007), *Rachel Carson: Legacy and Challenge* (2008), *Wild Comfort: The Solace of Nature* (2010), and *Moral Ground: Ethical Action for a Planet in Peril* (2010). She has traveled widely to the wild places of the world, most recently to the Galapagos Islands in the spring of 2014. Her son is a wildlife biologist in the Pacific Northwest.

JOHN A. MURRAY has written or edited forty-five books, including ten with university presses. Most can be found at goodreads.com or at rare book sites such as Alibris and Abe Books. Among his works is *Writing About Nature: A Creative Guide*, also published by University of New Mexico Press, which has been used as a text by professors at American colleges and universities for over twenty years. He has been an editor for the *Bloomsbury Review* since 1986. He was the founding editor of the world nature series with Oxford University Press in 1989 and the founding editor of the Sierra Club nature writing annual in 1993. As an editor, he has published over two hundred writers, including three authors who have received a Nobel Prize (V. S. Naipaul, Derek Walcott, and Jimmy Carter) and seven Pulitzer recipients. His books have received the Colorado Book Award (2001) and the Southwest Book Award (2002). He has taught at the University of Denver, Regis University, the University of Alaska, the Oklahoma Arts Institute, the Yellowstone Institute, and the Rocky Mountain College of Art and Design. He directs the United States Literary Award program.

DOUG PEACOCK was one of Edward Abbey's closest personal friends. He served as a Green Beret combat medic in Vietnam. Abbey wrote about his backcountry adventures in the desert Southwest with Doug Peacock in such books as *Cactus Country* (1973) and based fictional characters in his novels *The Monkey Wrench Gang* (1975) and *Hayduke Lives* (1989) on his confrere. Doug Peacock is the author of many fine works of non-fiction, including *Grizzly Years: In Search of the American Wilderness* (1990), *Baja* (1991), *Walking It Off: A Veteran's Chronicle of War and Wilderness* (2005), *The Essential Grizzly: The Mingled Fates of Men and Bears* (2006), and *In the Shadow of the Sabertooth: A Renegade Naturalist Considers Global Warming, the First Americans, and the Terrible Beasts of the Pleistocene* (2013). He lives near Emigrant, Montana, at the headwaters of Yellowstone River and close to the great wilderness areas and historic national parks of the northern Rockies that he loves and to the preservation of which he has devoted his residence on Earth.

GLENN VANSTRUM is a medical doctor, essayist, novelist, screenwriter, classical pianist, surfer, and underwater photographer. He has practiced medicine as an emergency room physician in California and Hawaii and as a cardiac anesthesiologist on a heart-transplant team in California. He takes every fourth week off so that he can surf and enjoy the salt water as much as possible. Vanstrum lives with his wife, two sons, and a golden retriever in a home overlooking the Pacific Ocean in La Jolla, California. He is the author of *The Saltwater Wilderness* (2003), which he illustrated with his own underwater photographs taken on trips around the world, as well as several short story collections and novels, a screenplay, and a highly regarded textbook on anesthesiology. Vanstrum is a trained musician and an accomplished classical pianist and has performed in California and elsewhere in the country. His latest surfing adventures and upcoming music concerts are chronicled on his website.

Index

Abbey, Clarke (last wife),131, 181, 194, 197

Abbey, Edward: alcoholism and other significant issues, x; literary craft and place in the guild, 1–3; mental illness, 4–5; humor, 6; relations with other authors 7–8; approach to essay, 10–11; in the Southwest, 13–16; relations with Joseph Wood Krutch, 16–17; effect of life events, 18–19; freedom as theme in writing, 20; as philosopher and thinker, 27–32; on immigration, 43–49; as an idiosyncratic thinker, 51–56; last trip to the Grand Gulch BLM Primitive Area in southeastern Utah, 57–62; Alaskan trips and relation to Alaska, 65–70; relationship between *Desert Solitaire* and *Monkey Wrench Gang*, 71–79; as a singular member of the guild, 83–89; as a close personal friend, 91–95; as a comrade in the Southwest, 97–105; as an outlaw persona in his times, 107–22; as a complex intellectual figure when met in person, 123–62; as a representative writer and activist in his century, 163–64; as a mentor, 167–70; as an intellectual companion on a journey abroad,

171–80; a posthumous evaluation of the author's virtues, shortcomings, and ultimate legacy, 181–95.

Abbey, Joshua (son), 6

Abbey, Mildred (mother), 6

Abbey, Paul Revere (father), 86

Abbey, Renee (third wife), 123, 131

Abbey, Rita (first wife), 15

Abbey's Road, 126

Adams, Ansel, 135, 138

Adams, John Luther, 155

Alexander, Genoa Rose, 10, 167–70, 207

Alcock, John, 10, 43–49, 207

Allegheny Mountains, 86

American Academy of Arts and Letters, 85

anarchy, 32, 26, 89, 100, 129

Anthony, Susan B., 4

Appalachia, 37, 89

Aravaipa Canyon (Arizona), 161

Aristophanes, 198

Aristotle, 2, 150

Arpaio, Joe, 45

Atacama desert (Chile), 171–80

Auer, Tom and Marilyn, 5

Auman, Lisl, 148

Austin, Mary, 12

Avedon, Richard, 140

AWP (Associated Writing Programs),
  153–54
Aztec Peak, 87

Babi Yar, 156
Balzac (novelist), 183
Basho, 15
Bate, Walter Jackson, 124
Beethoven, Ludwig von, 16, 79, 93
Berlin, 157
Berry, Wendell, 7, 8, 37, 39, 74, 131,
  132, 183
Best of Abbey, 168
Beyond the Wall, 67
Big Sur, 85
Blake, William, 189
border patrol, 111
Borges, Jorge L. (writer), 187
Bowden, Charles, 10, 107–22, 207
Bowra, Maurice, 12, 13
Brahms, 199
Branch, Michael, 10, 35–42, 208
Brower, David, 135, 138
Burns, Jack, 102–3
Burroughs, John, 87, 154, 192
Burton, Richard, 4, 126

Cabeza Prieta National Wildlife
  Refuge, 95
Calahan, James, 45
Camus, Albert, 2, 14, 123, 129, 163,
  181, 184, 192, 194
Carr, David, 9
Carson, Rachel, 3, 41, 77
Carter, Jimmy, 136, 143
Carver, Raymond, 155
Cassady, Carolyn, 130
Cassady, Neal, 160
Castaneda, Carlos, 131
Catlin, George, 20, 132
Chase, Alston, 7
Chatham, Russell, 141
Chatwin, Bruce, 174
Chaucer, Geoffrey, 198

Chavez, Cesar, 41
Childs, Craig, 11
China, 7
China Lake, 12
Ciudad Juarez (Mexico), 110
Clark, Captain William, 20, 132
Coleridge, Samuel, 199
Collins, Judy, 142
Commander Cody (band), 148
Cooper, James Fennimore, 6
Coover, Robert, 187
cranes, 114
Crumb, R., 153
Cunningham, Imogene, 12

Dana, Richard Henry, 1, 139
Darwin, Charles, 20, 115
Datz, Hyman, 136
Da Vinci, Leonardo, 11
DeFillipo, Frank, 137, 138
Defoe, Daniel, 136
Delicate Arch (Utah), 71
Descartes, 2
Desert Solitaire, 60, 65, 68, 73, 83,
  91, 92, 95, 136, 137, 150, 173, 176,
  177, 180, 189
Dharma Bums (novel), 128
Dickens, Charles, 183
Dillard, Annie, 7, 37, 134, 135
Dixon, Maynard, 12
Douglas, Kirk, 84, 159
Drummond, William, 11
Dubos, Rene, 2, 55
Dylan, Bob, 130, 149, 151, 152

Earth First!, 36, 51, 91
Einstein, Albert, 20
Eliot, T. S., 199
Ellsberg, Daniel, 127
Emerson, Ralph Waldo, 2, 6, 19, 52,
  186
Erhlich, Gretel, 7

Faulkner, William, 89, 130

Flaubert, Gustave, 183
Fletcher, Colin, 7
Flett, Charles, 137
Fool's Progress, The, 197, 198, 199
Foreman, Dave, 21
Frankl, Viktor, 5

Galapagos Islands, 89
Gallup, NM, 12
Garcia, Jerry, 148
Gart Brothers, 141
Ghandi, 139
Ginsberg, Allen, 128, 129, 131, 149,
   150, 151, 192
Glen Canyon, 103
Goethe, 129
Goia, Dana, 155, 189
Good News (novel), 103
Gorbachev, Mikhail, 35
Grand Gulch Primitive Area, 57
Grenada, 140
Grey, Zane, 12
Guthrie, A. B., 151
Guthrie, Woody, 130

Haines, John, 11, 132, 153–57, 183,
   188, 189, 192
Hall, Donald, 190
Harrison, Jim, 77, 190
Havasu, 169
Hayduke Lives (novel), 103
Hemingway, Ernest, 3, 148, 182, 193
Hepworth, James, 191
Hesse, Herman, 161
Hetch Hetchy Dam, 85
Hildebrand, John, 155
Hinkley, John, 139
Hoagland, Edward "Ted," 7, 10,
   83–89, 155, 208
Holbein, Hans, 162
Holocaust, 157
Home, PA, 92
Honig, Esther Rose, 10, 171–80, 209
Hopper, Dennis, 13, 123

Hoshino, Michio, 157
Howl (poem), 128
Hugo, Victor, 139
Hyde, Phillip, 18

Ibsen, Heinrich, 158
Idaho, 6
Iraq, 7
Irving, Washington, 152
Island in the Sky (Utah), 63
Ives, Charles, 107, 108, 110, 116, 121

Jackson, William Henry, 126
Jaehnig, Mattheus, 148
James, Henry, 137
John, Elton, 130
Johnson, Josephine, 134
Johnson, Samuel, 31, 124, 164, 199
John the Baptist, 15
Journey Home, The, 123
Joyce, James, 4, 193
Judea (in Biblical times), 15

Kant, Immanuel, 2
Keats, John, 19
Kennedy, John F., 131
Kerouac, Jack, 4, 128
Kerry, John, 152
Kesey, Ken, 74, 155, 191
Kierkegaard, Søren, 151
King, Stephen, 150
Klett, Mark, 58, 60, 61
Krugman, Paul, 9
Krutch, Joseph Wood, 1, 16, 17, 19,
   20, 52, 185
Kumin, Maxine, 134

Lamm, Richard D., 137
Landon, Brook, 75
Lawrence, D. H., 13
Lawrence, T. E., 183
Least Heat-Moon, William, 162
Lennon, John, 130, 149
Leopold, Aldo, 152

Levi, Primo, 194
Lewis and Clark, 20
Lincoln, Abraham, 21
Locke, John, 150
Loeffler, Jack, 10, 97–106, 209
Lopez, Barry, 7, 8, 134, 187
Lord, Nancy, 10, 65–70, 209
Los Alamos, NM, 12
Luhan, Mabel Dodge, 14
Lyon, Thomas J. (scholar), x, 6, 126
Lyons, Raymond, 140

Mailer, Norman, 140
Mandela, Nelson, 153
Mann, Thomas, 161
Mapplethorpe, Robert, 131
Maricopa County, AZ, 45
Marquez, Gabriel, 7, 162
Massachusetts Bay Colony, 120
Matthau, Walter, 84, 159
Matthiessen, Peter, 7, 182
McCarthy, Cormac, 182, 192
McGuane, Thomas, 190
McGurl, Mark, 190
McKee, Leslie, 27
McKibben, Bill, 66, 69
McMurtry, Larry, 135
McPhee, John, 132, 135, 160
Meine, Curt, 10, 51–56, 209–10
Melville, Herman, 1, 11, 71, 139, 198
Mercury Café, 5, 123
Merton, Thomas, 188
Meyer, Jeffrey, 4
Michener, James, 140
Milton, John, 183, 199
Minteer, Ben A., 10, 57–64, 210
Mitchell, David, 182
Momaday, N. Scott, 157
Monkey Wrench Gang, The, 30, 37,
    51, 66, 67, 68, 69, 72, 73, 75, 83,
    85, 87, 103, 123, 143, 189
Montaigne (essayist), 3, 10, 163
Moore, Kathleen Dean, 10, 27–34, 210
More, Thomas, 162

Mormon (faith), 27
Mount Hermon (school), 191
Muir, John, 2, 11, 41, 66, 84, 87, 152
Murie, Adolph, 15
Murray, John (publisher), 152
Murray, John A., ix–xi, 1–25, 123–63,
    181–96, 210

Nabhan, Gary, 18
Neruda, Pablo, 175, 179
Neutra, Richard, 12
Nichols, John, 101
Nixon, Richard, 140, 148, 149

Obama, Barack, 9, 152
O'Keeffe, Georgia, 12, 123
Olson, Sigurd, 15
Omar (victim of desert), 44
O'Neill, Eugene, 4, 182
One Life at a Time, Please, 84, 107
Oracle, AZ, 92
Orlovsky, Peter, 128
Owachomo Bridge, 81

Packer, George, 8
Paine, Thomas, 41
Parker, Charlie, 115
Parkman, Francis, 3
Patriot Act, 150
Peacock, Douglas, 10, 91–96, 211
Petersen, David, 182
Pilate, Pontius, 10
Plato, 31
Poe, Edgar Allen, 199
Portland, Oregon, 27
Powell, John Wesley, 133, 173
Powell's Books, 27
Proust, Marcel, 136
Pruitt, William (biologist), 158
Putin, Vladimir, 153
Pynchon, Thomas, 77

Questa, NM, 13

Ramke, Bin, 192
Reagan, Ronald, 134–35, 137, 138, 139
Rexroth, Kenneth, 39
Richardson, Robert, 154
Risner, Henry C., 125
Risner, Jerry, 125
Robbins, Marty, 12
Rogers, Stephen, 157
Rogers, Will, 153
Roosevelt, Theodore, 174
Ruch, James, 125
Rukheyser, Louis, 142
Russell, Bertrand, 7
Russia, 94

Sagebrush Rebellion, 133
San Juan River, 27
San Pedro (Chile), 171
Sarvis, Al, 181
Schoenberg, 76
Scott, Sir Walter, 139
Sea of Cortez, 86
Shakespeare, William, 3, 79, 192–93
Smyth, Paul, 191
Snowden, Edward, 127
Snyder, Gary, 7, 37
Socrates, 194
Solzhenitsyn, Alexander, 3, 7, 153, 162
Sons of Liberty, 4
Steadman, Ralph, 153
Stegner, Wallace, 11, 135, 157, 185
Steinam, Gloria, 7
Steinbeck, John, 151
Sterling, Terry, 43
Stevens, Ted, 155
St. Francis, 19, 22
St. Kitts (island), 167–70
Stone, Robert, 155
Superstition Mountains, 97
Swift, Jonathon, 1, 5
Swigert, Jack, 138

Tao (philosophy), 100

Taos, NM, 13, 14
Teale, Edwin Way, 15
Tertullian, 14
Thompson, Hunter S., 3, 4, 7, 11, 16, 136, 139–53, 186, 187, 188, 189, 190, 192, 193
Thoreau, Henry David, 2, 3, 11, 15, 19, 21, 32, 38, 41, 52, 66, 85, 88, 125, 173, 185
Timberg, Craig, 110
Time Exposure, 126
Tohono O'odham Indians, 43
Tolstoy, Leo, 3, 129, 183, 198
Trumbo, Dalton, 159
Turkey Pen Ruins, 58
Twain, Mark, 3, 6, 132, 182
Twining, Ed, 123, 124, 136, 162

Uinta Basin, 7
University of New Mexico, 9
Updike, John, 7, 183

Valle de Luna (Chile), 171–80
Vanderjaght, Bruce, 149
Van Dyke, John, 12, 16
Vanstrum, Glen, 10, 71–79, 211
Vasari, Giorgio, 11
Vietnam, 101
Villa, Pancho, 117
Voltaire, 139
Von Humboldt, Alexander, 174

Wallace, David Rains, 185
Washington, D.C., 35
Whitman, Walt, 2, 39, 84
Wildgans, Anton, 5
Williams, Terry Tempest, 18, 134
Williams, William Carlos, 155
Wilson, Douglas, 124, 133, 161, 162
Winter, Johnny, 148
Winthrop, John, 120
Wolfe, Tom, 7, 67, 138
Woodstock, 148
Wordsworth, William, 2, 19, 21, 125

Wright, Frank Lloyd, 12, 160

Yevtushenko, Yevgeny, 156
Young, Brigham, 126
Yukon River, 86

Zevon, Warren, 148
Zion National Park (Utah), 72–73
Zwinger, Ann, 7